Gerald Stahl

THE
LONELIEST
CONTINENT

THE STORY OF
ANTARCTIC
DISCOVERY

THE
LONELIEST
CONTINENT

by Walker Chapman

NEW YORK GRAPHIC SOCIETY PUBLISHERS, LTD.
GREENWICH, CONNECTICUT

The author and publisher wish to thank the following for permission to use selections from their titles:

Selections reprinted by permission of Dodd, Mead & Company from SCOTT'S LAST EXPEDITION by Robert Falcon Scott. ©, 1913, 1941, by Dodd, Mead & Company.

Selections reprinted by permission of Wm. Heinemann Ltd., from THE HOME OF THE BLIZZARD by Sir Douglas Mawson. ©, 1915, by Wm. Heinemann Ltd.

Selections reprinted by permission of Wm. Heinemann Ltd., from THE HEART OF THE ANTARCTIC by Sir Ernest Shackleton. ©, 1909, by Wm. Heinemann Ltd.

Selections reprinted by permission of The Macmillan Company from SOUTH by Sir Ernest Shackleton. ©, 1920 by The Macmillan Company, Renewed 1947 by Raymond Swinford Shackleton and Edward Arthur Alexander Shackleton.

Selections reprinted by permission of John Murray Publishers, Ltd. from SOUTH POLE by Roald Amundsen. ©, 1912 by John Murray Publishers, Ltd.

Selections reprinted by permission of G. P. Putnam's Sons from ALONE, DISCOVERY, and LITTLE AMERICA all by Richard E. Byrd. ALONE © 1938, DISCOVERY © 1935, LITTLE AMERICA © 1930, all by G. P. Putnam's Sons.

CONTENTS

And now there came both mist and snow,
And it grew wondrous cold:
And ice, mast-high, came floating by,
As green as emerald.

And through the drifts the snowy clifts
Did send a dismal sheen:
Nor shapes of men nor beasts we ken—
The ice was all between.

The ice was here, the ice was there,
The ice was all around:
It cracked and growled, and roared and howled,
Like noises in a swound!

COLERIDGE: *The Rime of the Ancient Mariner*

1 TERRA AUSTRALIS INCOGNITA

ACROSS THE WHOLE SOUTHERN HEMISPHERE OF A MAP of the world made in the fifteenth century there stretches a single grim word: BRUMAE, "fogs." So much, and no more, was known of the geography of that hemisphere five hundred years ago.

The southland was mysterious and unknown. No vessel had ever penetrated its forbidding, enigmatic latitudes. Europe was the known world, and what lay beyond Europe was Terra Australis Incognita—"The Unknown Southern Land."

Men had speculated about the existence of that strange land for thousands of years. As early as 400 B.C., Greek philosophers had decided that the world must be a sphere. And, with that fondness for neatness and symmetry that they often displayed, the Greeks argued that there must be land to the south, balancing the known lands of the north. To the northland, the

1

Greeks gave the name *Arktikos,* because that part of the world lay under the constellation Arctos, the Bear. Through Arctos there ran an imaginary line, the Arctic Pole, on which all the heavens seemed to turn. It was easy enough to imagine a fixed point *opposite* the Arctic—an *Antarctic* Pole.

From the earliest, then, the Greeks argued for the existence of an Antarctic region to give the known world balance. Aristotle, following such earlier thinkers as Thales and Pythagoras, divided the world into five zones: the torrid zone, lying along the equator; two temperate zones, lying just to the north and south of the torrid zone; and two frigid zones, the Arctic and Antarctic, at the poles of the earth. Imaginary lines marked the boundaries between one zone and the next: the two tropic circles between the torrid zone and the temperate zones, the Arctic Circle between the north temperate zone and the north frigid zone, the Antarctic Circle between the south temperate, and the south frigid.

Of course, no one went to look. All this was theory, the work of armchair geographers. Those seamen who ventured out of the Mediterranean did not go far. Some, perhaps, traveled as far north as England, and got a taste of the Arctic cold beyond. Others went southward toward Africa, and one bold Phoenician sailor may even have circumnavigated the Dark Continent.

It was thought that only the temperate zones could be inhabited. At the poles were the snowcaps, eternally frozen, everlastingly dead. And round the middle of the world were the blazing tropics, where no man could survive, an endless Sahara of fearful heat. There could well be life in the south temperate zone, the Greeks thought—but no one in the north would ever know, for how could men cross the terrible tropics?

Ancient geography reached its culmination about A.D. 150, with the work of an Egyptian named Claudius Ptolemy, who wrote in Greek. No traveler himself, Ptolemy had access to the great library at Alexandria, and he studied and summed up the reports of voyagers and the ideas of earlier geographers. Alexandria was then the greatest commercial center of the world, and to its harbor there came merchants from many lands. From them, Ptolemy learned of the zone of fire that lay south of Egypt, and of the zone of ice north of Europe. What lay beyond the burning torrid belt? Why, another temperate zone, of course, Ptolemy said. He imagined—and drew elaborate maps of—a vast southern continent. The whole bottom of the world was one huge land mass, according to Ptolemy; Africa and Asia were joined, beyond the torrid zone, and in that Terra Australis Incognita lived civilized men, forever cut off from the Greek and Roman world by the tropics.

The rise of Christianity put an end to such speculations. The attitude of the new church toward knowledge was sounded by St. Basil in the fourth century, when he asked, "Of what importance is it to know whether the earth is a sphere, a cylinder, a disc or a concave surface? What is of importance is to know how I should conduct myself towards myself, towards my fellow man, and towards God."

At the same time, St. Augustine disposed of the idea that there could be a southern habitable continent. This "fable, that there are antipodes—that is to say, that on the opposite side of the Earth, where the sun rises when he sets to us, men plant their footsteps opposite to our feet—it is by no means to be believed," he said. After all, man had been created only once—when God brought Adam into being. If, as the geographers said, no mortal could cross the tropics, how could human beings have reached the southern land? Had God created a separate race of men there, not descended from Adam? Unthinkable!

Men have always loved to think about the unthinkable. Although Ptolemy's writings remained locked up in dusty libraries, although the Church officially discouraged talk of a spherical earth and an inhabited southland, the ideas persisted. Bede, that learned English churchman of the eighth century, openly wrote of the old five-zone theory of the earth: a northern, "uninhabitable by reason of cold"; a temperate; a tropic, "torrid and uninhabitable"; a brumal or winter zone, temperate and inhabited; and finally the "austral [southern] zone around the southern turning point [pole] which is covered with land and is uninhabitable by reason of the cold."

Imaginative men turned their thoughts southward and tried to envision the creatures who lived there. The south, they said, was an abode of monsters, a place of terror. Medieval maps labeled the unknown places, *"Frigida," "Perusta"*—"frozen," "burned." The tropical ocean boiled like a pot under the sun, one map maker said. To the south lay the "ocean unknown to the sons of Adam," while farther beyond, the icy breath of the polar seas brought death to the bottom of the world.

It was a vast and mysterious place, this unknown southern continent, bounded at the north by a zone where the sun melted all, at the south by bitter cold. The gulf between that continent and the known world was terrifying and impassable, a haunted sea, where not only heat but fearsome spirits drove men back. Medieval geographers told how, as one entered the torrid zone, the sea became covered with darkness, the waves towered to mountainous heights, the wind dropped to a deadly calm, the water itself sizzled away to reveal loathsome monsters writhing in the mud. Most ghastly, the hand of the Devil thrust itself up through the boiling sea, groping for wandering ships; one medieval map shows an island named Hand of Satan. "Unknown to the sons of Adam, having nothing which belongs to our race"—so the map maker Lambert of St. Omer described the southern lands in A.D. 1130.

The maps teemed with monsters out of the blazing zone and the glacial blackness beyond. A fourteenth-century map now in the British Museum gives us a whole circus full of bizarre dwellers in the southern land, creatures not of the line of Adam. First we see the territory of the Androphagi, "cannibals that each other eat." Then the Garamantes, in whose land the waters boil by day and freeze by night. Their neighbors are the Farici, eaters of raw flesh, especially flesh of panthers and lions. Next are the Monoculi, who run swiftly though they have only a single leg and a single eye; when the sun grows too strong for them, they raise their one foot as an umbrella over their heads. Still more remote are the Virgogici, the insect-eaters; and the soft-voiced Troglodytes, devourers of serpents.

And then the Antipodes, "who dance in ecstasy and have sixteen fingers"; adjoining these cheerful folk are a tribe "whose heads do grow beneath their shoulders," and their mouths in their breasts. The crowded map next shows us the Presumbani, who are earless, and then a race without tongues, and one without noses, and one sort of folk whose mouths are so small they can only take nourishment through a straw.

The travel book of John de Mandeville, written about 1370, added to the geographical sideshow. The book was supposedly a record of real travels, but later turned out to be simply a compilation of other men's writings, liberally larded with fantasy. "In a certain isle toward the south," Mandeville declared, "dwell folk of foul stature and of cursed kind that have no heads, and their eyes be in their shoulders. . . . And in another isle be folk of foul fashion and shape that have the lip above the mouth so great that when they sleep in the sun, they cover all the face with that lip." (A distorted report of Africa's lip-stretching Ubangis, perhaps?)

The haunted seas, too, swarmed with monsters and dragons. Eaters of men, devourers of ships, hideous things with scales and fins and many heads, the sea beasts were untroubled by the great heat of the tropical ocean. Such baleful beasts as the Scolopendra, with fiery face and eyes twenty feet around, waited hungrily for mariners so foolish as to approach.

This was the nightmare world of medieval geography. The long unhappy dream began to end in 1410, when the books of Ptolemy were at last translated into Latin and given wide circulation in Europe. Ptolemy, though he had been far from accurate in his vision of the world, was at least a man of science, not a teller of tales. He had depended more on the reports of travelers than on the workings of his own imagination.

Influenced by Ptolemy, the new geographers attempted to cast out the demons and take a more realistic approach. One of the first of these new geographers was Pierre d'Ailly (1330–1420), whose *Cosmographic Compendium* of 1413 was destined to have a great influence on the thinking of Christopher Columbus.

"The earth is spherical," D'Ailly stated flatly, "and the Western Ocean is relatively small." He cited ancient evidence to show that it should be possible to sail westward and reach the Indies without difficulty.

When it came to sailing southward, though, D'Ailly was still gripped by medieval ideas: "Beyond Thule, the last island of the Ocean, after one day's sail the sea is frozen and stiff. At the Poles there live great ghosts and ferocious beasts, the enemies of man. Water abounds there, because those places are cold, and cold multiplies vapors."

The revival of Ptolemy brought with it a revival of the idea of Terra Australis Incognita, the continent of dreams, the enormous, temperate southern land lying between the tropics and the South Pole. However, this was no longer an age of dreaming, but of doing. Bold men in bobbing wooden vessels beat southward into the forbidden zones, half afraid of monsters but determined to behold with their own eyes the wonderful southern land.

The search for the southern continent began in earnest in the middle of the fifteenth century. If, as Ptolemy had said, India and Africa were joined in the south to Terra Australis, then it should be possible to reach the southern land simply by sailing down Africa's coast, through the burning zone, into a temperate clime.

Between 1418 and 1460, Prince Henry the Navigator, the farseeing Portuguese geographer, sent ship after ship southward. Each expedition ventured just a bit farther than the last, down Africa's western coast. At first, only the trackless wastes of the Sahara were visible from shore; but by the middle of the century, Portuguese vessels had crossed the equator, and had found green and fertile lands south of Africa's bulging western hump.

In 1488, a Portuguese seaman named Bartholomew Diaz performed a major piece of surgery on Ptolemy's Terra Australis. Diaz, his frail craft driven by raging storms far beyond the previous farthest south attained, came to land's end. To the south lay open sea. He turned eastward, rounding the southern tip of Africa. Thus he amputed one great lobe of the vast supposed southern continent. In 1497, Vasco da Gama sailed completely around Africa and reached India, demolishing forever the possibility that an unknown southern land thrust northward into that part of the world.

Columbus, meanwhile, had sailed westward across the Atlantic. He found islands which he thought were the East Indies (they were the islands of the Caribbean), and he saw signs of a great land mass lying to the south. Was this Terra Australis?

New expeditions went forth. In 1501, a Portuguese expedition left Lisbon, crossed the Atlantic, and reached the coast of the New World about five degrees of latitude south of the equator. The only report of this voyage was set down by a certain Florentine merchant and astronomer who happened to be aboard. His name was Amerigo Vespucci. His letters describing the voyage received such wide circulation that the New World soon was known by a name derived from his: America.

The Portuguese landed on the east coast of Brazil, near the present town of Natal. It was obvious to them that they had arrived at no mere island, but a huge continental land mass, for they sailed southward for more than two thousand miles without seeing an end to land. This, then, must be Ptolemy's southern continent, they thought. There was no blazing impassable tropic. There were no monsters. Did the new land extend all the way to the Pole?

Vespucci's account tells of journeying to a latitude of 52° S. Strange new constellations glittered in the sky. "There arose a tempest of so much violence upon the sea that we were compelled to haul down all our sails, and we scudded under bare poles before the great wind . . . the nights were very long, so that on the 7th day of April we had a night which was 15 hours long." Eventually they came to a rocky coast, without signs of life, and then the storms forced them to turn back.

This account has been challenged by later geographers, and it now seems likely that the Portuguese ships got no farther south than 32° S. Even this, though, was a greater distance beyond the equator than anyone had gone before. The question still remained: Was newly discovered America an offshoot of the southern continent?

A Portuguese skipper named Ferdinand Magellan, sailing on behalf of Spain, settled that question in 1520. Magellan's mission was to get around the American continent, if possible, and sail westward to China and Japan. He followed South America's coastline downward, probing at every bay and river mouth, hoping to find a strait that carried through to the far side of the continent. If necessary, he would sail right to the Pole.

It was unnecessary. At a latitude of 52° S., a channel appeared, deep and broad, with salty water and a strong current. Magellan and his little fleet passed through, and found that it was a genuine strait cutting from ocean to ocean. To their left as they passed through—that is, to the south—the sailors could still see land. It seemed, to Magellan, to be continental land, perhaps the northernmost prong of Terra Australis. He gave it the name of Tierra del Fuego, "Land of Fire."

Magellan had shown that South America was not joined to the southern continent. He had helped to strengthen the belief in the existence of that continent, though. Now the map makers were convinced that south of Magellan's Strait there lay a huge body of land. Rumor grew, as rumor will, that Tierra del Fuego was populated by giants eleven feet high, and by fierce elephants and sea lions. Not for many years, however, did any navigator dare to venture south of the strait to see what was really there.

That bold buccaneer, Sir Francis Drake, was the first to do so, in 1578. He was not searching for Terra Australis at the time. Queen Elizabeth had sent him off in an attempt to halt the spread of Spanish influence in the New World, Spain and England then being deadly enemies. Drake's assignment was to find and sail through the Strait of Magellan into the Pacific, and to explore the western coastline of South America, establishing friendly relations with the natives and opening new markets for English goods. On August 17, 1578, Drake's ship entered the strait. Seven days later, according to Francis Fletcher, chaplain of the expedition, "we found great store of fowl which could not fly, of the bigness of geese, whereof we killed in less than one day 3,000 and victualled ourselves thoroughly therewith." Thus occurred the first recorded meeting between Englishmen and penguins.

It took Drake's fleet eighteen days to clear the 360-mile strait. A day after they emerged into the Pacific, the English ships were struck by a storm. Drake's flagship, the *Golden Hind*, was carried far to the south. The little craft was driven relentlessly by frosty winds, until at last Drake regained control well to the south of Tierra del Fuego, and found himself among a group of islands.

Francis Fletcher noted in his journal: "At length we fell in with the uttermost part of the land towards the South Pole, and had certainly discovered how far the same doth reach Southward from the coast of America aforenamed. The uttermost cape or headland of all these islands stands near in the 56th degree, without which there is no main nor island to be seen to the Southwards, but that the Atlantic Ocean and the South Sea meet in a large and free scope."

This meeting place of the oceans now bears the name of Drake Passage. The "uttermost cape" of which Fletcher wrote was probably Cape Horn, the very tip of South America.

Drake had thereby shown that the land Magellan had seen was no new continent, but merely a small piece of South America cut off from the mainland by the strait. Beyond Drake Passage was only open sea, so far as the eye could tell. Another great lobe of Terra Australis had been chopped away.

So the makers of maps had to revise their work. The most famous map of the day was the world map of Abraham Ortelius, first published in 1570 at Antwerp. It showed an enormous land mass which Ortelius called Terra Australis Nondum Cognita, "Southern Land Not Yet Known," which began just south of the Strait of Magellan, and spread over large portions of the Atlantic, Pacific, and Indian oceans. Much of what we now know to be the island region of Polynesia was included in this southern continent. The map showed open sea south of Africa, because the Cape of Good Hope passage had been known for nearly a century. Now, thanks to Drake, open water had to be added south of Drake Passage.

Terra Australis, though, by no means disappeared. It continued to occupy a colossal place on the new maps. The dream of a vast new continent was too attractive to abandon. It was a time of exploration, of outward expansion and conquest. Spain and England, the two great naval powers now that Portugal had come upon hard times, were out to carve up the world between them—and the Netherlands, newly independent and full of vigor, joined the two greater powers in the quest for new lands.

The Spaniards in particular dreamed of a southern continent somewhere in the Pacific, to the south and west of Chile. In 1567, the Spanish Viceroy of Peru sent out an expedition in search of this land, under the command of Alvaro de Mendana and piloted by a Portuguese, Pedro Fernandez de Quiros. They found no continents, but they did discover an island group, which Mendana named the Solomon Islands, for he hoped to find "the gold of Solomon" in that part of the world. An earlier Spanish voyage had discovered a great land mass, running for some hundreds of miles, which was thought to be an outcropping of Terra Australis, and which was given the name of New Guinea.

These two voyages led many to feel certain of the existence of the southern continent. Thus in 1578, the same year in which Drake disposed of the idea that Tierra del Fuego was the tip of Terra Australis, the Englishman George Best was writing:

"Terra Australis seemeth to be a great firm land, lying under and about the South Pole, being in many places a fruitful soil, and is not yet thoroughly discovered, but only seen and touched on the north edge thereof, by the travaile of the Portingales [Portuguese] and Spaniards in their voyages to the East and West Indies. . . . It is thought this Southland about the Pole Antarctic is far bigger than the Northland about the Pole Arctic."

The job of surgery went on. Voyage after voyage hacked away at the mythical Terra Australis. In 1615, two Dutch navigators, Schouten and Le Maire, revisited the region Drake had unwillingly entered. They rounded South America's southernmost tip, giving the ultimate cape the name of Cape Hoorn (Horn) after the Dutch town whose merchants had sponsored their voyage. Other Dutch voyagers followed this route into the Pacific, establishing trading connections for the wealthy Dutch East India Company.

Meanwhile, in 1605, Pedro Fernandez de Quiros—who had been Mendana's pilot nearly forty years before—made a new trip into the Pacific, heading for New Guinea. Bad weather sent him off course, and he came to a high headland that he named Austrialia del Espiritu Santo. He jumped to the usual conclusion: that this was another projection of Terra Australis. "To God alone the praise and glory!" Quiros declared as he took possession in the name of the Pope and the King of Spain. "O Land so long sought for, believed in by so many, so earnestly longed for by me!"

Alas, Austrialia del Espiritu Santo was no continental mass, but only an island of the group now called the New Hebrides. Worse, Quiros' second-in-command, Torres, went off on a voyage of his own that took him completely around New

Guinea—cutting it, too, off the rapidly shrinking southern continent.

Torres had seen land to the south of New Guinea. So had various Dutch seamen exploring that part of the Pacific about the same time. Gradually, it became clear that a land much larger than New Guinea lay to the south, and once again the cry of "Terra Australis!" went up. In 1642, the Dutch captain, Abel Tasman, spiked that theory by sailing past the southern side of the new land mass and proving that it was yet another island, but a giant island—a continent, in fact. Though at first men called it New Holland, it quickly came to be known as Australia, "the Southern Land"—a southern continent, but not *the* southern continent.

It was evident now that the polar continent, if it existed at all, could not extend very far north of the South Pole. Open water had been found south of Africa, South America, and Australia. Roaming buccaneers and merchantmen had ventured into high latitudes without seeing even a hint of the supposed southern land.

The first known landfall in the true Antarctic regions was made in 1675. An English merchant named Anthony de la Roché, rounding Cape Horn on his way back to Europe after a trading journey in the South Seas, was caught by a gale and blown eastward to a snow-covered island, mountainous and stormy and uninhabited, which was probably the island now called South Georgia, at a latitude of about 55° S. In the twenty years that followed, such English pirates as Bartholomew Sharpe, Ambrose Cowley, and Edward Davis reported being carried into latitudes above 60° S., and seeing floating ice and no sign of land. Storms and extreme cold discouraged them from making any explorations.

The dream of a fertile, inhabited, wealthy southern continent refused to die. Quiros, after his 1605 voyage, had written ardently of the "land of gold and silver, cattle and grain, the richest fruit and the healthiest climate, a land without venomous beasts or insects, peopled by gentle natives," that he was certain lay to the south. Now new searchers came—Frenchmen.

The French had come late to exploration. While the Spanish and Dutch and English were carving out overseas empires in the Pacific, the French had concentrated on their North American possessions. True, a pioneering French merchant named Binot Paulmier de Gonneville had followed Vasco da Gama's route around Africa in 1503, and, blown off course, had discovered a large island which he named Southern India. For more than two centuries afterward, the French were inactive on the southern seas, but in 1737 a young captain, Bouvet de Lozier, was able to persuade the French East India Company to give him two ships to search for Gonneville's "Southern India."

Bouvet sailed southward from the Cape of Good Hope. At 48°50′ S., he encountered floating ice, and as he forged on southward, the icebergs increased in size and number. He felt that Southern India could not be far, since icebergs break off from land. But there was no sign of Gonneville's huge tropical island, for Bouvet was on a false trail; "Southern India" had probably been Madagascar, off the east coast of Africa and not in southern waters at all.

On New Year's Day, 1739, steep, snow-topped mountains

loomed out of the fog. Bouvet attempted to make a landing, but rough water drove him back. So thick was the fog that it was hard to tell whether he had found an island or a continent, but the first seemed more likely. Bouvet charted its location as 55° S. and about 28° east of the Canary Islands. As for what lay beyond, he felt it could hardly be attractive; he visualized a remote, unapproachable continent, ringed by a belt of floating icebergs, inhabited only by seals and penguins.

For the next thirty years France did little about southern exploration. Bouvet's descriptions of flat-topped icebergs, 200 to 300 feet high and up to 10 miles in circumference, did not encourage other expeditions, even though the presence of seals and penguins on the icebergs, and the icebergs themselves, indicated some sort of land beyond. But then the Seven Years' War (1756–63) stripped France of most of her North American possessions. At once, it became urgent that France repair her empire by claiming new land elsewhere. The English were already in the field; Charles Byron, in 1764, and Samuel Wallis and Philip Carteret, in 1766, had been sent by the British Admiralty to look in the South Atlantic and South Pacific for the undiscovered continent which "there was reason to believe might be found."

They found nothing but scattered islands. A French expedition to the Pacific under Bougainville, in 1767, added more lovely tropical islands to the maps, but no southern continent. Finally, in January, 1772, the French made one last valiant attempt to find the elusive land.

Two small vessels sailed southward under the command of Yves Joseph de Kerguelen-Tremarec. Kerguelen chose a route that lay east of Bouvet's, and he, too, hoped to find Gonne-

ville's "Southern India." On February 12, fog-shrouded land
was sighted in 49°40′ S. Kerguelen dubbed his discovery
South France, and hastily returned to Paris with this glowing
report:

"The lands which I have had the happiness to discover
appear to form the central mass of the Antarctic continent . . .
and the land which I have called South France is so situated
as to command the route to India, the Moluccas, China, and
the South Seas. . . . No doubt wood, minerals, diamonds,
rubies, precious stones and marble will be found. . . ."

In March, 1773, Kerguelen returned to South France with
instructions to establish trade relations with the natives of the
southern continent, and to explore its coast between 40° and
60° S. He arrived in December, the middle of the summer
there, and went ashore. He found no natives, no wood, no
diamonds, no rubies—nothing, in fact, but fog and snow and
storm. Nor was South France part of a continent, he realized
now. It was merely a small, insignificant, barren island in the
midst of an icy sea. Disillusioned, Kerguelen sadly renamed
South France the Land of Desolation, and journeyed somberly
homeward. Posterity has given him one small consolation: his
Land of Desolation now bears the name Kerguelen Island.

The time was at an end when every voyage into high latitudes set up a false cry of discovery of a southern continent.
A man had joined the search who belongs in the very highest
rank of explorers, with Columbus and Magellan and Vasco da
Gama. It was Captain James Cook who put to rest at long last
the tantalizing hope for an inhabited, fertile Terra Australis.

2 COOK CROSSES THE CIRCLE

YORKSHIRE-BORN JAMES COOK, THE SON OF A FARM laborer, hardly seemed marked for greatness when he came into the world in 1728. He went to sea, as many boys did, and served as an apprentice on a lowly coal-hauling brig, the *Freelove*. Then, for ten years, he held posts on merchant vessels trading along England's east coast and the Baltic. Eventually he became mate of the *Friendship*, and was offered command of the vessel.

He turned down the opportunity. Instead, with the bold decisiveness that marked every aspect of his life, Cook volunteered for the Royal Navy, preferring the bottom rank of able seaman in the navy to a captaincy on a merchantman. It was June, 1755. He was twenty-seven years old. He "had a mind to try his fortune that way," he explained.

Cook joined H.M.S. *Eagle*, and in six weeks had won promotion to the rank of master's mate. In those days, the captain's role on board ship was to maintain discipline and hold authority, while the actual job of navigating was left to the master, an experienced seaman who had picked up the skills of the trade. The captains of the navy were usually men of high social position; the masters, generally, were of lower degree.

Before long Cook was serving as master of H.M.S. *Solebay.* He took part in the capture of Quebec from the French during the Seven Years' War; for the next three years, until 1762, Cook served with the Royal Navy squadron based at Halifax, Newfoundland, and somehow, between battles, managed to teach himself mathematics, astronomy, and marine surveying. His senior officers began to speak of "Mr. Cook's genius and capacity." After the war, he was placed in command of the surveying vessel *Grenville,* and passed the next five years making navigational charts of the western and southern coast of Newfoundland. In 1766, an eclipse of the sun took place, and Cook made careful observations of it, which he forwarded to the Royal Society in London, the most important English scientific body.

The Royal Society was impressed. Cook's meticulous results marked him as "a good mathematician and very expert in his business." It happened that the Royal Society was then planning to send an expedition into the South Pacific to carry out certain astronomical and scientific observations. What better man to head the expedition, it was asked, than James Cook?

Cook returned to England in 1768, having established a fine reputation both as a surveyor and as a sailor. He still had a rank no higher than master, for he lacked the social qualifications a higher officer was thought to need. Nevertheless, he

was picked to lead the South Seas expedition, and given the
rank of lieutenant. On August 25, 1768, Cook sailed from
Plymouth, aboard H.M.S. *Endeavour*.

What interested the Royal Society most keenly was a transit
of Venus, due to take place in 1769. Venus would then be
visible as a black spot crossing the sun's disk—a rare astronomical event, and one which would yield important scientific
information if observed properly. The best place to observe
the transit would be the South Pacific—specifically, the island
of Tahiti. But there was more involved in the plan than that.
Nothing less than a search for the still unknown southern continent was intended.

The prime mover here was a hot-tempered, stubborn, can-
tankerous Scot named Alexander Dalrymple. A Fellow of the
Royal Society, he was not only an astronomer but a student of
geographical lore, and he was firmly convinced that somewhere in the Pacific there lay an undiscovered continent,
stretching from temperate regions to the South Pole. Dalrymple stirred up enough public interest in a South Seas expedition to make it a reality. His dream was to command the
voyage himself, but this was not to be. The Royal Navy positively refused to let a civilian command a military expedition.
Many years before, on a similar voyage of scientific research,
the astronomer Halley had been given command of a naval
ship, and the results had been disastrous, ending in mutiny.

So Dalrymple had to stay home. Command went to Cook
instead—which made him the target of Dalrymple's unending
hatred.

Cook was gone from 1768 to 1771 on this first voyage. He
rounded Cape Horn, performed the astronomical observations

at Tahiti, charted and circumnavigated the islands making up
New Zealand, journeyed up the east coast of Australia to discover the Great Barrier Reef, and completed his trip around
the world by coming home via New Guinea and Java. The
achievements in many fields of science were great, and so
were the geographical results.

One important result was Cook's conviction that the vast
southern continent imagined by Quiros and Dalrymple was a
myth. "As to a southern continent," Cook wrote, "I do not
believe any such thing exists, unless in a high latitude." His
voyage, he said, "must be allowed to have set aside the most,
if not all, the arguments and proofs that have been advanced
by different authors to prove that there must be a southern
continent—I mean to the northward of 40° S., for what may
lie to the southward of that latitude I know not. Certain it is
that we saw no visible signs of land, according to my opinion,
neither in our route to the northward, southward, or westward,
until a few days before we made the coast of New Zealand."

Dalrymple refused to give up. In violent language, he insisted that Cook was wrong. Since there were large bodies of
land north of the equator, there must be large bodies of land
to the south also; otherwise the earth would not remain poised
on its axis. Dalrymple let it be known that if *he* had been
chosen to lead the expedition, in place of Cook, "I would not
have come back in ignorance."

In 1772, Dalrymple published a book renewing his argu-
ment. "The number of inhabitants in the southern continent is
probably more than 50 millions," he estimated. Imagining a
continent stretching from Chile to Australia, he observed,
"This is a greater extent than the whole civilized part of Asia,

from Turkey to the eastern extremity of China. There is at present no trade from Europe thither, though the scraps from this table would be sufficient to maintain the power, dominion, and sovereignty of Britain, by employing its manufacturers and ships."

He managed to create enough talk of a southern continent so that the Royal Navy decided on a second expedition. Once again, Dalrymple failed to get control of it. Command went a second time to his hated rival, Cook.

This time he was given two ships, the *Resolution* and the *Adventure*. Like the *Endeavour* of his first voyage, they were sturdy little coal-carrying vessels of the kind in which Cook had spent his early years at sea. Profiting by the experience of the first voyage, Cook planned everything with great care, giving special attention to the problem of provisions. Scurvy, which we now know is a vitamin-deficiency disease, was the plague of mariners who went on long voyages. Cook laid in great supplies of pickles, sauerkraut, and preserved vegetables, believing that they would help prevent outbreaks of scurvy. (During the voyage, Cook also took aboard supplies of fresh fruits, which he found were even more useful for this purpose.) The value he placed on cleanliness aboard ship was also unusual for 1772.

Cook's instructions specifically called for him to search for the southern continent. The British Admiralty knew, by this time, of the expedition of Bougainville and of two later French voyages, and were eager to forestall the French if possible. Cook was to travel first down Africa's west coast to the Cape of Good Hope, and then to continue southward until he reached land. If he found an inhabited southern continent, he was to be friendly to the natives, showing them "every kind of civility and regard."

He sailed from Plymouth on July 13, 1772. Aboard were astronomers, naturalists, and other scientists. The two ships carried provisions for two years. By late November they had reached Capetown and were heading southward, following Bouvet's course of thirty-five years before.

On December 10, in 50°40′ S., the explorers saw their first icebergs. Some were flat on top, straight-sided, majestic in their solidity. Others were fantastically hollowed and carved into grotesque shapes by the action of the water. Day and night, the officers of the watch searched for land, but time and again they sighted "land" that turned out to be just another iceberg. Bouvet Island was nowhere to be found; the fog and mist were too thick. One of the scientists aboard the *Resolution* gloomily noted in his journal, "We were almost perpetually wrapped in thick fogs, beaten with showers of rain, sleet, hail and snow, surrounded by innumerable islands of ice against which we daily ran the risk of being shipwrecked."

Cook cruised onward toward the Pole. Icebergs and floating ice floes were everywhere. Now and then, Cook sent boats out to collect ice and bring it on board; when melted, it turned into perfectly drinkable fresh water. The fact that the icebergs were of fresh, and not salt water, indicated more strongly than ever that land lay to the south.

On January 11, they saw some penguins on an ice floe. An entry in Cook's journal on the same day tells us: "Mr. Forster shot an albatross, whose plumage was of a color between brown and dark gray." The calm notation gives us chills today, perhaps—but Coleridge, who would one day set down in immortal verse the dangers of slaying albatrosses on Antarctic journeys, was still in his cradle, and Cook knew nothing of the Ancient Mariner and the curse that beset him.

Six days later—on January 17, 1773—Cook achieved something no man in all recorded history had done before. He crossed the Antarctic Circle and entered the south frigid zone. The entry in his journal is as unsensational as ever: "On the seventeenth, between eleven and twelve o'clock, we crossed the Antarctic Circle in the latitude of 66 degrees 36 minutes 30 seconds south. The weather was now become tolerably clear, so that we could see several leagues around us; and yet we had only seen one island of ice since the morning. But about 4 P.M., as we were steering to the south, we observed the whole sea in a manner covered with ice. . . ."

The ships continued southward a few hours more, but then it became obvious that they could go no farther. They had reached 67° S., and ahead of them stretched the ice pack, as far as anyone could see. Cook retreated above the Circle, and sailed eastward for the next two months, passing to the south of the island Kerguelen had discovered, and so proving that it was no part of an Antarctic continent. In the middle of March, the brief Antarctic summer neared its end, and Cook's ships headed for New Zealand. They arrived on March 25, having sailed twelve thousand miles without seeing land.

The explorers spent the rest of 1773 in the tropics, visiting Tahiti and other islands and making various scientific observations. Toward the end of November they headed southward again, crossing the Antarctic Circle for the second time five days before Christmas. The earlier southward plunge had been made due south of Africa, in eastern longitudes. Now they sailed southward from New Zealand, far to the west on the other side of the world. Here, they were able to travel much farther south before the icebergs became troublesome. After they had crossed the Circle, the ice thickened. Cook maintained a southeasterly course along the edge of the pack ice, but when he reached 147°30′ W., he could go no farther. On December 22, after making a latitude of 67°31′ S., Cook was forced to stand for the north again.

The weather was fierce. Though it was midsummer, the temperature never rose above freezing. The wind was strong and cold, and fog was a constant companion. Several times the ships nearly were frozen into the ice fields; in the fog, deadly icebergs came looming up out of nowhere; more than once, Cook noted in his log that they "had received several hard knocks from the larger pieces, which, with all our care, we could not avoid."

The icebergs at 67° S. were awesome: "Very high and rugged, forming at their tops many peaks; whereas the most of those we had seen before were flat at top, and not so high, though many of them were between 200 and 300 feet in height, and between 2 and 3 miles in circuit, with perpendicular cliffs or sides astonishing to behold." A few birds accompanied them, petrels and gray albatrosses, to break the forbidding monotony of their surroundings.

The bad weather and hazardous conditions were wearing down the nerves of Cook's men, if not of the iron-willed Cook himself. He took his crew on a northeastward course, as high as 47°50′ S. This detour proved that there were no southern continents between New Zealand and Cape Horn, despite Dalrymple's optimism.

By the middle of January, Cook's ships were on the poleward side of the sixtieth parallel once more, heading south. Icebergs appeared again, but, strangely, as the ships continued southward, the air grew warmer and the icebergs less numerous. On January 26, 1774, the *Resolution* crossed the Circle for the third time. Cook was in 109°31' W. now, considerably to the east of his first two entries into the frigid zone. There was little ice to be seen here, but those on board were too weary by now to rejoice. George Forster, one of Cook's naturalists, probably spoke for most of the voyagers when he noted darkly in his journal: "A gloomy, melancholy air loured on the brows of our shipmates, and a dreadful silence reigned amongst us. . . . The hour of dinner was hateful to us." Cook, though, grew more cheerful as they drew nearer the South Pole.

On January 30, at four in the morning, it was possible to see unusually bright, snow-white clouds over the horizon to the south. Cook knew that this was caused by the reflection of sunlight against an unbroken field of ice, and so the journey was at an end again. (The sun was shining at four in the morning because at that time of year there is almost no night in high southern latitudes.)

By eight in the morning, they were at the edge of the ice. It extended beyond the reach of sight. "Ninety-seven ice hills were distinctly seen within the field, besides those on the outside, many of them very large, and looking like a ridge of mountains, rising one above another till they were lost in the clouds," Cook wrote. "The outer or northern edge of this immense field was composed of loose or broken ice close packed together, so that it was not possible for anything to enter it."

They had attained a position of 71°10′ S., in 106°54′ W. The South Pole was still many hundreds of miles beyond them, but no human beings had ever been so close to it before. It was time to turn back. "I will not say it was impossible anywhere to get farther to the south," Cook wrote. "But the attempting it would have been a dangerous and rash enterprise, and what I believe no man in my situation would have thought of."

It was Cook's opinion, shared by those on board, that the field of ice extended right to the Pole. He felt that there might well be land ahead, but wholly covered by ice, and hardly worth the risk of attempting. He added this thought:

"I, who had ambition not only to go farther than anyone had been before but as far as it was possible for man to go, was not sorry at this interruption, as it in some measure relieved us, at least shortened the dangers and hardships inseparable from the navigation of the southern polar regions. Since, therefore, we could not proceed one inch farther to the south, no other reason need be assigned for my tacking and standing back to the north."

There was at least one other reason, though. A diet of salted meat and rotten biscuits had left nearly everyone on board desperately weakened and sick, despite all Cook's careful planning. There had been no scurvy, and no deaths, but Cook's men were heartily weary of the polar regions and longed for a warmer clime.

They sailed northward between 100° and 90° W., looking for the supposed continent lying just off South America's western coast. It failed to appear, so they turned westward, hunting for Davis Land, another alleged continent seen by a buccaneer in mid-Pacific a century before. Davis Land turned out to be little Easter Island, the strange land of giant stone heads. The tired voyagers replenished their provisions there, then headed for happy Tahiti, arriving in April and resting for a month.

May saw Cook on the way again, grimly determined to complete the job of exploding Dalrymple's dream. Having shown that no southern continent of any value lay south of Africa or in the eastern Pacific, Cook headed now for the site of Quiros' Austrialia del Espiritu Santo. He showed it to be an unimportant island group, which he named the New Hebrides, and wiped another "continent" off the map. Then he turned southward for one last thrust into the Antarctic before going home.

Beginning at 160° W., Cook sailed eastward at about 55° S., meeting neither ice nor land until he was in the neighborhood of Tierra del Fuego, on December 17. They spent Christmas at anchor off an island there, then headed southward to round Cape Horn. Cook went in search of the Gulf of St. Sebastian, a great bay in the coastline of Dalrymple's imaginary continent, but, of course, only open water could be found. Early in 1775, Cook came upon a fair-sized island, covered with snow, which almost certainly was the one seen by Anthony de la Roché in 1675 and rediscovered at least once since then. Cook explored the island's coast, landed at three places, and took possession in the name of King George III. He called it the Isle of Georgia; its name today is South Georgia.

It was hardly a cheerful place. Perpendicular ice cliffs rimmed it, and, Cook observed, "pieces [of the ice] were continually breaking off, and floating out to sea. . . . A great fall happened while we were in the bay, which made a noise like cannon."

Inland, the island was "not less savage and horrible. The
wild rocks raised their lofty summits till they were lost in the
clouds, and the valleys lay covered with everlasting snow. Not
a tree was to be seen, nor a shrub even big enough to make a
toothpick. The only vegetation we met with was a coarse,
strong-bladed grass growing in tufts, wild burnet, and a plant
like moss, which sprung from the rocks."

There were penguins, too—and thousands of seals. The
shores swarmed with them. Cook noted the fact down, and it
proved to be one of the most important discoveries he had
made on the whole journey.

When he had satisfied himself that South Georgia was truly
an island, and no part of any continent, he moved on, naming
the southeastern tip of the island Cape Disappointment. The
disappointment, he remarked, "did not affect me much; for
to judge of the bulk by the sample it would not be worth the
discovery." After discovering a couple of other small isolated
islands, Cook turned northward again on February 7, and
made a second search for Bouvet Island. He failed to find it—
nor did anyone else, in fact, until 1898. By March, he was in
Capetown, catching up on old newspapers after the three-year
journey. The wanderers were home in England by the end of
July.

Dalrymple had been demolished. The map of the southlands
had been wiped clean of legendary continents, and left blank
for the next explorers. Cook reported himself "well satisfied
no continent was to be found . . . but what must lie so far to
the south as to be wholly inaccessible on account of ice." He
had no yearning to hunt for it, nor did he think anyone else

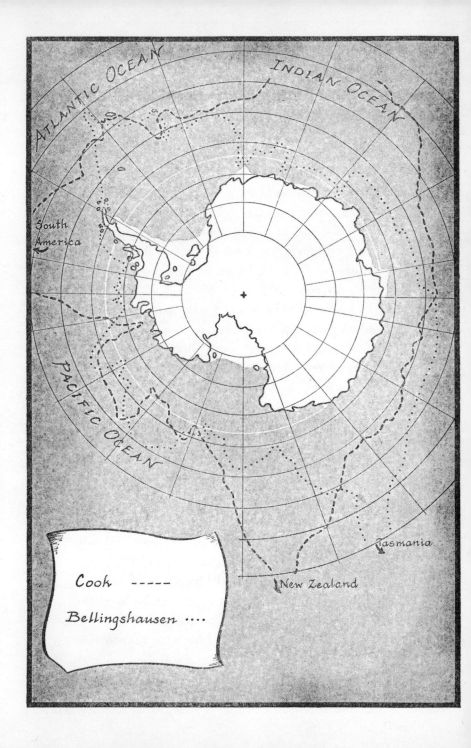

ATLANTIC OCEAN

INDIAN OCEAN

South
America

PACIFIC OCEAN

Tasmania

New Zealand

Cook ‑ ‑ ‑ ‑ ‑

Bellingshausen ‥‥

would take the trouble to do so: "The risk one runs in exploring a coast, in these unknown and icy seas, is so very great,
that I can be bold enough to say that no man will ever venture
farther than I have done; and that the lands which may lie to
the South will never be explored."

He wrote with obvious distaste of "Countries condemned to
everlasting rigidity by Nature, never to yield to the warmth
of the sun, for whose wild and desolate aspect I find no words;
such are the countries we have discovered; what then may
those resemble which lie still further to the south?" If anyone
cared to explore them, Cook said, "I shall not envy him the
fame of his discovery, but I make bold to declare that the
world will derive no benefit from it."

Cook never ventured again into what he called the "inex-
pressibly horrid" Antarctic regions. In 1776, he was at sea
once more, heading northward this time to explore the western
coast of North America and the islands of the North Pacific.
Two years later, on a Hawaiian beach, the greatest explorer
since Magellan met his death, dying as Magellan himself had
died—murdered by the natives of a Pacific isle.

Captain Cook stands as a towering figure in the story of
Antarctic discovery. The first to cross the Circle, the first to
penetrate as far as 70° S., Cook glimpsed the outlying ice
fields surrounding the Antarctic continent, and correctly
guessed the nature of the bleak wasteland that lay beyond. He
had blotted Dalrymple's sunny southern continent from the
maps forever.

Cook was wrong, though, in thinking that no man would
ever attempt the southern voyage again. Nor was he right in

saying that "the world will derive no benefit" from such explorations. The next men to tackle the frozen wastes did so not out of the pure love of exploration that had motivated Cook, but for the sake of private profit. They went to the land of ice in search of fortunes.

3 THE SEALERS FIND A NEW CONTINENT

COOK HAD REPORTED SEEING SEALS ON SOUTH Georgia, and whales in many parts of the southern seas. Whales were big business in the eighteenth century; petroleum was not yet being used for fuel, and there were, of course, no electric lights. The homes of Europe were lit by whale-oil lamps. Whaling ships had fished the northern waters around Europe so thoroughly that whales were scarce in them. News of new whaling territory far to the south was exciting indeed.

Seals, too, suddenly took on pound-and-shilling, dollar-and-cent importance. Not only was seal oil as good for lighting as whale oil, but the pelts of the seals were worth money. That much had been discovered on Cook's third voyage. After the great captain's death, his second-in-command, James King, had continued on to Canton, China. Aboard were seal pelts that the English had picked up by trading with the Indians of

America's Pacific Northwest. The Chinese merchants eagerly snapped up the pelts at high prices, and the Asian fur trade was born.

The English were quick to send whalers to the Antarctic waters, in search of whale oil, seal oil, and those profitable seal pelts. The newly born United States, too, got into the seal-hunting business. Lusty, brawling seamen out of New England headed to the far south in quest of seals.

The early years of the sealing industry are shrouded in impenetrable mystery. An explorer like Cook kept careful records of his journeys, and openly published his journals each time he returned to England. The sealers, though, were in it for the money; they kept information about the richest sealing grounds strictly to themselves. We do know, at least, that an American captain named Edmund Fanning went south in the corvette *Aspasia* on a seal-hunting mission in 1800. Not long after, a Boston ship, *The States,* visited the Falkland Islands, off the coast of Argentina, and slaughtered 13,000 seals. The sealers filled their hold with seal oil, crammed their 13,000 pelts aboard, and sold them in New York for fifty cents apiece, $6,500. The New York buyer then shipped the pelts back around Cape Horn and on to China, where they fetched a price of $5 a pelt, $65,000 in all, from Cantonese merchants!

A new industry had emerged. By 1815 or so, there were some two hundred American and British sealing vessels cruising the cold waters south of Cape Horn.

Sealing was a brutal, cold-blooded operation, and the men who manned the ships were the toughest to go to sea since the days of the Elizabethan buccaneers. Sailing in ice-filled seas, gliding between uncharted rocks hidden by mist and

snow, they made their landings on lonely, barren islands where
thousands of friendly, harmless seals had come to mate. The
seals offered no defense as the sealers went among them, club-
bing them to death. The men worked caked with grease, wading in rivers of blood. It was cruel work, and attracted cruel
men. Since England and the United States had been at war
from 1812 to 1815, meetings at sea between American and
British sealers were hardly friendly.

Island after island was stripped of its seals. One sealing
vessel alone killed 100,000 seals in five years. As the known
islands were depopulated, the sealing men had to search out
new territories. The spokesman for the American sealing industry was Edmund Fanning, of Stonington, Connecticut, who
grew wealthy in the grim trade, discovered several islands in
the South Pacific, and sailed three times around the world. In
1812, Fanning persuaded the President of the United States
to commission an exploring voyage to find new seal islands in
the Southern Hemisphere. Two vessels were provided, but the
journey had to be called off when war broke out with England.

Fanning was sure that other islands, and "extensive land,"
lay beyond South Georgia. The first unquestionable discovery,
though, was made by an Englishman, Captain William Smith.

Smith, who had learned the tricks of navigating in icy
waters while hunting whales off Greenland, was now a merchant captain voyaging from Montevideo to Valparaiso in his
brig *Williams*. In February, 1819, while rounding Cape Horn,
he met with rough head winds, and decided to steer southward
in search of better weather. On the eighteenth, he thought he
saw land through falling snow. The skies cleared the next day,

and he became certain of his discovery. He charted his position as 62°40′ S., 60° W., and continued on to Valparaiso.

He informed the English authorities there of his discovery, but failed to rouse any great interest. It must have been no more than a large iceberg, Smith was told. On his return journey around the Horn in June, he failed to relocate his landfall, and when he arrived in Montevideo he received the same unenthusiastic treatment from the English.

There were some American sealing men in Montevideo, though, who were keenly interested indeed. They thought Smith might well have found new sealing territory, and offered him large sums of money for the exact location. Smith had not officially taken possession of the land in the name of the English king, however, and, as he wrote, he "resisted all offers from the said Americans, determined again to revisit the new-discovered land."

In October, sailing from Valparaiso, Smith found his island again and claimed it, sending his first mate ashore to take formal possession. He gave it the name of New South Britain, but this was later changed to New South Shetland, because the island was in the same longitude as the Shetland Islands off the coast of England. It was a barren, disagreeable place, covered with ice—but along its shores were seals in abundance.

Smith returned triumphantly to Valparaiso. There was a ship of the Royal Navy then in port, the *Andromache*, and Smith told her captain that he had found a new sealing land. The captain, William Shirreff, promptly chartered Smith's boat in the name of the King. Smith was named master and pilot, and Shirreff sent his own master, Edward Bransfield, aboard as commanding officer. Bransfield's orders were to return to New South Shetland, to survey its coasts and harbors, and "to observe, collect, and preserve every object of natural science." In case the brig should be trapped in the ice, she was stocked with twelve months' provisions. On December 20, 1819, Bransfield and Smith sailed southward out of Valparaiso, bound for New South Shetland and the other islands of the South Shetland group.

While this voyage was getting under way, American sealers were as busy as ever in Antarctic waters. Edmund Fanning was still the leading figure of the industry—but now Fanning had a young protégé, Nathaniel Palmer.

Nat Palmer was born in 1799 in the little port of Stonington, Connecticut. His father was a shipbuilder, and young Nat grew up in the shipyard, listening to the tales of the workmen, many of them retired sailors. His eyes widened at their stories of adventure, and he determined to go to sea himself.

He had his chance early. During the War of 1812, a great British fleet blockaded Stonington. In defiance of the blockaders, men of Stonington ran the blockade at night in light sloops, slipping out to run supplies along the American coast from New York to Boston. At the age of fourteen, Nat Palmer shipped aboard one of the blockade runners, learning the ways of the sea at first hand under the most dangerous possible conditions.

Palmer was a swift learner. When the war ended, he stayed in his trade, and by the age of eighteen he was master of a coasting vessel, with a brilliant local reputation as a navigator.

Edmund Fanning, a Stonington man himself, was getting up an expedition to search for new sealing grounds in southern waters. Fanning, the organizer, did not plan to go himself. He had hired a veteran sealing captain, James Sheffield, and put him in command of the brig *Hersilia*, brand-new, "coppered and fitted out in the best manner." In 1819, Fanning asked nineteen-year-old Nat Palmer to sign on as second mate, and Palmer proudly accepted.

The *Hersilia* stopped at the Falkland Islands to pick up fresh meat and vegetables before continuing into more southerly waters. Another ship, the British-owned, British-manned *Espiritu Santo*, arrived at the Falklands a couple of days later, and Young Nat, as he was known, struck up a friendship with the English skipper. The Englishman told Palmer that he was "bound to a place where there were thousands of seals," but, of course, he refused to reveal the location.

Palmer and Sheffield decided to do some searching. They set out after the *Espiritu Santo*, and early in February, 1820, entered a harbor in the South Shetlands. The *Espiritu Santo* was already there, its crew busily salting down seal skins. Her captain hid his dismay well enough, telling Palmer, "There are plenty of seals for all."

When Palmer returned to Connecticut later that year, he was able to tell Fanning that he had pried from the English the whereabouts of valuable new sealing grounds, the South Shetlands. There was talk of sending an American military expedition to the South Shetlands to drive out the British sealers and take exclusive possession, and Secretary of State John Quincy Adams seems to have seriously considered the idea for a while, but no such action was ever taken. As for Palmer, he became a local hero, and when a new sealing expedition was organized, Nat was promoted not merely to first mate but to captain.

The *Hersilia*'s sealing operations had been highly profitable. Now the Stonington sealers organized a full-scale armada that would descend on the South Shetlands and carry off as many seal pelts as possible. There were five ships in all, under the over-all command of Captain Benjamin Pendleton, another experienced sealing man. Nat Palmer was placed in command of the sloop *Hero*. He was not quite twenty-one years old, but he had no difficulty making his authority felt aboard ship. The *Hero*, only 47 feet long and 17 feet wide, had the job of exploring to seek out undiscovered seal beaches, and of acting as a supply ship bringing provisions from the bigger vessels anchored in deep waters to the sealers working on shore.

By October, 1820, the Stonington fleet had reached the Falkland Islands. Palmer led the way southward, sighting the South Shetlands on November 10. While the men of the other ships got to work hunting seals, Palmer in the *Hero* went looking for new beaches, and found an excellent natural harbor on a nearby island. The sea had entered the crater of an extinct volcano there, forming a neat, circular harbor with water several hundred feet deep. It is now known as Deception Island.

The fleet transferred its activities to this harbor. Captain Pendleton looked southward from a high point on the island and thought he saw land. He asked Nat Palmer to have a look.

On November 16, Palmer noted in the log of the *Hero*, "Got under weigh; at ten we were clear from the harbor; stood over for the land." The next day he recorded, "Found the sea filled with immense icebergs. . . . Laid off and on until morning—at 4 A.M. made sail in shore and discovered—a strait—trending SSW and NNE—it was literally filled with ice and the shore inaccessible—we thought it not prudent to venture in ice. . . ."

Palmer withdrew rather than risk his tiny ship in such rough waters. He sailed along the coast of the newly discovered land for a day, and then returned to the Shetlands. Palmer offers no other details of this trip. However, Edmund Fanning, writing thirteen years later, supplies more information. Fanning said that while the *Hero* lay in "Yankee Harbor," on Deception Island, Palmer saw from the top of a mountain on a clear day a range of mountains far to the south. The *Hero* set out, and on November 16 came to "an extensive mountain country, more sterile and more dismal if possible, and more heavily laden with ice and snow than the South Shetlands. There were sea-leopards on its shore but no fur seals. The main part of its coast was ice-bound, although it was midsummer in this hemisphere, and landing consequently difficult."

It is possible to reconstruct Palmer's voyage of November 16, 17, and 18, however, even from this skimpy evidence. What he saw from Deception Island was another island now called Trinity Island. He came to the entrance to what is now known as Orleans Strait, which divides Trinity Island from— the mainland of Antarctica itself.

On this evidence, Nat Palmer is hailed by many American geographers as the discoverer of the world's loneliest continent. Many accounts of Antarctic exploration credit the boyish skipper with the accomplishment. It has become part of the American legend of adventure and boldness.

There is only one thing wrong. The best available evidence shows that another man spied Antarctica first, ten months before Palmer's voyage. It is one of the touchiest points in the whole story of Antarctic discovery, for it seems almost unpatriotic for an American to admit that an Englishman deserves the credit that in the United States has gone to Nat Palmer.

We have to go back to December, 1819. William Smith has discovered the South Shetlands and has reported the fact to Captain Shirreff of H.M.S. *Andromache*, in Valparaiso. Shirreff has chartered Smith's brig, the *Williams*, and has placed his own master, Edward Bransfield, in command.

Bransfield's orders were to visit the newly discovered land. "You will ascertain the natural resources for supporting a colony and maintaining a population," he was told. "If it be already inhabited, [you] will minutely observe the character, habits, dresses and customs of the inhabitants, to whom you will display every friendly disposition."

The voyage south was uneventful. The *Williams* reached the South Shetlands on January 16, 1820, Bransfield going ashore on an island he named King George Island to plant the British flag and take possession. For some days, the small craft explored the islands of the group, meeting no inhabitants other than seals and penguins. The inhabitants were friendly. Hampered by fog, Bransfield was unable to tell whether he was exploring a continuous peninsula or a group of islands, but he thought—rightly—that it was probably the latter.

January 27 saw the *Williams* sailing past Deception Island, where the following November the Yankee sealers would anchor. Bransfield bore sharply to the southwest and entered a region of mist and fog, where treacherous icebergs threatened the ship at every point. But on January 30, the haze suddenly cleared and land could be seen ahead.

The only eyewitness account of this voyage, written by Thomas Bone, a midshipman aboard the *Williams,* was published in November, 1821, in an English magazine called the *Literary Gazette.* Midshipman Bone wrote that at four in the afternoon, a chain of islands appeared. "The whole of these," he said, "formed a prospect the most gloomy that can be imagined, and the only cheer the sight afforded was in the idea that this might be the long-sought Southern Continent, as land was undoubtedly seen in latitude 64°, and trending to the eastward."

A round island was named Tower Island. A stretch of land beyond it was given the name Trinity Land. Since some thirty-one icebergs loomed before the ship, Bransfield did not attempt to go farther south, but instead sailed eastward along the northern coast of Trinity Land, which soon became lost in the fog. A day or two later, the fog cleared and two lofty mountains were sighted. Bransfield's farthest south was 64°30′ S. The *Williams* continued to cruise the coasts of the newly discovered territories until March 21, when the onset of the Antarctic winter forced Bransfield to head northward.

The charts Bransfield made leave no doubt of his accomplishment. About January 30, 1820, the men of the *Williams* were the first to sight the last undiscovered continent of our planet. Bransfield's Trinity Land is the northern tip of a narrow peninsula that juts out of Antarctica like a finger pointing toward Cape Horn. The two high mountains Bransfield saw now bear the names Mount Bransfield and Mount Jacquinot.

So far as the official American view goes, all that Bransfield discovered was the large island off the mainland, known as Trinity Island. It remained for Nat Palmer, the following November, to find the strait separating Trinity Island from the mainland region known as Trinity Land. Thus it was Palmer, not Bransfield, who commanded the first expedition that saw Antarctica proper, as far as the United States is concerned.

Perhaps it is not a very important point. What really matters is that sometime in the year 1820, the Antarctic continent was unquestionably discovered, though not landed upon. Of course, no one yet could know that the jutting finger of the peninsula was only a tiny outlying segment of a much vaster continent.

Nat Palmer had no knowledge of Bransfield's work when he reached the shores of Trinity Land in mid-November. So far as he knew, he was the discoverer, and he returned to the South Shetlands to bring the happy news to his fellow captains. On the way back, Palmer became involved in one of the strangest incidents in the whole history of the polar exploration.

Almost constant fog shrouded the *Hero* as she headed for Yankee Harbor. On a night of thick mist, the sloop was becalmed not far from the newly discovered continent, and Palmer came on deck to stand the watch. He struck one bell to toll the time, and was startled to hear the sound of an answering bell. An hour later, the same thing happened; Palmer tolled two bells, and heard a reply out of the fog!

"I could not credit my ears," Palmer said later. "I thought I was dreaming."

No other ships could have been nearby, Palmer believed. Certainly none of the Stonington fleet would have left the safety of Yankee Harbor to come down here, and no other craft was known to be in Antarctic waters. Yet each hour came the ghostly echo of Palmer's bells from across the water. Finally, in the morning, the fog began to clear. Palmer saw that his little sloop lay between a frigate and a sloop-of-war. When Palmer hoisted the American flag, the strange ships ran up the Russian colors.

What were Russians doing at the bottom of the world?

The Russian frigate sent a boat to the *Hero*, inviting Palmer to go on board. He found that the Russian vessels were two discovery ships sent out by Emperor Alexander of Russia on a voyage round the world. The expedition was under the command of Captain Fabian Gottlieb von Bellingshausen.

There are several versions of the meeting between Palmer and Bellingshausen—unfortunately, none of them by Palmer himself. One report appeared in 1833, in Edmund Fanning's book *Voyages Around the World*. According to Fanning, Palmer went aboard Bellingshausen's ship, the *Vostok*. The commander of the other Russian ship, the *Mirnyi*, served as interpreter.

Bellingshausen asked if Palmer knew anything about the islands just to the north. "Captain P. replied," wrote Fanning, "he was well acquainted with them, and that they were the South Shetlands." He offered to pilot the Russians to Yankee Harbor, where the other four American sealing ships would gladly offer any assistance that was needed.

Bellingshausen thanked Palmer kindly. But, he explained—so said Fanning: "Previous to our being enveloped in the fog, we had sight of those islands, and concluded we had made a discovery, but behold, when the fog lifts, to my great surprise, here is an American vessel apparently in as fine order as if it were but yesterday she had left the United States; not only this, but her master is ready to pilot my vessels into port; we must surrender the palm to you Americans!"

According to another account, set down by one Frank T. Bush in 1844, Palmer then went on to describe his discovery to the south. Bellingshausen "arose much agitated" and begged Nat to fetch his logbook from the *Hero*. Palmer did so, and the Russian commander carefully examined Palmer's records, and after a while exclaimed:

"What do I see and what do I hear from a boy in his teens: that he is commander of a tiny boat the size of a launch of my frigate, has pushed his way towards the Pole through storm and ice and sought the point I in command of one of the best appointed fleets at the disposal of my august master have for three long, weary, anxious years, searched day and night for."

Putting his hand fondly on the youthful skipper's head, the downcast Russian continued, "What shall I say to my master? What will he think of me? But be that as it may, my grief is your joy. Wear your laurels. With my sincere prayers for your welfare, I name the land you discovered in honor of yourself, noble boy, Palmer's Land."

What we have here is a good example of how a story can get distorted and altered through telling and retelling. In order to find out what really happened when Russian explorers met American sealers at the bottom of the world early in 1821, we have to turn to the account of Fabian von Bellingshausen himself.

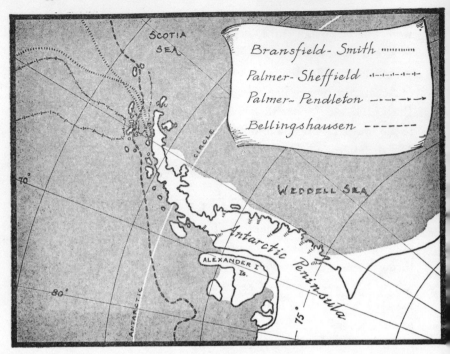

Alexander I, Czar of Russia early in the nineteenth century, had become a passionate seeker after knowledge for its own sake. And Russia, a backward and undeveloped country, was trying to become an important maritime power. Russia needed harbors, but all the good harbors of the known world were already controlled by other nations. By 1819, it seemed like a worthy idea to send out a Russian expedition of discovery, with a double purpose: "to help in extending the fields of knowledge," and to investigate "the possibilities of establishing future sea-communications or places for the repair of ships."

Two ships were to go to the far north, and two to the far

south. Command of the Antarctic expedition was entrusted to a celebrated Russian captain named Rashmanoff, but when he begged off on a plea of ill health, Fabian von Bellingshausen was chosen.

There was not much time to get organized. Czar Alexander had given his imperial command on March 25, 1819, but his Minister for Naval Affairs, the Marquis de Traversey, did not find out there was supposed to be an expedition until the middle of the following month. The expedition was scheduled to sail in July. On May 5, Bellingshausen was notified he was to take command.

He was forty-one years old, and had had a distinguished naval career. Dignified and aristocratic, he was a capable leader, a skilled seaman, and a wise and moderate person. Rushing halfway across Russia, Bellingshausen finally reached the gathering expedition on June 3, and his first act was to order the lofty masts of his 130-foot corvette *Vostok* (East) cut down, to make the ship more maneuverable in rough weather. Hastily, he assembled a crew, taking with him an astronomer and an artist. Two German naturalists were supposed to join the expedition at Copenhagen, but they backed out at the last moment.

Bellingshausen suggested that two Russian scientists be invited to replace them. But no qualified Russians were available. He sailed at the end of July without any naturalists, and reached London on August 9. The Russians spent a month there, purchasing charts and instruments, and vainly trying to persuade English naturalists to join the expedition. Perhaps made wary by Cook's grim account of the southern regions a generation before, England's scientists stayed back from the opportunity to a man. Regretfully, Bellingshausen headed south without any naturalists, though he knew that their absence would weaken the value of his expedition.

At Rio de Janeiro, in September, he encountered the Russian Arctic expedition, then heading northward. Bellingshausen continued down the South Atlantic, reaching South Georgia two days after Christmas, and meeting two British sealing vessels there. After visiting and charting some minor islands in the vicinity, the *Vostok* and *Mirnyi* sailed south again, and on January 27, 1820, became the first ships to cross the Antarctic Circle since Cook's second voyage. (Bransfield, who at the same moment was nearing Trinity Land well to the west, had not had to cross the Circle to find the peninsula.)

A day later, the two ships were in latitude 69°21' S. and longitude 2°14' W., and—though they did not know it—the Russians were only twenty miles from the coast of Antarctica. But their way was blocked by "a solid stretch of ice running from east through south and west," and the path ahead was wrapped deep in fog. If the Russians had chanced it, they would have been the first explorers—by forty-eight hours—to lay eyes on the Antarctic mainland. Instead, they turned away.

As Bellingshausen cruised through the icy waters, he carried out many scientific experiments even without his naturalists. He tested a new deep-sea water bottle containing a thermometer, and showed that the water at 200 fathoms was colder and saltier than at the surface; he had pieces chipped off icebergs for study; and, as the nights grew colder, he made observations on the formation of ice in salt and fresh water.

On February 17 and 18, Bellingshausen was again close to the mainland, and this time the weather was clear. He saw ice cliffs descending to the water's edge, and toward the interior, the ice "sloped upwards towards the south to a distance so far that its end was out of sight even from the masthead." On the eighteenth, he saw ice-covered mountains far off. Too cautious, though, he refused to conclude that he was looking at a continent. The mountains might merely be giant icebergs, he felt.

For more than a month afterward, Bellingshausen sailed eastward through Antarctic waters, following the track of Cook, but remaining well to the south of his route. No one had ever been in these seas before, and Bellingshausen was the first to skirt the Antarctic ice pack in latitudes of 60° to 63° S., between 41° and 87° E. Between January and March, the two Russian ships covered one-eighth of the circumference of the earth, seeing nothing but occasional drifting ice. Late in March, they headed for Australia as the fierce winter weather descended.

Six months later, after a cruise of the South Pacific that charted seventeen new islands, Bellingshausen was ready to try the Antarctic again. On September 21, he put in at Sydney, Australia, where the Russian Minister had a dispatch for him, informing him of Smith's discovery of the South Shetlands the year before. Early in November, 1820, after their ships had been overhauled, the Russians were at sea again and on December 9 they crossed the sixtieth parallel and entered unknown seas.

For two months and three days, the expedition remained south of 60° S., covering 145 degrees of longitude, or nearly half of the earth's circumference, and remaining within sight of the Antarctic ice pack all the while. Not even Cook had shown such endurance. Bellingshausen crossed the Antarctic Circle again and again, being driven back repeatedly by icebergs as he tried to get beyond 69° S. On January 1, 1821, the Russians reached their farthest south—69°52′ S., in 92° 10′ W.

Three weeks later they discovered land, the most southerly land yet discovered. "A black patch through the haze" was spied, and then, Bellingshausen wrote, "The sun coming out from behind the clouds lit up the place and to our satisfaction we were able to assure ourselves that what we saw was land covered with snow. Only some rocks and cliffs, where the snow could not hold, showed up black. Words cannot describe the delight which appeared on all our faces at the cry of 'Land! Land!' Our joy was not surprising, after our long monotonous voyage, amidst unceasing dangers from ice, snow, rain, sleet, and fog. We had no reason to suppose that we should find land in this quarter, because we had not encountered the usual signs of it, such as floating seaweed and penguins."

They soon realized that they had discovered an island, nine miles long and four miles wide, that rose some 4,000 feet above the surface of the sea. They gave it the name of Peter I Island, after the Russian Czar who had first brought their land out of its medieval isolation. Bellingshausen thus became the first captain to sight land within the Antarctic Circle. Peter I Island, at latitude 69° S., longitude 90° W., lay far southwest of the region where Bransfield and then Palmer had explored.

Ice-filled sea lay all about. The Russian explorers made their way southeasterly, and on January 29 sighted more land, extensive and mountainous. So rough was the ice pack that the ships could not come within forty miles of the shore, but in the unusually clear weather they had a good view of the land. Bellingshausen named it Alexander I Land, after the reigning Czar, and wrote: "I call this discovery 'land' because its southern extent disappeared beyond the range of our vision. The shore was covered with snow, but there was no snow on the slope of the mountain and on the steep cliffs." Later exploration, however, has shown what Bellingshausen discovered was actually a large island, cut off from the true Antarctic mainland by a narrow, ice-covered sound some two hundred miles in length. His position at the time of discovery was about 69° S., 73° W.

The Russians had now very nearly circumnavigated the entire Antarctic continent. All that remained to close the circle was to continue eastward for a look at the newly discovered South Shetlands.

Bellingshausen explored this group thoroughly, giving many of the islands Russian names. But Bransfield had already charted and named the islands, and his names have remained in use. It was while making this exploration that Bellingshausen had his celebrated meeting with Nat Palmer.

Bellingshausen's account of the meeting is the only eyewitness report that was written. Unfortunately, Bellingshausen's report remained untranslated from the Russian until 1945. Now that it is available, we can see that the standard account of the meeting—by Edmund Fanning—was incorrect in many respects. (We have to assume that Bellingshausen, a sober and reliable keeper of records, is more to be trusted than Fanning, who in any case got his information secondhand.)

Fanning had written that the meeting took place "on the

Hero's return passage to Yankee Harbor," which would have put it late in November, 1820. Bellingshausen's log dates the meeting at February 5, 1821, so it must actually have occurred while Palmer was making a second voyage to the mainland. On that day, Bellingshausen sighted a "high island, with steep cliffs." He gave it the name of Teille Island, after a Russian military hero, but it already bore a name. It was Deception Island, and the Yankee sealers lay at anchor there. Continuing past, the Russians entered the strait separating Deception Island from its neighbors in the Shetlands group, and it was there that they encountered Nat Palmer and the *Hero*.

The ships hailed each other and Palmer went aboard the *Vostok*. Fanning says that Bellingshausen questioned the American about the South Shetlands, but obviously there was no need for him to do so. He knew all about William Smith's discovery, and he had just spent some weeks charting those islands. Instead, he asked about the sealing ships. The Stonington fleet had evidently been joined by other British and American ships, for, Bellingshausen says: "There were as many as eighteen vessels about at various points, and not infrequently differences arose amongst the sealers, but so far it had not yet come to a fight. Mr. Palmer told me that the above-mentioned Captain Smith, the discoverer of New Shetland, was on the brig *Williams* and that he had succeeded in killing as many as 60,000 seals, whilst the whole fleet of sealers had killed 80,000."

The Russian captain and the American captain discussed the sealing industry for a while, and the difficulties of navigation in the surrounding waters. Then, Bellingshausen says simply, "Mr. Palmer soon returned to his ship, and we proceeded along the shore."

That is all. No mention of Bellingshausen's grief or surprise, no mention of the dubbing of the peninsula Palmer's Land. The more dramatic parts of the story seem to have been invented by Fanning. It is a pity, in a way.

So ends this tale of three skippers. Bellingshausen, his epic journey done, returned to Russia in July, 1821, after the most important voyage of exploration since Cook's. He had discovered two islands in the west, small Peter I Island and large, mountainous Alexander I, and he had carefully charted the small islands of South Georgia, the South Shetlands, and another outlying group, the South Sandwich Islands. For over a century—until Alexander I Land was proved to be an island, in 1940—Russia claimed that Bellingshausen was the true discoverer of Antarctica, for he had sighted what he thought was mainland there. (The Russians conveniently overlooked Bransfield and Palmer, who had unquestionably seen the mainland the year before.) In the east, Bellingshausen had been the first to see the continental coast of Antarctica, though he had not realized it.

Bellingshausen never made another such expedition, but his later naval career was a successful one, and in 1831 he attained the rank of admiral. He died in 1852, and his name is perpetuated by the Bellingshausen Sea, the body of water that touches the shores of Alexander I Island.

As for Nat Palmer, he returned to Stonington in May, 1821, three months after his meeting with Bellingshausen. Within five months, a Connecticut map maker had published a chart showing the South Shetlands with "Palmer's Land" south of

them. This map, prepared by William Woodbridge, was the
first ever published that showed any part of the Antarctic
continent.

In 1822, Palmer returned to the South Shetlands as master of
another sealer, the *James Monroe*. He explored his peninsula
once again, as far as 66° S., and, in company with a British
sealing captain named George Powell, who was almost as
youthful as Palmer himself, discovered an island group east
of the Shetlands. Palmer, who had his share of immortality in
Palmer Land, named the new islands Powell's Group. A few
years later, however, other explorers unjustly renamed them
the South Orkneys, and so they are known today. As we will
see, Palmer Land underwent an equally unfair change of name
later on.

Between 1822 and 1830, Palmer made several other exploring cruises in southern waters, never again revisiting
Palmer Land. When he was in his thirties, he turned to a less
hazardous trade, the design of ships. He won new fame as a
designer of clipper ships, those fast ocean-going sailing vessels that were so important to world trade in the middle of the
nineteenth century. In 1844, a Palmer-designed clipper, the
Houqua, set a world record by sailing from New York to
Hong Kong in eighty-four days, with Captain Nat in command. The man who had been hailed inaccurately as "the
discoverer of Antarctica" now added a better-earned title,
"father of the American clipper ship." He died in 1877, five
months older than the nineteenth century, and was buried in
his beloved Stonington.

What of Bransfield, the real discoverer of Antarctica? His
career is shadowy. He had never intended to discover any

continents. It was just a matter of luck that he had been in Valparaiso, master of the *Andromache*, when William Smith arrived with his tale of new-found land to the south. Obeying his captain's orders, Bransfield took the *Williams* south, found and explored an outlying projection of Antarctica, and returned to his naval duties. Then he slipped back into the obscurity from which he had come—just another capable officer of His Majesty's Navy, who had done nothing more than discover an unknown continent.

4 WEDDELL SAILS SOUTH

THERE WAS PLENTY OF ACTIVITY IN THE WATERS OFF the newly discovered continent in the next few years—most of it carried on by American and British sailors in search of seals. The sealing men went about their trade in a way that was not so much simple as simple-minded. They would anchor at a seal-inhabited island and slaughter every seal in sight. When the island had been totally depopulated, they would look for new grounds.

If they had been content to harvest their seals more carefully, they would not have been put to so much trouble finding new seal beaches. But what was the good of simply thinning out a flock, when a few weeks later another ship might come along and clean out every remaining seal? The sealers grabbed what they could, then went looking for more—and, because they did, new discoveries followed.

One of the sealers, Captain John Davis of New Haven, Connecticut, may have been the first man ever to set foot on the Antarctic continent. We cannot be sure, because of the vague way the sealing men kept their logs. Davis, exploring the South Shetlands for new sealing beaches, headed south-eastward from Deception Island in February, 1822. In latitude 64°01′ S., land became visible, and Davis' ship anchored in a large bay. The land beyond, Davis wrote, was "high and covered entirely with snow." A party of sealers went ashore in a small boat, found no seals, and returned. A snowstorm blew up and forced Davis to head out to open water, but he had seen enough to conclude, "I think this Southern Land to be a Continent."

From Davis' imprecise description, it seems likely that the place he came ashore was Hughes Bay, on the western side of Palmer Land. In any case, Davis was the first man to use the word "continent" in connection with the newly discovered land. He could be guessing, though, since no one had yet seen enough of Antarctica to tell how far the large land mass extended.

While Davis and other sealers were roving the waters down the western side of Palmer Land, some going nearly as far as the Bellingshausen Sea, another skipper was making a unique voyage to the east. He was James Weddell, a Scot who captained the sealing ship *Jane*.

Like Cook, Weddell came from the working classes. Orphaned when a boy, he was apprenticed aboard a coal-carrying ship, and then served for a while on a merchant ship that traded in the West Indies. In 1808, angered by some action of his captain, Weddell knocked the man down, and found himself handed over to the Royal Navy to learn discipline.

He learned. He was quickly promoted to midshipman and then to master, and his commanding officer called him "one of the most efficient and trustworthy officers I have met with in the course of my professional life." In 1816, after the war with the United States, the British cut their navy down, and Weddell was allowed to return to the merchant service. When news came in 1819 of the discovery of the South Shetlands, he signed on in command of the brig *Jane*.

Weddell was the first British captain after Smith himself to reach the South Shetlands. He spent the season of 1820–21 there, charting and exploring, finding new islands and helping to remove from the charts a mythical group, the Aurora Islands, which a Spanish ship had claimed to sight in 1762. (Weddell proved that the Spaniards had seen icebergs aground on an outcropping of rocks.)

On this voyage, one of Weddell's men had the good fortune to meet a mermaid. The strange being, Weddell was informed, "had a human face of reddish hue and long green hair," its body being shaped like that of a seal below the waist. Mermaid and sailor stared at each other for two full minutes, the mermaid making a "musical noise," and then it "disappeared in an instant." Some further looking revealed that the imaginative sailor had met a friendly, noisy seal of a kind never before seen. Weddell was able to capture a specimen and bring its skin home for study, and the species is known as the Weddell seal to this day.

Weddell returned to the sealing grounds in 1821–22, and and again in 1822–23. This time, he was joined by another small ship, the *Beaufoy*, commanded by an Irishman named Matthew Brisbane. The *Jane* carried twenty-two men, the *Beaufoy* thirteen, as they set out on what would prove to be a history-making voyage.

In January, 1823, they visited and charted the islands known as Powell's Group, now the South Orkneys. Then they sailed southward, keeping close together. Floating ice made the progress "very teasing and unprofitable." They got as far as 64°58′ S. without finding new sealing islands. Weddell offered a reward to the man who first sighted land, and there were many false alarms. The cry of "Land!" went up when iceberg or fog banks were seen, and once even a floating dead whale, "very much inflated," led to a claim for the reward.

On February 4, after some fruitless tacking back and forth, Weddell and Brisbane decided simply to sail due south until they encountered land or until massed ice packs drove them back. Six days later another false alarm was sounded, and "land" turned out to be a huge iceberg containing so much dark soil that it looked like a rock in the distance. It was a good sign, at least, that land lay somewhere ahead. The sailors, who would receive no pay if they came home without a cargo of seal pelts, grumbled at the disappointment. Some talked of wanting to go back to the more certain sealing grounds to the north. Weddell kept the course southerly.

Though only a sealing captain, not an explorer like Cook or Bellingshausen, Weddell "was well aware that the making of scientific observations in this unfrequented part of the globe was a very desirable object." And so he lamented "my not being well supplied with the instruments with which ships fitted out for discovery are generally provided." He did have a pair of thermometers, which he used to make regular temperature observations. But an accident broke both thermometers on February 16, when Weddell was south of the seventieth parallel, and after that no records could be made.

Humpback and finback whales kept the two little vessels company. The summer weather was beautiful, there was no ice to be seen, and the sea was "literally covered with birds of the blue petrel kind." Weddell had entered a vast ice-free sea to the east of Palmer Land and, a little to his surprise, he found himself getting into higher latitudes than had ever been achieved before. Cook had come no closer to the Pole than 71°10′ S. By the eighteenth, Weddell was at 73° S., with no obstacles ahead.

"Nothing like land was to be seen," Weddell wrote on February 20. "Three ice-islands were in sight from the deck, and one other from the mast-head. On one we perceived a great number of penguins roosted. Our latitude at this time . . . was 74°15′ [S.], and longitude 34°16′45″ [W.]" Although the sea ahead lay open, a strong wind from the south prevented further progress. The season was late, and a thousand miles of ice-strewn sea had to be retraced. Provisions were running low. Weddell feared that if he kept going south, he would be caught by winter and frozen into the pack, and no one had ever spent a winter in the Antarctic. To be trapped by the ice meant certain death. "I could not determine otherwise than to take advantage of this favorable wind for returning," Weddell wrote.

A little ceremony was held. "Our colors were hoisted, and a gun was fired, and both crews gave three cheers." Then the two ships turned back, having gone 214 nautical miles closer than Cook to the South Pole. It would be many years before anyone matched Weddell's accomplishment.

In one way, no one has ever done the same thing again. The sea that Weddell found so easy to enter, and which now bears his name, has never again been so approachable. Everyone who has followed Weddell's course has met with a solid shelf of ice covering the water to a distance hundreds of miles north of Weddell's halting point. This has tended to cast some doubt on Weddell's voyage. But he was too truthful, too reliable a man to have invented the episode. The year 1823 must have been an unusually mild one in the Weddell Sea, with little ice to bar the lucky voyagers.

Lucky, that is, so far as exploration went. But they had found no land and no seals. Weddell and Brisbane had a hard journey northward, getting badly battered by the pack ice that was forming as winter approached. They spent the rest of 1823 sealing in the South Shetlands and the islands of Tierra del Fuego, and returned to England in May, 1824. Weddell published an account of his trip, called *A Voyage Towards the South Pole*, in 1825, and it became so popular that a second edition was needed.

Not much is known of Weddell's career after his one great voyage. He may have made another sealing trip between 1831 and 1833, and he died in London in 1834, at the age of forty-seven. His daring plunge southward will always remain one of man's boldest ventures into the unknown.

Other sealers followed the pioneers, and by 1830 the Antarctic seas were positively crowded. Many of the British ships belonged to the firm of Enderby Brothers, the largest of the

English whaling companies. The Enderbys were as interested
in geographical progress as they were in profits, and they instructed their captains to make scientific observations in the
course of their voyages.

The best known of the Enderby skippers is John Biscoe,
like Weddell a retired Royal Navy master, who joined Cook
and Bellingshausen on the small roster of men who had circumnavigated Antarctica. Biscoe left England in July, 1830,
with the schooner *Tula,* accompanied by the little cutter, the
Lively. They crossed the Antarctic Circle on January 22,
1831, entering eastern waters that had already been visited by
Bellingshausen a decade before. Biscoe had no way of knowing this, since Bellingshausen's journal had not yet been published, even in Russia.

The edge of the pack must have retreated in those ten years.
Biscoe was able to sail well south of the Russian's course. In
February, "an appearance of land" was sighted—the ice
cliffs of the distant continent—but it was impossible to approach. As the two ships drew near, they became trapped in
a bay eight miles in diameter, ringed with deadly teeth of
floating ice, and it took a week to wriggle out again.

A month later, land appeared again, and Biscoe saw the
dark fangs of mountains rising above the ice. The *Tula* and
Lively edged through the pack and, as they neared shore, they
were greeted by a sudden display of the Aurora Australis, "the
Southern Lights." "Nearly the whole night," Biscoe wrote,
"the Aurora Australis showed the most brilliant appearance,
at times rolling itself over our heads in beautiful columns,
then as suddenly forming itself as the unrolled fringe of a

curtain, and again suddenly shooting to the form of a serpent, and at times appearing not many yards above us."

The lovely sight abruptly vanished and the region was swept by a suddenly rising gale. Biscoe's ships were driven a hundred miles out to sea by icy winds. When the storm lifted, Biscoe, aboard the badly battered *Tula*, was unable to find the *Lively*. She had vanished from sight.

Gamely, Biscoe headed coastward again for a second look at shore. He named the stretch of land ahead Enderby Land, after his employers. It lay in 66° S., 47° E., and was the first continental stretch of Antarctica to be discovered other than Palmer Land. With winter already arriving, Biscoe did not linger. The land was inaccessible, heavy gales blew constantly, and many of his men were sick. "The vessel," he wrote, "is very uncomfortable in bad weather, and ships a great deal of water, and is now on her outside, both hull and ropes, where the spray can reach, one mass of ice."

The *Tula* headed for Tasmania. By April, only three men aboard could work; the rest were down with scurvy. The ship reached the port of Hobart in May. There, Biscoe learned that the *Lively* had survived the storm, and had reached port safely near Melbourne, Australia—but all on board except the captain, one seaman, and a cabin boy had died of scurvy during the terrible voyage.

After meeting James Weddell in Hobart and exchanging sea stories with him, Biscoe replenished his crews and returned to the Antarctic in October, 1831. Biscoe spent three months getting a cargo of seal oil, then set out westward down Palmer Land, unknowingly following Bellingshausen's track once again. On February 14, 1832, Biscoe sighted land in 67°

S., 72° W., and named it Adelaide Island, after England's queen. "It has a most imposing and beautiful appearance, having one very high peak running up into the clouds," he wrote. Most of the island was "buried in a field of snow and ice of the most dazzling brilliance." He claimed that Adelaide Island was "the farthest known land to the southward," but, of course, he did not know of Bellingshausen's Alexander I Land farther on.

Fog drove Biscoe back and he turned northward after a glimpse of the mountains of Alexander I Land. On February 17 and 18, he sailed past a group of small islands off Palmer Land, now called the Biscoe Islands. Behind them he could see the lofty, snow-covered mountains of the mainland. On February 21 he made a landing on what he thought was the mainland itself, though it was really Anvers Island, off the central stretch of Palmer Land.

Biscoe proceeded to give this stretch of coast the name of Graham Land, after Sir James R. G. Graham, then Britain's First Lord of the Admiralty. Mysteriously, the entire peninsula was soon being called Graham Land by the British, thus ignoring two earlier names that it already had. Bransfield, the real discoverer of the mainland, had called the northern part of the peninsula Trinity Land. After Palmer's visit ten months later, the same area appeared on American maps as Palmer's Land or Palmer Land. Now the name of Graham, an unpopular British politician who had nothing to do with Antarctic discovery, was allowed to eclipse the two earlier names.

The confusion continued to exist for more than a hundred years. The United States, insisting that Palmer was the first to sight the mainland, used the name Palmer Peninsula. Great

Britain clung to Graham Land as the name, and so it appeared on all British maps, in all British books on Antarctica, and even on a set of postage stamps issued for use in a post office on the peninsula. The British did give Palmer some credit, retaining the name of Palmer Archipelago for the islands off the western shore of the peninsula.

Palmer Land, Palmer Peninsula, and Graham Land were therefore all the same place. Early in 1964, however, the United States and the English-speaking nations active in Antarctica—Great Britain, Australia, and New Zealand—agreed on a compromise. The peninsula first seen by Bransfield, visited soon after by Palmer, and more thoroughly explored a decade later by John Biscoe, would be known as the Antarctic Peninsula. The northern part of the peninsula would retain the old name of Graham Land, and the southern part that of Palmer Land, but the peninsula as a whole would bear the new official designation. (This did not completely settle the problem, though. Chile and Argentina, which both have territorial claims there, have given the peninsula names honoring their national heroes: respectively, O'Higgins Land and San Martin Land. But at least the English-speaking nations are now in agreement on the peninsula's official name.)

Biscoe returned to London in January, 1833. Though he had covered thousands of miles in Antarctic waters, he came home with relatively little in the way of seal oil or furs, and Enderby Brothers took a heavy loss on the voyage. But Biscoe's discoveries were honored by a gold medal from the Royal Geographical Society, and the Enderbys, encouraged by his achievements, planned further voyages of Antarctic exploration.

At least one of the later Enderby skippers deserves mention here. In 1838, John Balleny sailed southward from New Zealand and discovered, 450 miles off the Antarctic coast, the islands that bear his name. He also was the first to see the section of the Antarctic coastline called Sabrina Land, named for Balleny's ship *Sabrina*. On this voyage, Balleny spied an iceberg in which was embedded a block of dark stone four yards high and two yards wide. Its presence in the sea could be explained only by saying that it must have broken off from land, and so Balleny was the first to show that there was definitely land, and not simply drifting ice, within the Antarctic Circle south of New Zealand.

A continent was taking shape. The sealers, nibbling at the fringes of Antarctica, had discovered a long stretch of land south of Cape Horn—the Antarctic Peninsula—and two strips of seeming coastline on the other side of the world—Enderby Land and Sabrina Land. Were they linked? What lay between these outlying regions?

The day of the sealers was almost over. Now, once again, there came missions of pure exploration to the bottom of the world, and Antarctica grudgingly yielded a few more of her secrets.

5 TO THE MAGNETIC POLE

A NEW AGE OF SCIENCE WAS DAWNING. SINCE THE downfall of Napoleon in 1815, Europe had been at peace, and mankind had a rare interlude of tranquility in which to think about the mysteries of the world.

One of those mysteries was the earth's magnetic field. It had long been known that some magnetic force drew the needle of a compass toward the ends of the earth. The compass needle, though, did not point exactly toward the geographical poles. It was attracted, not due north or south, but to the so-called magnetic poles, which were at a fair distance from the true geographical poles. It also appeared that the magnetic poles were not fixed, but wandered through various positions from time to time.

The great German scientist Alexander von Humboldt, himself a celebrated explorer, led the campaign for expeditions that would map the earth's magnetic field for the first time. He talked the governments of the world into setting up a row of magnetic observation stations that stretched from Europe to China and across into North America. Another German, Johann Karl Friedrich Gauss, showed mathematically that the earth's magnetic field followed a specific north-south pattern. In 1831, a British expedition led by an officer named James Clark Ross had reached the North Magnetic Pole in the frozen wastes of the Arctic. Now Gauss was able to predict through his equations that the South Magnetic Pole was located in the Antarctic, at about 66° S. and 146° E. By 1835, the Royal Geographical Society and other British learned groups were calling for a government-sponsored expedition to discover the actual location of the South Magnetic Pole.

Within a few years, not one but three such expeditions were in the field. Britain sent James Clark Ross, the discoverer of the North Magnetic Pole, to look for its Antarctic counterpart. France commissioned the explorer Dumont d'Urville to do the same. And the United States of America made its first venture in large-scale exploration when it dispatched a naval squadron under Lieutenant Charles Wilkes to investigate the Antarctic region.

The French were the first to get under way. While the governments of Great Britain and the United States wrangled about the minor details of their respective expeditions, Dumont d'Urville took to the sea, in September, 1837.

Jules Sebastien Cesar Dumont d'Urville was one of the most interesting men who ever headed an Antarctic expedition. From childhood, he was studious and scholarly, fascinated by many branches of science. Though he chose the navy for his career, he was a student of linguistics, the science of language, and of ethnology, the science of human culture. In 1820, while serving with the fleet in the eastern Mediterranean, D'Urville visited the island of Melos and was taken to see an old armless statute that had recently been unearthed. Captivated by its beauty, he wrote home insistently requesting funds to ship it to Paris, and so it is because of D'Urville that the Venus de Milo can be seen at the Louvre today.

Returning to Paris in 1821, D'Urville helped to organize the Paris Geographical Society, and urged France to send out a round-the-world exploration party. From 1822 to 1825, and again from 1826 to 1829, D'Urville was at sea, carrying out important investigations including a detailed study of the culture of the people of the South Pacific islands.

Political upheavals in France between 1830 and 1835 left D'Urville temporarily out of favor. He spent the time planning an elaborate new journey of discovery to the South Pacific, and eventually won government support for the idea. By this time, though, British agitation for an expedition to the South Magnetic Pole had reached the ears of France's King Louis Philippe. The King, seeing that D'Urville had an expedition ready to go, decided to steal a march on the British. He tacked on to D'Urville's route a detour by way of the Antarctic.

D'Urville, whose real interest lay in studying the island peoples of the Pacific, was anything but enthusiastic about making a side trip to those icy, lifeless waters. But he bowed to the royal command, since he had no choice, and told the Paris Geographical Society rather glumly, "If the enterprise is bold and perhaps impracticable for certain spirits, it is at least honorable to attempt it, and whatever be the result it must at least give occasion for interesting observations."

He was given two ships, the *Astrolabe* and the *Zelee*. Since the expedition planned to spend most of its time sailing tropical waters, no attempt was made to fit the ships out against the rigors of an Antarctic voyage. They had wide ports intended to house guns, and in any high sea, icy water would cascade into the holds. D'Urville himself was in poor health, so the expedition did not have a very promising beginning.

The first task was to enter the Weddell Sea and try to get south of Weddell's mark of 74°15′ S. The ships had only reached 63°39′ S., though, when the ice pack blocked their way. Annoyed, D'Urville spent two months skirting the edge of the ice, and finally decided that Weddell had simply invented the whole story of his voyage. Thoroughly disgusted, D'Urville retreated to the South Shetlands and spent the Antarctic summer exploring the by-now-well-explored Antarctic Peninsula.

He charted the area carefully, naming a mountain after Bransfield and giving the whole peninsula its fourth name in less than twenty years, Louis Philippe Land. He also discovered a large island at the extreme northwest tip of the peninsula, naming it Joinville Island. (It is now known to be two islands in reality, and they are called Joinville Island and D'Urville Island.)

On March 5, D'Urville left Antarctic waters without much regret and spent the rest of 1838 as well as the following year cruising the South Pacific. Then, perhaps feeling guilty about the minor accomplishments of his Antarctic work, he turned southward again at the end of 1839 for a second try.

Abandoning the Weddell Sea idea, D'Urville went in search of the South Magnetic Pole from the other side of Antarctica —the region south of 60° S., between 120° and 160° E. No one had explored here before, so far as D'Urville knew—though actually Balleny had been there in 1839.

On January 19, D'Urville sighted land: a vertical cliff of ice towering hundreds of feet, broken in places by deep inlets where the ice had fallen into the sea to drift off as icebergs. D'Urville gave it the name of Adelie Land, after his wife, and sent a boat toward shore to take possession. It was impossible to make a landing, but the French sailors reached an island in the ice-filled waters just off shore. There, while squawking penguins protested the invasion, the French flag was unfurled and D'Urville claimed Adelie Land for France. "Our enthusiasm and joy," he wrote, "were such that it seemed to us that we had just added a province to French territory, by this wholly pacific conquest. . . . We regarded ourselves, therefore, at once as being on French soil."

D'Urville collected a few rock samples for scientific study, naming the little island Point Géologie. Then the French expedition moved on. They knew that the South Magnetic Pole lay to the east, and that they could not be far from it. The ships' compasses were spinning wildly, indicating that they were near the Magnetic Pole, while the "dip needle," an instrument that showed the direction of magnetic force more accurately than an ordinary compass, confirmed the fact.

On January 29, 1840, while continuing eastward, D'Urville became involved in one of those strange Antarctic meetings that seem to defy all probability. The American expedition under Wilkes had reached the Antarctic by this time, so there were other ships sailing those waters. But the Antarctic continent has a coastline sixteen thousand miles long. What were the odds against ships of the two expeditions meeting?

It happened. The *Astrolabe* and *Zelee* were about 65° S. and 135° E., shrouded in fog. Suddenly there appeared a fast-moving man-of-war flying the Stars and Stripes. It was the *Porpoise,* one of Wilkes' ships. A curious misunderstanding occurred. The American ship, under full sail, was apparently going to be blown past the French vessels without a chance for a meeting. To keep up with the *Porpoise,* D'Urville ordered the sails of his ships to be raised. The American commander, Lieutenant Ringgold, interpreted this to mean that the French wanted to keep their explorations a secret and were going to flee. So he changed course quickly and soon vanished in the fog, without having halted to exchange a few words as was customary when explorers met at sea.

Both sides were annoyed. Ringgold, as a matter of fact, had thought the ships belonged to the British expedition under James Clark Ross. He was, he said, "preparing to cheer the discoverer of the North Magnetic Pole," when the two ships hoisted the French flag, made sail, and rudely began to slip away "without exchanging the usual and customary compliments incidental to naval life." Wilkes himself, when he heard of the incident, was surprised at the "cold repulse." D'Urville, though, declared afterward, "We had no object in keeping secret the results of our operations." The days when navigators had to hide their discoveries from rival nations were past, he said.

After the misunderstanding, D'Urville abandoned his journey toward the South Magnetic Pole. An icy coast blocked the advance. There was no way to land and trek toward the Pole. The French turned back, having charted a previously unknown stretch of coast with great accuracy, and by November, 1840, they arrived in their native land after an absence of more than three years.

There was one other odd conflict with the Wilkes expedition. Wilkes had proudly announced that he had discovered land on January 19, 1840. He claimed to be the first to have sighted this stretch of Antarctica. But then D'Urville's report appeared, with the claim that he, too, had sighted the same region the day before! A matter of national pride was at stake, trivial, perhaps, but very important to the commanders involved.

It turned out that Wilkes had been first after all. D'Urville, in his voyage, had crossed the 180th meridian, the International Date Line, but had failed to advance the date in his log. His "January 18" was actually January 19, as he was embarrassed to discover on adding things up. So the French discovery had taken place on the same day as Wilkes'—but ten hours later!

Of all the great voyages of polar exploration, none ever came into being for a stranger reason than that of Wilkes. Captain Cook had gone to the Antarctic because Alexander Dalrymple believed there was an enormous, fertile continent to be found there. Charles Wilkes made *his* Antarctic journey —at least indirectly—because an eccentric retired soldier thought there were holes in the Poles.

The soldier was John Cleves Symmes, born in New Jersey in 1780. After a fine military career, Symmes left the army in 1816, taking up residence in Kentucky and devoting himself to the perfection of a strange theory about the earth. In April, 1818, Symmes sent a manifesto to five hundred institutions of learning and to government officials in the United States and Europe. It contained a certificate of Symmes' sanity, and made this claim:

"The earth is hollow, habitable within; containing a number of concentric spheres; one within the other, and . . . it is open at the pole twelve or sixteen degrees."

Symmes' idea of gaping holes at the ends of the earth, through which explorers might enter the habitable spheres within, might have died a quick death as just another crackpot notion, except that Symmes was energetic and diligent. He toured the United States, telling people that there was an opening 4,000 miles in diameter at the northern end of the world, and one 6,000 miles in diameter at the southern end, and people listened to him with great seriousness. He spent years compiling "proofs" of his theory, and urged the government of the United States to send out polar expeditions that would make contact with the interior of the earth, which, he said, was "inhabited by human beings . . . of various grades of civilization, none, however being much civilized. . . ."

Symmes sounded sincere and convincing. Again and again he petitioned Congress for funds for an expedition, but Congress paid no heed. Symmes spent his savings and injured his health promoting his great idea, and by 1824 he was nearly ready to abandon his one-man crusade. He had made many converts, but no one could help him organize an expedition.

Then, in 1825, the Symmes crusade fell into the hands of an aggressive young promoter named Jeremiah N. Reynolds. Today, perhaps, someone like Reynolds might become a public-relations man or a television executive. Born ahead of his time, he had to find other uses for his talents.

Dynamic and ambitious, Reynolds had already worked as a lumberjack (he told his fellow workers, "I assure you the time is coming when you will feel proud that you ever rolled logs with Jeremiah N. Reynolds"), as a schoolteacher, and as a small-town newspaper editor in Ohio. There Symmes met and hired him for an 1825–26 lecture tour. Reynolds delivered his first lecture in Pennsylvania in October, 1825, and was so successful in putting across the hollow-earth "message" that before long he was the star of the team, Symmes dropping into obscurity.

Whether Reynolds really believed there were holes in the Poles, we cannot tell. He *seemed* sincere as he promoted Symmes' idea. In short order, Reynolds was a public figure better known than Symmes himself, and he began to demand an Antarctic expedition that would verify the Symmes theory.

Shrewdly, Reynolds joined forces with important men of science in America who, while wanting nothing to do with Symmes, were nevertheless eager to see an American voyage of exploration to the Antarctic. He also contacted the major sealing men, such as Edmund Fanning and Nat Palmer, and got their support, too. They were less interested in discovery for its own sake, but Fanning in particular, as we have seen, had been petitioning the government for an expedition since 1812, for the purpose of finding new sealing grounds.

Reynolds thus was able to apply pressure in Washington from many angles. By 1827, he had President John Quincy Adams sympathetic to the idea of an expedition, and the fol-

lowing May the House of Representatives passed a resolution
calling on the Navy Department to send a small vessel to the
Pacific and to the Antarctic region. The sloop *Peacock*, under
command of Captain Thomas Ap Catesby Jones, was chosen
as the exploring vessel, and a naval lieutenant named Charles
Wilkes got the task of purchasing scientific and nautical instruments for the voyage.

Now began a fantastic political wrangle. The Navy Department had acted on the House resolution without waiting for
the Senate also to approve it. The Senate, miffed at this, voted
against the plan and canceled the expedition. Reynolds and
Fanning thereupon organized a privately backed voyage themselves, and in 1829 the *Seraph* and the *Annawan*, two sealing
vessels, headed southward under the command of those veteran
skippers, Benjamin Pendleton and Nat Palmer. Reynolds himself went along as a "scientist."

The expedition was a failure. No new land was sighted, few
seals were taken, and the crew nearly mutinied. Nor was
Symmes' polar opening discovered. One of the scientists
aboard, James Eights, did manage to make some valuable
studies of the shellfish living on the shores of the South Shetlands, but that was about the only accomplishment of the trip.
When Reynolds returned, he again took up the cudgels for a
full-scale government-sponsored expedition. No more was
heard about Symmes and his hollow-earth idea. That wild
scheme had simply served to get Reynolds started. Now he
pursued his own course.

Reynolds and Fanning bombarded Congress with petitions.
The years dragged on without action. In 1835, finally,
$150,000 was appropriated to finance a voyage. While Con-

gress debated, Reynolds spoke before the House, ringingly describing American explorers "pushing their adventurous barks into the high southern latitudes, to circle the globe within the Antarctic Circle, and attain the Pole itself;—yea, to cast anchor on that point where all the meridians terminate, where our eagle and star-spangled banner may be unfurled and planted, and left to wave on the axis of the earth itself!"

Congress was impressed. The appropriation was doubled to $300,000. President Andrew Jackson expressed the hope that the expedition would sail before his term ended, in March, 1837. Thomas Ap Catesby Jones once again was chosen to head the expedition. But Congress, in 1837, was not very different from the Congress of today, and soon the enterprise was bogged down in a political morass. Months went by while Congressmen feuded with government officials over the details of the expedition. Martin van Buren replaced Jackson in the White House. Captain Jones, wearied by the long delay, resigned his command and went home at the end of 1837.

Finding a new commander was not easy. Few experienced naval officers cared to go chasing Jeremiah Reynolds' wild geese in the icy desolation of the Antarctic. When all the first-line officers in the navy had respectfully declined the appointment, the government turned in despair to a junior officer, Charles Wilkes, and offered him the job.

Wilkes was born in New York City on April 3, 1798. He had gone to sea at seventeen, aboard a merchant ship, and three years later entered the United States Navy. Following the example of Cook, Wilkes taught himself mathematics and surveying, and by 1826 his skills had won him the rank of lieutenant. He was in charge of obtaining scientific instru-

ments in 1828 and again in 1836 when it seemed as though
an Antarctic voyage would sail. He had expected to be respon-
sible for the astronomical and physical-science aspects of the
expedition, but he hardly thought he would end by commanding the whole squadron.

Since Wilkes was only a lieutenant, there were problems in
getting officers to serve under him. Another lieutenant, William L. Hudson, was persuaded to become Wilkes' second-in-
command even though he was Wilkes' senior in point of service. "It is not to be endured," the Secretary of the Navy told
Wilkes, "that the purposes you are sent to attain are to be
defeated by the fantastic claims of rank."

The long-delayed expedition took to the sea on August 18,
1838. There were four naval vessels: the sloops-of-war *Vincennes* and *Peacock,* the brig *Porpoise,* and the supply ship
Relief. They were accompanied by two pilot boats, the *Sea
Gull* and *Flying Fish.* Wilkes' flagship, the 780-ton *Vincennes,*
dwarfed the little vessels of Cook and Bellingshausen. Wilkes
had 83 officers and a crew of 345 men, of whom 15 would die
and 47 desert before the expedition was over. In addition, he
took a dozen civilian scientists and artists. One civilian who
did not go was Jeremiah N. Reynolds, who had campaigned
for thirteen years to get the expedition under way. He had
made too many political enemies, and, like Dalrymple the
century before, he was left behind, loudly protesting his
treatment.

Wilkes was a capable and strong-willed man, determined to
triumph over any obstacle of nature or human weakness that
lay before him. But the political confusion surrounding his
expedition had forced him to go to sea with a fleet of aging,

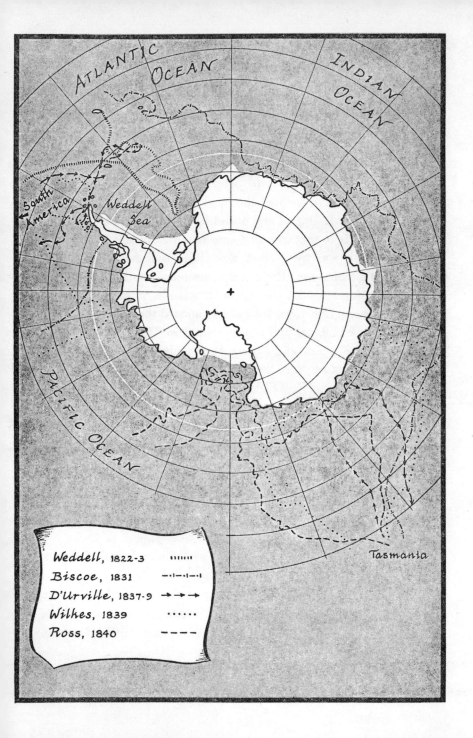

ATLANTIC OCEAN

INDIAN OCEAN

South America

Weddell Sea

PACIFIC OCEAN

Tasmania

Weddell, 1822-3	·······
Biscoe, 1831	-·-·-·-·-·
D'Urville, 1837-9	→→→
Wilkes, 1839	······
Ross, 1840	- - - -

creaky, inadequate ships. Nor did he carry the sort of equipment he thought a polar expedition should have had. He knew
that if he had insisted on a better-equipped expedition, new
Congressional action would have been necessary, and the
project might have been strangled in red tape without ever
getting under way. As he set sail, he wrote gloomily in his
journal, "It required all the hope I could muster to outweigh
the intense feeling of responsibility that hung over me. I may
compare it to that of one doomed to destruction."

Still, it was the largest expedition that had yet ventured
into the Antarctic. There was some reason to be hopeful.

In March, 1839, the northern islands of the South Shetlands came into view. Wilkes was aboard the *Porpoise*, having
left the *Vincennes* and *Relief* behind in Tierra del Fuego. He
sent the *Peacock* and *Flying Fish*, under Lieutenant Hudson,
over to explore from the Bellingshausen Sea on the west side
of the Antarctic Peninsula, as far as 106° W., where Cook had
made his farthest south. Wilkes himself, with the *Porpoise* and
Sea Gull, attempted to enter the Weddell Sea, east of the
peninsula.

Like D'Urville—of whose voyage the year before Wilkes
knew nothing—the Americans found the Weddell Sea ice-
filled, and could not go far. They sailed down the eastern
coast of the peninsula, trying to reach the shore through the
drifting ice. "I have rarely seen a finer sight," Wilkes wrote.
"The sea was literally studded with these beautiful masses,
some of pure white, others showing all the shades of opal,
others emerald green, and occasionally here and there some
of deep black, forming a strong contrast to the pure white."

Landing was impossible. Wilkes' crew suffered terribly

from cold and dampness, and the shoddy clothing and cheap
provisions supplied by dishonest American contractors began
to show their weaknesses. Southwesterly gales blew icy water
through the wide-open gun ports of the *Porpoise*. The decks
of both ships were weighted down by ice, and the rigging froze
iron-hard. By March 5, with scurvy beginning to break out
and the hulls of the ships themselves starting to rot and
crumble, Wilkes swung round and headed for safe harbor
in the South Shetlands.

The other part of the expedition, meanwhile, had nearly
broken Cook's record for southern attainment in western longitudes. The *Peacock* and the *Flying Fish* had become separated in dense fog. Hudson's *Peacock* struggled on through
dangerous waters as far as 68° S., 95°44′ W., and there the
little *Flying Fish* reappeared with the news that she had
slipped through the ice as far as 70° S. 107° W., all but
matching Cook's record of 71°10′ S., before meeting a solid
ice wall 20 feet high.

The Antarctic winter had arrived. Wilkes took three of the
vessels to Valparaiso. The *Relief,* though, which had not gone
south of Tierra del Fuego, was so slow that she had to be left
behind, and Wilkes sent the *Flying Fish* and the *Sea Gull* to
accompany her on her journey around Cape Horn. When it
became clear that the *Relief* was useless and had to be sent
home, the two small pilot ships headed round the Horn to join
the three vessels already at Valparaiso. During a storm on
April 26, they became separated, and the *Sea Gull* was never
seen again. A search failed to find her, and Wilkes sadly concluded she had been lost with all hands.

With his remaining four ships, Wilkes headed into the

Pacific, visiting Samoa, Fiji, the New Hebrides, and other islands. At the end of November, 1839, the fleet assembled at Sydney, Australia, to prepare for a second thrust into the Antarctic.

By this time, word of the proposed British expedition under Ross had reached Australia. The people of Sydney had read the details of Ross' plans, taking particular note of his careful preparations for Antarctic conditions. When they came out to see the American fleet, they were horrified to see how poorly equipped it was for the task ahead. Wilkes wrote, "They enquired whether we had compartments in our ships to prevent us from sinking? How we intended to keep ourselves warm? What kind of antiscorbutic [scurvy remedy] we were to use? And where were our great ice saws? To all of these questions I was obliged to answer, to their great apparent surprise, that we had none, and to agree with them that we were unwise to attempt such service in ordinary cruising vessels; but we had been ordered to go, and that was enough and go we should." Most of the Australians, Wilkes remarked, "considered us doomed to be frozen to death."

In the shipyards of Sydney, Wilkes had his battered, rotting ships repaired as well as possible, and on December 26, 1839, they headed southward again. The ships tried to keep together, but on January 1 the *Flying Fish* was left behind when a high wind came up, and the little pilot ship was not seen again until the end of the cruise. On January 15, Wilkes came upon the Balleny Islands, though without knowing that John Balleny had discovered them the year before. The sea was strewn with ice now. Wilkes, in the *Vincennes*, spent anxious

hours listening "to the low and distant rustling of the ice" as
the bergs became more numerous.

Four days later the Americans saw Antarctica proper.
Wilkes, in the *Vincennes*, entered a large bay beyond which
high land could be seen, while Hudson, in the *Peacock*,
reached "an immense mass which had every appearance of
land, seen far beyond and towering over an ice island. It bore
southwest and had the appearance of being 3,000 feet in
height, looking gray and dark, and divided into two distinct
ridges throughout its entire extent, the whole being covered
with snow."

They were at about 67° S., 155° E. About ten hours later
and some four hundred miles to the west, D'Urville would
sight his Adelie Land. Wilkes gave the name of Cape Hudson
to the point of land they saw, in what is now known as Oates
Land. The three ships continued westward.

Moving now through a belt of giant icebergs, the ships were
in constant danger. Wilkes could not help being awed by the
beauty of the ice masses that threatened his life. "Some of the
bergs," he wrote, "were of magnificent dimensions, one third
of a mile in length, and from 150 to 200 feet in height, with
sides perfectly smooth as if they had been chiselled. Others,
again, exhibited lofty arches of many-colored tints, leading
into deep caverns, open to the swell of the sea, which, rushing
in, produced loud and distant thunderings. The flights of birds
passing in and out of these caverns recalled the recollections
of ruined abbeys, castles, and caves. . . . If an immense city
of ruined alabaster palaces can be imagined, of every variety
of shape and tint, and composed of huge piles of buildings
grouped together, with long lanes or streets winding irregu-

larly through them, some idea may be formed of the grandeur
and beauty of the spectacle."

The ships worked westward, often separated from one
another. On January 24, the *Peacock* found herself menaced
by ice closing in on her bows, and while trying to escape
smashed her rudder. The ship went out of control and a sudden high wind blew her against an iceberg. Down crashed the
rotten timbers of the upper masts. Other collisions with the
ice left the ship shaken and crippled, but somehow Hudson
managed to guide her through the ice and into open water.
Further exploration in the *Peacock* was obviously impossible,
and with great skill Hudson brought her back to Sydney by
February 21.

Wilkes knew nothing of the *Peacock's* fate. He continued
westward with the *Vincennes* and *Porpoise*, skirting the coast
and sighting land now and then. On January 30, the *Porpoise*
had her unhappy little meeting with D'Urville's ships. That
same day, Wilkes and the *Vincennes* emerged from thick fog
and a violent snowstorm to see land once again. They entered
a bay with water only 180 feet deep, ringed with rocks and
walls of ice. Taking magnetic observations, Wilkes concluded
that the South Magnetic Pole lay 230 miles inland, due south
of this point, but there was, of course, no way to go ashore.
Mountainous land stretched for sixty miles from east to west.

Wilkes calculated his position as 66°45′ S., 140°30′ E, and
wrote in his journal, "Now that all were convinced of its
existence, I gave the land the name of the Antarctic Continent."

The voyage nearly ended at this point. Wilkes' hard-driving
discipline and the foul weather had left the crewmen fatigued

and ill. The ship's doctors told Wilkes that if they did not turn back, there would soon be so few sailors able to work that the lives of all would be endangered. Wilkes shook the doctors off. "It was my duty to proceed," he wrote, "and not to give up the cruise until the ship was totally disabled, or it should be evident to all that it was impossible to persist any longer."

Another commander might have been faced with a mutiny after making such a decision. Wilkes, stern and tough, never relaxed his authority. The *Vincennes* advanced westward, with the *Porpoise* trailing far behind. Wilkes' goal was Enderby Land, somewhere far to the west.

The shore remained unapproachable because of the ice barrier. Mountains and cliffs could be seen, though, and little doubt remained that what they were skirting was the edge of a mighty land mass that deserved the name of continent. By mid-February, the *Vincennes* was past Biscoe's Sabrina Land, but the season for exploration was ending, and Wilkes soon had to admit that Enderby Land could not be reached on this trip. On February 16, the *Vincennes* encountered a great peninsula of ice jutting out into the sea, blocking all advance. Wilkes had no choice but to turn north—that is, away from the Antarctic mainland. (At the bottom of the world, all directions away from the mainland are north.) He called the obstacle Termination Land, and plotted his position as 97° 37' E.

By March 11, 1840, the *Vincennes* was back in harbor at Sydney, her epic voyage over. She found the *Peacock* already there, undergoing repairs. It had earlier been arranged that if the expedition became separated, everyone would meet at the Bay of Islands, New Zealand, and when Wilkes and Hudson got there on March 30, they found the *Porpoise* and the long-lost *Flying Fish* waiting for them there.

The weary wanderers reached the United States on June 10, 1842. Wilkes had carried out the most important Antarctic cruise thus far. He had skirted the coast of Antarctica for 1,500 miles—proving beyond doubt that the polar region was a vast continent, not a group of detached islands. He had carried out useful magnetic observations, and his team of scientists had made enough discoveries to fill nineteen huge volumes of text and eleven more of plates. Yet Wilkes received no hero's welcome when he returned after almost four years at sea. He met with a stormy reception, and, as we will see, the reward for his services was court-martial and disgrace.

The whole outcry for an expedition to look for the South Magnetic Pole had begun in England. But first France and then the United States got expeditions off to sea, while the English went on debating the wisdom of the idea.

The thought that the United States, so recently an English colony, might surpass the mother country in polar exploration finally got things moving. An anonymous pamphlet published in London in 1837 flamboyantly called on Great Britain to "follow up the glorious track" of "our immortal countryman Cook," stressing the disgrace "that we, who date a thousand years of naval supremacy, allowed a nation but of yesterday, albeit gigantic in her infancy, to snatch from us our birthright on the ocean."

By the summer of 1838, plans for a British expedition were well under way. The command went to a logical choice:

James Clark Ross, already the discoverer of the North Magnetic Pole. Born in 1800, Ross had joined the Royal Navy at the age of twelve, sailing aboard the ship of his uncle, Admiral Sir John Ross. In his late teens, Ross transferred to the command of Sir Edward Parry, a great Arctic explorer, and in 1827 Ross and Parry took part in an unsuccessful attempt to reach the North Pole. Two years later, Ross was sailing with his uncle again, on a four-year expedition to the Arctic. It was on this trip that the younger Ross located the North Magnetic Pole, on June 1, 1831, and raised the British flag there.

No one alive was better suited to take command of the British expedition. Handsome and high-minded, with a stern sense of duty and a total unwillingness to accept defeat in anything he did, Ross was beloved by his men for his kindness and generosity, and could inspire unusual efforts under the harshest of conditions.

The two ships he was given were the *Erebus* and *Terror*. They were strong, small wooden sailing vessels, slow and clumsy but well designed for Antarctic work. They had decks of double thickness, watertight bulkheads to prevent flooding in case of iceberg damage, and thick, sturdy hulls. Ross took command of the *Erebus*, and another veteran of Arctic exploration, Francis Crozier, commanded the *Terror*. No civilian scientists were taken, but the four medical officers had all had training in such fields as zoology, geology, and botany, and they were expected to make scientific observations as time permitted.

Ross' orders were first to set up stations for magnetic research on the Atlantic island of St. Helena and at the Cape of Good Hope, and then to continue toward the Antarctic in search of the South Magnetic Pole. He was to chart such known regions as the Antarctic Peninsula and Enderby Land, as well as all newly discovered land.

The expedition left England on September 25, 1839. The two magnetic observatories were duly set up, and Ross proceeded as far south as Kerguelen Island, getting there at the end of May for more magnetic studies. It was winter in the southern hemisphere, so no Antarctic work could be done, and Ross headed westward round Cape Horn for his next scheduled port of call, Hobart, Tasmania.

The Governor of Tasmania was Sir John Franklin, another veteran of Arctic research, and he welcomed the explorers royally. By a strange twist of fate, Franklin was destined to take the *Erebus* and *Terror* to the Arctic himself five years later, losing his life on the voyage and touching off the greatest search of the nineteenth century.

Ross spent four months at Hobart, preparing for the polar journey. Troubling news reached him there: both Wilkes and D'Urville, he learned, had been exploring in the very region where Ross planned to search for the South Magnetic Pole!

Angry and disturbed, Ross decided it was foolish to "follow in the footsteps" of other expeditions. On his own authority, he drew up new plans for the voyage, resolving to explore far to the east of Wilkes, around the longitude of 170° E., where Balleny had found open sea two years before at 69° S.

It was a lucky change of plan, for it led Ross to great new discoveries. At the time, though, he could only grumble at the "embarrassing situation" in which Wilkes and D'Urville had placed him by selecting "the very place for penetrating to the southward" that they knew he was about to attempt. He blandly overlooked the fact that the other two expeditions had received their orders long before his plans had been made public.

On November 12, 1840, the *Erebus* and *Terror* left Hobart, and by January 5 they were at the edge of the great ice belt that encircled the continent. More than a hundred miles of ice floated on the sea ahead of them—a barrier which every other commander had termed impenetrable. Never before, though, had two ships so well designed for such work gone south. Ross sent his vessels battering ahead into the ice field. Their rounded bows smashed the close-packed floes apart, cutting a clear channel. Now and again, the ships would shudder as their hulls struck giant floes, but they withstood the sort of buffeting that would have broken up Wilkes' craft in moments.

On January 9, dark sky was seen ahead—"water sky." In the Antarctic, a bright sky means sunlight reflected off fields of ice, a dark sky means open water. Soon the ships broke out of the pack and found themselves in an ice-free sea. Antarctica lay ahead. Their position was 69°15′ S., 176°15′ E.

It was one of the great moments of exploration. For the first time, ships had penetrated this unknown sea, and a virgin continent was in view. Ross set the course for due south, hoping to find the Magnetic Pole, which his instruments told him was not far off.

Crossing the open water, he caught sight of land to the south, a hundred miles away. Awe-inspiring mountains soared to staggering heights. Their "lofty peaks," Ross write, "perfectly covered with eternal snow, rose to elevations varying from seven to ten thousand feet above the level of the ocean. The glaciers that filled their intervening valleys, and which descended from near the mountains' summits, projected in many places several miles into the sea."

Ross named each feature as it appeared, giving geographical immortality to contemporary British political figures. A high mountain became Mount Sabine; a jutting cape, Cape Adare. The new land posed a problem for Ross. The South Magnetic Pole, his goal, lay some 500 miles to the southwest, he believed. The land just ahead blocked any direct southward advance, unless he could find a strait or channel somewhere that led to the interior. The other alternative was to sail westward—but that would take him into the area where Wilkes and D'Urville had been in 1840.

He preferred the unknown. Hoping that what lay before him was only a large island, not an impassable continent, Ross continued southward. On January 11, the *Erebus* and *Terror* were only a few miles offshore. Ross and his men stared in wonder at the great glaciers, frozen rivers inching silently and slowly toward the sea. The land was cold, lifeless, forbidding. Fallen blocks of ice, beaten and swirled by the pounding surf, bordered the beach and made going ashore impossible. On the morning of the twelfth, Ross and Crozier made a landing on the rocky shore of a small island just off the coast, and claimed the region in the name of England's youthful Queen Victoria. They gave the island the name of Possession Island, and the mainland was dubbed Victoria Land. As the flag-raising ceremony took place, hundreds of curious penguins crowded round, commenting in hoarse cries on the strange procedure.

Rounding Cape Adare, Ross discovered that it was possible to continue south after all. They went forward, with the coastline now to the right of them. New mountains could be seen, some as high as 14,000 feet above sea level. By January 22, the two ships had reached 74°20′ S., surpassing the record Weddell had set on the other side of the continent. The Magnetic Pole, Ross calculated, was now only about 250 miles away, but there was still no channel leading westward toward it, so he continued south.

On January 27, an island was discovered at 76°8′ S., and named for Sir John Franklin. Joseph Hooker, one of the ship's doctors, went ashore to collect rock specimens, and as he jumped from the boat he landed in the water, getting an icy Antarctic baptism. The shivering Dr. Hooker collected his rocks hastily and beat a quick retreat to the warmth of his ship.

At midnight, another island came into view, topped by several massive peaks. The ships approached. Ross saw what seemed to be clouds of steam at the summit of one of the mountains. As they came even nearer, they gaped in disbelief and astonishment at what was perhaps the most unlikely possible sight here in this silent, icy wasteland: an active volcano!

Flames belched from the summit. Smoke rose high. The dull glare of molten lava lit up the sky. Dr. Hooker, perhaps still a little chilly from his dunking, hurried to his notebook and set down his reaction: "All the coast one mass of dazzlingly beautiful peaks of snow which, when the sun approached the horizon, reflected the most brilliant tints of golden yellow and scarlet; and then to see the dark cloud of smoke, tinged with flame, rising from the volcano in a perfectly unbroken column,

one side jet-black, the other giving back the colors of the sun.
. . . This was a sight so surpassing everything that can be
imagined . . . that it really caused a feeling of awe to steal
over us at the consideration of our own comparative insignificance and helplessness, and at the same time, an indescribable
feeling of the greatness of the Creator in the works of His
hand."

Ross named the volcano Mount Erebus. It was 12,400 feet
high, and its plume of smoke sometimes reached 2,000 feet
above the crater's rim, falling back in misty clouds. Beside it
stood a 10,900-foot peak, apparently also a volcano though
inactive, which was named Mount Terror. Ross gave the island
the name of High Island; it is now known as Ross Island. It
was unbelievable that in the bowels of the white-mantled continent there should smolder a volcanic furnace, but the fantastic sight was no dream.

Still questing toward the South Magnetic Pole, Ross hoped
that he could sail round the island of volcanoes and head
westward and northward toward his goal. As the ships sailed
southward looking for a westerly passage behind the island,
something came into view that was, if anything, even more
astounding than the live volcano. Stretching eastward from the
island, Ross saw, was a long, low white line spanning the sea
as far as the eye could reach. "It presented an extraordinary
appearance, gradually increasing in height as we got nearer
to it, and proving at length to be a perpendicular cliff of ice,
between 150 and 200 feet above the level of the sea, perfectly
flat and level at the top and without any fissure or promon-
tories in its own seaward face."

They had discovered the mighty wall of ice known today

as the Ross Ice Shelf, or Ross Barrier. A vast apron of ice, more than 700 feet thick and as great in size as California, the Ross Shelf lies between the Antarctic shore and the open sea, today called the Ross Sea. It floats on the water, rising hundreds of feet above the turbulent waves to form an impassable, unscalable barrier.

There could be no further southward progress, Ross knew, "We might with equal chance of success try to sail through the cliffs of Dover, as to penetrate such a mass." Ross considered going ashore and traveling overland, past "the brilliant burning mountain" toward the South Magnetic Pole to the west. In his innocence he had no idea of the hardship of land travel in Antarctica. But he was spared the awakening, because there was no possible way to climb the flat face of the Barrier. All he could do was turn eastward and sail along the Barrier until some channel appeared.

Day followed day, and no break in the Barrier was seen. On February 2, they attained their farthest south of the trip, 78°4′ S., the closest men had yet come to the South Pole. The Barrier there was 160 feet high; they had already followed it for 250 miles. A few days later, at 173° W., the ice wall was only 50 feet high, and it was possible to catch a glimpse of the upper surface—a flat sheet of snow sweeping off to the horizon.

On February 5, in 167° W., ice made further eastward progress impossible. Ross turned back toward the coast of Victoria Land. February 16 saw the ships passing Mount Erebus again—it staged a magnificent eruption for the occasion—and, after a look into a deep sound that Ross named for one of his officers, McMurdo, the expedition gave up the hunt for a passage to the Magnetic Pole and returned to Tasmania for the winter.

The way back took them westward into the region Wilkes had visited in 1840. Wilkes had helpfully sent charts of his voyage to Ross, but the charts were sketchy and inaccurate, and Ross was unable to find any trace of the mountains Wilkes had claimed to see at about 167° E. In fact, on one day the British found themselves sailing "very nearly in the center of the mountainous patch of land laid down in Lieutenant Wilkes' chart as forming a part of the 'antarctic continent.' " Ross concluded that Wilkes had mistaken distant fog banks for land, and that a two-hundred-mile stretch of coastline charted by the American had "no real existence."

The *Erebus* and *Terror* reached Tasmania in April, 1841, and spent six months undergoing minor repairs and refitting. In November, Ross began his second Antarctic voyage. He still hoped to find some way around the eastern end of the Barrier, and so he entered the polar regions at 146° W. Drifting ice and heavy fog made this new venture dangerous, and the ships moved cautiously, working to and fro in the pack and advancing only a few miles a day. In the middle of January, while the *Erebus* and *Terror* were dodging warily through ice-choked waters, a fierce gale blew up and the explorers found themselves exposed to the full fury of an Antarctic storm at sea.

"Soon after midnight," Ross wrote, "our ships were involved in an ocean of rolling fragments of ice, hard as floating rocks of granite, which were dashed against them with so much violence that their masts quivered as if they would fall at every successive blow; and the destruction of the ships

seemed inevitable from the tremendous shocks they received."
The rudder of the *Terror* was ripped away by the ice, that of
the *Erebus* badly damaged. Decks and timbers groaned and
creaked as heavy ice floes pounded the ships. Through the
twenty-eight hours of the storm, "the ocean rolled its mountainous waves, throwing huge masses one upon another, and
then again burying them deep beneath its foaming waters,
dashing and grinding them together with fearful violence."

The storm subsided as abruptly as it had appeared. The
carpenters hurried to make repairs, and by January 24 the
ships were whole again. Four days later they calculated their
position at 67°39', 156° W. They had forced their way
through the pack for 800 miles. More than seventy years
before, Cook had come nearly this far without entering the
pack at all. Once again, it was seen that the size of Antarctica's
encircling belt of drifting ice could vary greatly from year
to year.

On February 19, 1842, the great Barrier came into sight at
last. Because of the delay in getting through the pack, the
exploring season was nearly over. The days were short and the
temperature hovered around 19°. Whenever high wind blew
spray across the deck, it froze solid. One day a small fish was
thrown against the bows of the *Terror* by a wave; it froze solid
and was immediately buried in a block of ice. A sailor hacked
it out and presented it to one of the ship's doctors, who
thought it might be a species new to science. Before he could
study it, though, the ship's cat spied it and carried it off for
dinner.

After a brief survey of the Barrier region, cold weather
forced Ross to withdraw, and the ships sailed north toward the

Falkland Islands. Early in March, while heading through relatively ice-free seas, a snowstorm came up, and visibility
dropped to zero. Unexpectedly, a large iceberg appeared just
ahead of the *Erebus;* Ross tacked to avoid a collision, only to
find the *Terror* bearing down on him in the fog. The ships
cracked together with a terrific impact, masts shattering. Ross
wrote: "The ships hanging together, entangled by their
rigging, and dashing against each other with fearful violence,
were falling down upon the weather face of the lofty berg
under our lee, against which the waves were breaking and
foaming to near the summit of its perpendicular cliffs. Sometimes she [the *Terror*] rose high above us, almost exposing her
keel to view, and again descended as we in turn rose to the top
of the wave, threatening to bury her beneath us, whilst the
crashing of the breaking upperworks and boats increased the
horror of the scene."

Finally the two ships separated, slipping one at a time
through a channel between two walls of ice formed by drifting
bergs, and escaped from the danger. Moving slowly, the
crippled vessels reached the Falklands in April, having been
through a 137-day voyage of small accomplishment and great
peril.

After a winter spent around Cape Horn, the Ross expedition entered Antarctic waters for the third time in December,
1842. The plan this time was to explore the Weddell Sea. Ross
hoped to surpass Weddell's farthest south, and perhaps to
continue on to the South Magnetic Pole from this approach.

They came down along the eastern shore of the Antarctic
Peninsula, plagued all the way by fog, gale, and snow. Stopping at an island just off shore, they collected plants of nine-

teen different species, the first plant life seen in the Antarctic
—all of them simple mosses, algae, and lichens.

Ross was confident that his sturdy little ships, which had so
easily smashed through the pack ice of the Ross Sea at the
other side of the continent, would have no trouble with the
Weddell Sea pack. But trouble developed at once. On January 13, with the temperature at 23°, ice formed around the
ships and trapped them, so that it seemed they might be
forced to spend the entire coming winter in the Antarctic.
Luckily, an iceberg struck the floe in which they were caught
and broke it up, freeing them after four days as prisoners.
They beat their way strenuously into the Weddell Sea, but had
to halt at 65°13′ S. when the ice became impenetrable.
D'Urville, four years before, had been able to continue
another 75 miles, and Weddell in 1823 had sailed on for 550
miles more without encountering difficulties. Ross generously
avoided hinting that Weddell had exaggerated his achievement. Unlike D'Urville, who had suspected fraud, Ross said,
"We must conclude that Weddell was favored by an unusually
fine season, and we may rejoice that there was a brave and
daring seaman on the spot to profit by the opportunity."

After skirting the edge of the ice for two more weeks, Ross
again turned north, and on March 11, 1843, left the Antarctic
region for the last time. Once more, he had accomplished little.
His first season's work had been the most important, and in
the two following seasons he had been too greatly hampered
by poor weather and by his own growing fatigue. On the way
north Ross attempted to find Bouvet Island, but was no more
successful than Cook had been, and the expedition continued
homeward, sighting England in September after an absence of

four years and five months. His great voyage of 1841 had not only taken men farther south than ever before, but had revealed the amazing Ross Ice Shelf, the grim barrier which in later years would prove to be the gateway to Antarctica.

Once again the fates of three men had crossed at the bottom of the world. Twenty years before, it had been Bransfield, Palmer, and Bellingshausen. Now three great captains, D'Urville, Wilkes, and Ross, had led three great national expeditions of discovery to the Antarctic.

Destiny had odd things in store for all three. D'Urville, who had returned to France in 1840, intended to spend many years editing a lengthy report on his voyage. But, in May, 1842, he took his wife and son to visit the palace at Versailles, and rode back to Paris after the outing aboard that new and still strange means of transportation, the railway. There was an accident; fire seared through the train; and the man who had sailed safely through the mists of the Antarctic died in the blaze, only a few miles from his home.

Ross, welcomed by England as the hero he was, became Sir James by Queen Victoria's command, took a wife, and was honored by the gold medals of several geographical societies. He retired from the sea and spent the remaining years of his life, to his death in 1862, editing the scientific reports of his expedition. His retirement was broken only once, in 1848, when he made a brief Arctic expedition in search of his old friends, Sir John Franklin and Captain Crozier. They had gone in the *Erebus* and *Terror* to look for the Northwest Passage across the top of the world, and had disappeared. Ross failed to find them, and never went to sea again.

The strangest fate awaited Wilkes. He had completed the greatest voyage of exploration in the brief history of the United States. Stopping at Honolulu on his way home, Wilkes learned that Ross had issued statements charging that some of Wilkes' most important discoveries were imaginary. The story reached the United States before Wilkes did, and he was met with the same charges when he docked at New York in June, 1842. He was accused of having uttered a "deliberate and wilful falsehood" when he claimed the discovery of land on January 19, 1840, and was told he would have to stand trial on a variety of other charges.

Wilkes tried to defend himself, insisting that Ross had misinterpreted his charts. The land east of 160° W. was Balleny's discovery, not his, and he had simply added it to the chart to be of assistance to Ross, he said. He himself had never claimed to have made such discoveries, and he was not even certain Balleny's information had been accurate.

He came to trial, charged with having exceeded his authority during the cruise, of having been unduly harsh to his crew, of having falsified his log, and even of "while yet a lieutenant wearing the uniform of a captain." These charges were brought by officers who had served under Wilkes on the voyage and who had built up grudges against him during the grinding exertions of the long journey.

They were foolish charges, and Wilkes was eventually found not guilty, except on the count of "illegal punishment of subordinates." He received a minor reprimand for this and, swallowing his bitterness at his unhappy homecoming, settled down to prepare the five-volume report of his expedition, which appeared between 1847 and 1849. After this, the technical volumes of the expedition's scientists began to appear, and Wilkes spent a total of eighteen years editing them and begging Congress for the funds to publish them. During those years Wilkes and Ross carried on a running feud that at times became quite ugly, each man accusing the other of deliberate falsehoods and poor judgment. Wilkes continued to maintain the continental nature of Antarctica, while Ross spoke of "various patches of land," seeing no proof that such widely separated regions as Enderby Land, Adelie Land, Victoria Land, and the Antarctic Peninsula were all part of the same continental mass.

Eventually the furor over Wilkes' voyage died down, and in 1855 he was finally given the rank of captain. When the Civil War broke out, the sixty-three-year-old Wilkes was called back to active service, and nearly managed to involve the United States in war with Great Britain. Commanding the sloop *San Jacinto,* he intercepted a British mail steamer, the *Trent,* that was carrying two Confederate commissioners to London. Firing two shots across the *Trent's* bow, Wilkes forced the British ship to halt, and took the two Confederates into custody. The British government protested, but settled for an official apology, and Wilkes was hailed in the United States for "great public service" and "adroit and patriotic conduct."

President Lincoln backed Wilkes' action. But soon he was embroiled in a series of quarrels with Lincoln's Secretary of the Navy, Gideon Welles. Stubborn and hotheaded as ever, Wilkes ignored Welles' instructions and carried on the war as he saw fit. The result was a second court-martial for the Antarctic hero. Wilkes was found guilty of disobedience of orders, insubordinate conduct, disrespect, and disrespectful language to a superior officer—Secretary of the Navy Welles. He was suspended from active duty for three years, but Lincoln reviewed the case and reduced the sentence to one year.

Wilkes never returned to active duty. In 1866, he was promoted to rear admiral on the retired list, and spent the remaining eleven years of his life in Washington, still working on the unpublished reports of his great voyage. After $350,000 had been spent on the publication of these volumes, Congress cut short Wilkes' funds, and some of the most important works never appeared. Those that did get printed were limited to one hundred copies apiece, most of which were destroyed by fire before they could be distributed. When he died, shortly before his eightieth birthday, Wilkes was considered a cranky, irritable, headstrong old man. His career had been turbulent and embittering—but he had coasted fifteen hundred miles of an unknown continent in rotten, leaking ships, and had made one of the most remarkable voyages in the annals of exploration.

6 THE CROWDED ANTARCTIC

THE THREE GREAT EXPEDITIONS OF 1838–43 RANG down the curtain on Antarctic exploration for many years. The British turned their energies toward Arctic voyages, spurred by the futile quest for Sir John Franklin. The United States was occupied in the turmoil that led up to the Civil War, and in the hard period of reconstruction afterward. And none of the other nations had ever been terribly interested in Antarctic research. The reports of Wilkes, Ross, and D'Urville had not kindled any great enthusiasm for visiting the useless, miserably cold Antarctic.

There were a few voyages. In 1845, H.M.S. *Pagoda* entered southern waters to complete Ross' magnetic studies, but did not sight land. Almost thirty years later, a British-sponsored scientific expedition aboard the *Challenger* visited the Antarctic seas. And in 1882 and 1883, Germany set up an observatory on South Georgia, making scientific discoveries but not adding new geographical knowledge. Those were the only three expeditions to the Antarctic regions until the closing years of the century.

The sealers, too, were gone. They had virtually wiped out the seals, and it no longer was profitable to venture south of Cape Horn. In their place came whalers. Ross in particular had sighted many whales, and fleets of whaling vessels now descended on the bottom of the world. They sought whales for their oil, and also for whalebone, needed in great quantities for use in women's clothing, and worth thousands of dollars a ton.

The *Challenger*, though it never came within sight of the Antarctic coast, was important for several reasons. It was the first steam-powered ship to cross the Antarctic Circle. And its researches backed up Wilkes' idea that Antarctica was a continent. By offshore dredging operations, the *Challenger* picked up fragments of granite, quartz, and other minerals that were only found along continental shores. Working from the data thus obtained, a *Challenger* scientist named John Murray spent twenty years plotting a picture of the Antarctic continent.

He based his theory on the dredged-up rocks and on the depth of the surrounding ocean. In a sort of scientific detective operation, Murray used his skimpy clues to portray the con-tinent in terms that later explorers would find had been surprisingly accurate. He mapped a roughly circular continent, with the Antarctic Peninsula jutting from it. From central highlands, he said, glaciers descended to form the flat-topped ice cliffs that rimmed the coastline. Where the ice sheet met the sea, great blocks of ice broke off to become the wandering icebergs of southern waters, sometimes many miles long.

Murray presented his findings to the Royal Geographical Society late in 1893. Half a century had gone by since Ross' homecoming, and many of England's leading men of science called for a new polar voyage, now that Murray had reawakened the old lure of the Antarctic.

Not scientists but whaling men revived the Antarctic dream, though. The whalers had had little luck in southern seas, and after 1874 had concentrated on the more productive whaling grounds off Greenland. Before long, the Right whale, chief source of precious whalebone, was all but extinct in the Arctic, and the whalers once again began to look south.

Four whaling ships sailing out of Scotland cruised the Weddell Sea in 1892, without much success. At the same time, a Norwegian whaler, the *Jason*, commanded by Captain C. A. Larsen, entered the same waters, taking no whales but finding enough seals to make the voyage worth while. Larsen returned the following year, going far south along the eastern coast of the Antarctic Peninsula. Several German whalers worked the waters west of the peninsula, getting as far south as Bellingshausen Sea without difficulty.

Meanwhile, a young Norwegian named H. J. Bull had been trying to organize an Australian whaling expedition. Arousing no interest down under, Bull returned to his native land and approached eighty-four-year-old Svend Foyn, the most powerful figure in the Norwegian whaling industry. Foyn—who was as interested in exploration as the Enderby Brothers had been —agreed to sponsor a combined whaling and exploring voyage to Antarctica's Ross Sea.

In September, 1893, the whaling ship *Antarctic* left Norway, commanded by Captain Leonard Kristensen. Bull was aboard. Another member of the party was a youthful Norwegian named Carstens Borchgrevink, who had been teaching languages and science in Australia. Borchgrevink was passionately eager to see Antarctica, and offered to pay his own way as a passenger. Captain Kristensen would have no passengers, however, and Borchgrevink finally wangled his way aboard by signing on as an ordinary seaman.

The *Antarctica* spent her first season sealing along the edge of the ice pack. After a winter in New Zealand, she sailed again on November 28, 1894, crossing the Antarctic Circle on December 21. The ship was a prisoner in the ice pack for almost three weeks, but finally broke out into the open water of the Ross Sea, and Cape Adare was sighted off Victoria Land on January 16. The expedition landed on Possession Island two days later, and Borchgrevink discovered lichen encrusting the rocks—the first plant life seen within the Antarctic Circle.

A few days of searching for whales produced no results. By January 24, the ship was again at Cape Adare, and this time polar history was made. Except for the doubtful and shadowy landing of John Davis in 1822, no one had actually set foot on the Antarctic continent itself. Now, a party went ashore, consisting of Bull, Borchgrevink, Captain Kristensen, and the *Antarctica's* second mate, Bernhard Jensen. Strangely, no one bothered to record which one was the first man actually to step ashore. They landed on a pebbly beach after rowing for an hour through loose ice. Bull wrote:

"The sensation of being the first men who had set foot on

the real Antarctic mainland was both strange and pleasurable, although Mr. Foyn would no doubt have preferred to exchange this pleasing sensation on our part for a Right whale, even of small dimensions."

A box painted with the Norwegian flag was raised on a pole. Fearless penguins gathered round, nipping at the heels of the seamen. Several of them were carried away, fighting and shrieking, for scientific study in Norway. Some rock specimens were chipped free, and Borchgrevink collected a few patches of lichen.

Bull suggested that the bay at Cape Adare could be used for landing full-scale parties of exploration. "Among the rocks of Cape Adare," he wrote, "a shelter could be found for the house, and the low promontory would furnish plenty of space for moving about. . . . If by ill luck the relief party did not succeed in fetching away the explorers during the second season, the penguin colony would afford an inexhaustible larder and stock of fuel."

It was a bold, provocative idea—establishing a base on the Antarctic mainland and spending an entire winter there! As the *Antarctic* pulled out of the bay, at least one member of the party, Carstens Borchgrevink, had already formed a plan to do just that.

While whalers made history in Antarctica, the British were once again debating the whys and wherefores of a new scientific expedition. A hundred and twenty years before, Alexander Dalrymple had urged such an expedition so vociferously that it finally came about. Sixty years later, Jeremiah Reynolds had done the same in the United States. Now, the crusading task was performed by Clements Markham, a scholar and traveler and president of the Royal Geographical Society.

Almost singlehandedly, Markham revived the idea of Antarctic exploration. In 1895, when he was sixty-six, he presided over the Sixth International Geographical Congress in London and brought to the platform such speakers as Sir Joseph Hooker, last survivor of the Ross expedition; John Murray of the *Challenger;* and young Borchgrevink, who had just returned from his voyage. Markham had the Congress pass a resolution declaring that "the exploration of the Antarctic Regions is the greatest piece of geographical exploration still to be undertaken."

Markham's enthusiasm was contagious. Although his own country was slow to respond, other nations took up the challenge. The next few years would see the Antarctic literally overrun by explorers of many lands.

The first expedition to leave was Belgian. An international crew manned the ship, a former Norwegian sealer that had been renamed the *Belgica.* The leader of the expedition, Adrien de Gerlache, was an officer of the Belgian Navy. The first mate was a Norwegian named Roald Amundsen, a muscular twenty-five-year-old who dreamed of reaching the North Pole, and who had signed aboard simply to get experience in cold-weather navigation. Five of the sailors were also Norwegians. The captain, George Lecointe, and the magnetic observer, Emile Danco, were Belgian; two of the other scientists were Polish and one a Rumanian. At Rio de Janeiro an American joined this ship as surgeon and photographer. He was Dr. Frederick Cook, who threw in his lot with the Belgians after his attempt to promote an American expedition had failed. Disgrace lay in Dr. Cook's future, for, in 1909, he falsely claimed to have reached the North Pole, was exposed as a liar, and later went to prison for a different fraud. His service on the *Belgica*, though, was untarnished and valuable.

The *Belgica* spent half the short summer season observing the natives of Tierra del Fuego, and did not head south until January 13, 1898—late in the season for polar work. The ship explored the west coast of the Antarctic Peninsula, making some twenty landings and accurately surveying the region for the first time. In February they steamed farther south, but pack ice forced the ship away from the coast and out into the Bellingshausen Sea. On February 28, at 70°20′ S., a gale came up and broke the pack, creating several narrow channels leading ahead. Against the advice of the others, de Gerlache insisted on continuing.

By March 4, at 71°30′ S., even de Gerlache had had enough. Winter was coming, and he gave orders to turn north again. Too late: the pack had closed behind the ship. The *Belgica* was frozen in! They had not planned it that way, but the explorers were going to be the first men to endure a winter in the Antarctic.

The ship was fairly new and had a rounded bow designed to ride up on the ice and break it with the ship's weight. There was no chance, though, to smash up the floe in which the *Belgica* was caught. The explorers were poorly prepared for their ordeal, lacking the equipment needed for a winter stay.

On May 16, the long night began. The sun disappeared below the horizon and was not to reappear for almost seventy days. Nothing broke the darkness but the silvery glitter of moonlight and the occasional weird radiance of the Aurora

Australis. Though the *Belgica* could not move, the floe that held her drifted constantly in random zigzags through the ice-choked waters. Cook wrote that they were "firmly stationed in a moving sea of ice, with no land and nothing stable on the horizon to warn us of our movements. Even the bergs, immense, mountainous masses, though apparently fixed and immovable, sail as we do, and with the same apparent ease. . . . It is a strange sensation to know that, blown with the winds, you are moving rapidly over an unknown sea, and yet can see nothing to indicate a movement."

Fierce storms assailed them. The ice floes ground and churned like giant teeth. Everlasting darkness blanketed the world. With the vanishing sun came gloom and then total despair. Depressed and melancholy, the homesick men suffered more from mental disturbances than from the severity of the cold. They began to irritate one another, and arguments flared in half the languages of Europe. On June 5, Danco, the magnetician, died of a heart ailment aggravated by tension and cold, and his death heightened the atmosphere of misery. Soon after, the ship's kitten died also, and the gloom deepened. "We live in a madhouse," one of the explorers wrote. Everyone aboard was seriously ill in mind or in body.

Dr. Cook tried every possible way to keep the men alive. He found that "everybody is alarmed and coming to me for medical treatment, for real or imaginary troubles." He persuaded the sick men to eat fresh seal and penguin meat instead of canned food. He ordered them to stand in front of a blazing stove to cure what he called "polar anemia," brought on by the absence of sunshine. "We were never hungry, always tired," Cook wrote. Any task, even keeping the log, became an exhausting effort. Feeling that the men needed exercise, Cook sent them out to walk a circular path on the ice around the ship. It came to be known as "madhouse promenade."

On July 22, the sun returned. Weak as they were, the explorers climbed the rigging to get a good view. About half past eleven in the morning, color suddenly glowed in the sky: "Gold, orange, blue, green, and a hundred harmonious blends," Cook wrote. Just at noon, the fiery rim of the sun appeared.

"For several minutes my companions did not speak," said Cook. "Lecointe and Amundsen were standing on an iceberg close to me. They faced the light and watched the fragment of the sun slide under the bergs, over hummocks, and along the even expanse of the frozen sea, with a worshipful air."

The return of sunlight did not bring immediate freedom. The ice still gripped the *Belgica* firmly. The spirits of the men rose, though, and one party felt strong enough to hike toward a large iceberg sixteen miles away, returning quickly when the ice began to break up. Springtime storms battered the imprisoned ship. On September 8, the temperature dropped to 45° below zero, the coldest they had endured so far. Cook wrote of sandlike snow driven into their faces like knives. He and Amundsen, both mindful of their polar ambitions, made sledge trips over the ice to gain experience.

Finally the summer thaw began. Open water could be seen in the distance, though the *Belgica* was still held fast as late as January 1, 1899. A horrible thought struck the men: what if they never got free during the short summer, and had to spend another winter like the last?

They set to work freeing themselves. Blasting seemed to
have little effect on the 10-foot-thick ice. Manning ice saws
they cut a canal 2,200 feet long, and were within 100 feet of
freedom when the wind shifted, blowing the canal closed. It
froze over, but two weeks later another shift of wind opened
it again, and on February 14 the *Belgica* finally steamed free.
Almost at once she was hemmed in between two threatening
icebergs of immense size. According to Amundsen, it was
Cook who saved the ship by suggesting that they drape the
hull with the skins of the penguins they had killed. For a day
and a night, the icebergs slammed against the sides of the
ship, but the penguin-skin "bumpers" cushioned the blows
and reduced the damage.

On March 28, 1899, the *Belgica* reached Tierra del Fuego.
The explorers had been locked in the ice for thirteen months,
drifting on a wandering westward course. They had discovered
no new lands, but they brought back the most detailed scientific observations of the Antarctic night that had ever been
made.

At the same time that the men of the *Belgica* were desperately fighting to break the grip of Antarctic ice after their
involuntary winter stay, other explorers in another part of the
continent were toiling to unload supplies for a planned winter
in the Antarctic. The leader was Carsten Borchgrevink, who
was about to make Bull's dream of a winter hut on the mainland a reality.

Borchgrevink sailed from England in August, 1898—but it
was not the government-sponsored British expedition that
Clements Markham had been working so hard to attain. The

government was still hesitating, and this was a private expedition, financed by the magazine publisher George Newnes. The ship, like the *Belgica,* was a Norwegian whaler, renamed the *Southern Cross* and fitted with powerful new engines. Her captain was Bernhard Jensen, who had been second mate on the *Antarctic.* Borchgrevink took along a meteorologist, a magnetic observer, two zoologists, and other scientists. More significantly, he carried dog teams for transportation, tended by two Finnish Lapps. Dogs had long been used to haul sledges in Arctic exploration, but this was the first time that they had been brought to the Antarctic.

By February 17, 1899, the *Southern Cross* had hammered her way through the Ross Sea ice pack and dropped anchor off Cape Adare. "We slowly moved towards the low beach whereon man had never attempted to live before," Borchgrevink wrote. "At 11 P.M. for the first time in the world's history, an anchor fell at the last *terra incognita* on the globe."

There was little ice in the bay, and the rocks of the Cape were bare and dark. Men went ashore and began to build a wooden hut. By March 2, the *Southern Cross* steamed away, bound for New Zealand to wait out the winter, and Borchgrevink and his nine comrades settled down for their willingly undertaken ordeal.

Winter gripped the Cape. "During the gradual shortening of the days," Borchgrevink wrote, "we experienced great depression, as if watching ourselves grow old. We were getting tired of each other's company and began to know every line in each other's faces . . . the days were now very dark, though the horizon toward the northwest was slightly crimson. The dark-

ness and the silence in this solitude roars in one's ears. It is
centuries of heaped-up solitude."

Before the sun disappeared, Borchgrevink and a companion
climbed to the summit of Cape Adare, 3,700 feet high. After
night fell on May 15, little exploration was done, despite the
presence of the dog teams. It was impossible to reach the
interior. The lofty mountains of Victoria Land hemmed them
in, and all they could do was chart and explore the region of
the bay itself.

There were seventy-five days of darkness. The temperature
fell 35° and more below zero. Ferocious blizzards hurled
blinding sheets of snow at the hut, and it was impossible to get
from the hut to the adjoining weather-observation stations,
even by crawling on all fours. The ten explorers did not suffer
the severe depression of the *Belgica* men, however, and their
health on the whole remained good—though Nicolai Hanson,
one of the zoologists, developed scurvy and died on October
14, early in the Antarctic spring.

The sun having returned on July 29, the penguins had come
back from their winter quarters, and they stood in solemn
array as Hanson was buried and a funeral service read. At the
end of January, the *Southern Cross* returned as scheduled,
bringing mail and newspapers, and the nine survivors went
aboard. They left their hut provisioned for any later travelers
who might come by.

The ship steamed southward along the coast, following
Ross' track. On February 10, Mounts Erebus and Terror
came into view, and then the great Ice Shelf appeared. Though
it was midsummer, the temperature dropped to 8° below
zero, but the sun was bright and the air clear. February 11

saw Ross' the farthest south surpassed. Then, at about 164° W., the *Southern Cross* came to a place where the ice wall dipped almost to the water. She moored alongside, and on February 19, another milestone was reached when Borchgrevink and an officer named Colbeck became the first men to set foot on the Ross Ice Shelf. They saw a smooth, flat stretch of snow-covered ice, so firm "it would serve as a road for a motor car." Borchgrevink and Colbeck, accompanied by a Finn named Savio, clambered into a dog-drawn sledge and made a short trip southward over the ice, reaching 78°50′ S., a new record. Borchgrevink's brief sledge trip was the forerunner of many that were to be made over the Shelf in the early years of the new century.

At one that afternoon, the *Southern Cross* steamed away, and had to fight her way through young, rapidly forming ice. She headed for Australia, and by the summer of 1900 Borchgrevink was in England. He had accomplished much. He had shown that it was physically possible to survive a winter on the Antarctic mainland, and that the Ross Shelf could be used as a jumping-off point for sledge journeys into the unknown interior. The edge of the Shelf had been charted, and it had been found to have receded thirty miles since Ross saw it. Useful weather records had been kept; new species of plants —and even the first live insects ever found in Antarctica— had been discovered.

In England, Clements Markham renewed his pleas for a large-scale government expedition. This time, the government paid some attention. But, once again, before Britain could act, a number of other expeditions had set out.

The first, which departed in October, 1901, was Swedish,

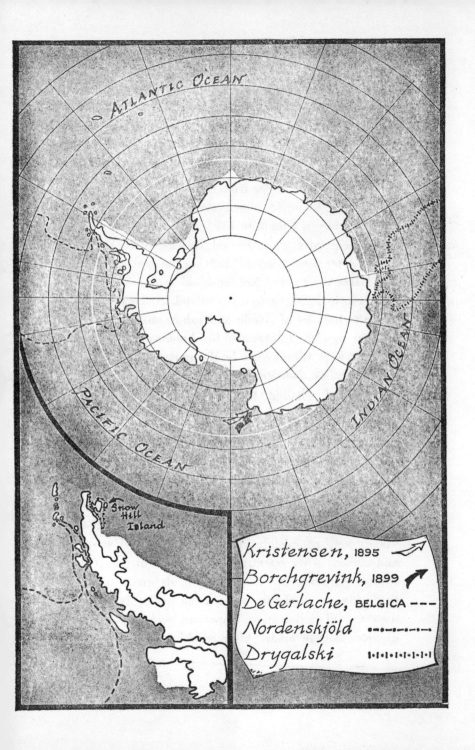

ATLANTIC OCEAN

PACIFIC OCEAN

INDIAN OCEAN

Snow
Hill
Island

Kristensen, 1895
Borchgrevink, 1899
De Gerlache, BELGICA ---
Nordenskjöld ·-·-·-·-
Drygalski |·|·|·|·|·|·|·|

and privately financed. Leader of the expedition was Otto Nordenskjöld, a geologist and mineralogist. Nordenskjöld, nephew of the Swedish Arctic explorer Baron Erik Nordenskjöld, had been born in 1869, and was just nine years old when his famous uncle made geographical history by conquering the Northeast Passage from Europe to the Bering Strait. The younger Nordenskjöld, who became a professor of geology at the University of Upsala in 1894, got his first taste of exploration a year later when he led an expedition to Tierra del Fuego. After three years of studying the geology of Patagonia and Tierra del Fuego, Nordenskjöld explored Alaska briefly, and then, in 1900, eastern Greenland. So he was well versed in the techniques of Arctic and sub-Antarctic exploration by the time he came to organize his Antarctic expedition.

There were twenty-nine in the party altogether, including nine scientists. Nordenskjöld's ship was the *Antarctic*, the three-masted whaling vessel with auxiliary steam power aboard which Carstens Borchgrevink had first visited Antarctica in 1895. Her captain this time was C. A. Larsen, who had already made two whaling voyages to the Antarctic in command of the *Jason*.

The Swedes sighted the South Shetlands on January 10, 1902. Nordenskjöld, accustomed as he was to icebound regions of the world, was startled to find that these sub-Antarctic islands were completely blanketed by ice and snow even in midsummer. After scientific observations of the 70-mile-wide strait separating the South Shetlands from the Antarctic Peninsula, the explorers coasted the peninsula and corrected the errors of earlier maps. Important geological and botanical discoveries were made. After reaching as far as 66° S., the ship turned back when it met thick pack ice, and retraced its path, rounding the northern tip of the peninsula on January 15 and cruising eastward into the Weddell Sea.

Nordenskjöld now attempted, as so many others had done, to follow Weddell's track southward. But, like the others, he met an impenetrable pack that stopped him south of 66° S.

The next part of the plan was to put a group ashore for the winter. Nordenskjöld chose as his winter base Snow Hill Island, in the Weddell Sea just off the eastern coast of the Antarctic Peninsula, in latitude 64°22′ S. Rich deposits of ancient fossil-shelled creatures called ammonites had been found in that area, and Nordenskjöld hoped to be able to determine the age of the rocks by study of the fossils they held.

On February 12, the party went ashore. Six men were left at Snow Hill Island: Nordenskjöld, the botanist Gosta Bodman, the surgeon and bacteriologist Dr. Ekelöf, Lieutenant Sobral of the *Antarctic,* and two of the ship's sailors. The *Antarctic* sailed away on February 21, intending to spend the winter at a South American port after it had laid down a depot at another point to the south for next summer's expedition.

Nordenskjöld and his five companions quickly set up the hut in which they would spend the winter. The *Antarctic* was supposed to return and pick them up the following summer— but they knew it might not be possible for the ship to get through the ice pack in time, and so they had furnished themselves with provisions for a two-year stay. Soon after the ship departed, the wintering party got an advance hint of winter: a savage storm pounded their hut, damaging it, and completely

demolishing the nearby observatory shack. Hasty rebuilding
was in order.

Once the living quarters were finished, the men were free
to undertake their scientific tasks. They carried out geological
and botanical studies, and made boat journeys to the nearby
islands. In April, a fifteen-day storm struck, with winds of
40 to 70 miles an hour almost steadily, and temperatures as
low as —13°. A storm in July was even fiercer. Within the
hut, though, the shore party remained comfortable and cheerful, even when the thermometer registered 32° below zero on
August 6.

The weather improved in September. On September 30,
Nordenskjöld, Sobral, and a seaman named Jonassen set out
on a sledge journey over the ice to the mainland of the peninsula. They took two sleds. One, loaded with 485 pounds of
provisions, was drawn by five powerful dogs, guided by
Jonassen. The other, loaded with 200 pounds, was to be "man-
hauled"—pulled by Nordenskjöld and Sobral. Though the
dog-powered sled was much heavier, the man-haulers had
trouble keeping up with it. After several attempts to match
the pace of the frisky dogs, Nordenskjöld and Sobral admitted
defeat and piled their sled on top of the other one. The dogs
were able to pull the greater load without strain—the first of
many such proofs that dogs were superb draft animals in
Antarctic conditions.

The temperature was ten below when the sledging party
set out, but the sunlight was bright and the air clear. The
party marched south over what is now known as the Larsen
Ice Shelf, covering 84 miles in seven days before a sudden
blizzard forced them to halt and make camp. They were in

sight now of the mountainous eastern coast of the Antarctic Peninsula, which Larsen, in 1893 on the first *Jason* voyage, had named Oscar II Land after Norway's king.

Struggling up a rising slope, they reached the mainland two weeks later, becoming the first to set foot on this side of the peninsula. Their way was made treacherous by crevasses in the ice—yawning abysses, concealed by flimsy bridges of snow. More than once, men and sleds sank into crevasses, but luckily they were able to pull themselves free. The sledgers halted at 65°48′ S., about one degree north of the Antarctic Circle. Bitter hurricanes lashed at them now; they suffered severely from snow blindness, their eyes being dazzled by reflections off the endless fields of white; and when Jonassen fell and injured his arm, it was necessary to turn back.

A strenuous, fatiguing return journey brought them to Snow Island safely, early in November. They had covered 400 miles in thirty-three days, 38½ miles on the final day alone. The men were exhausted—Nordenskjöld had lost more than fifteen pounds on the journey—but they had made useful geographical and geological discoveries. And now that the Antarctic spring was at hand, other scientific work could be resumed.

The shore party began to look forward to the return of the *Antarctic*. But the sea was blocked by ice, and it became obvious that the ship could not get through. Christmas saw the ice pack still thick. By February, with a second winter coming on, Nordenskjöld and his men resigned themselves to the fact that they would have to spend another year on Snow Island. They hurriedly set out to hunt penguins and seals to augment their dwindling supply of canned food.

The second winter was milder than the first, but nerves

were getting frayed in the island hut, and there were moments of doubt and pessimism. Clothing started to wear out. Irreplaceable items such as coffee, sugar, and tea were rationed in case a *third* winter had to be spent on the island. In October, 1903, Nordenskjöld undertook a second sledging expedition, this time into the unexplored region to the north and west of the base. Seven pups had been born during the year, so their "dog power" was greatly enhanced. Taking Jonassen with him, Nordenskjöld sledged in a circle around the coast of James Ross Island, a large island adjoining Snow Hill Island, and entered a bay known as Erebus and Terror Gulf.

The two Swedes halted at the headland of a frozen sound, giving names to the newly discovered islands and mountains they saw. While they were discussing a possible route back to Snow Hill, Jonassen pointed to a dark spot in the distance.

"What's that strange thing there close by the land?" he asked.

"Some penguins, I suppose," Nordenskjöld replied.

The "penguins" continued to advance, and Nordenskjöld, peering at them through his field glasses, gasped in bewilderment as he realized that they were men hurrying forward on skis. At least, he *thought* they were men, though they might well have been creatures from some other planet. At last they were close by. Nordenskjöld, in his account of the meeting described them as "two men, black as soot from top to toe; men with black clothes, black faces and high black caps, and with their eyes hidden by peculiar wooden frames, which are so attached to the face that they remind one of black silk masks with pierced pieces of wood for the eyes." Their long beards

FIG. I.
Capt. James Cook.

FIG. II.
*Admiral Fabian Gottlieb
von Bellingshausen.*

Fig. III. *Weddell seals.*

Fig. IV.
James Weddell.

FIG. V.
Nathaniel Palmer.

FIG. VI.
Lt. Charles Wilkes.

FIG. VII. *Ad-miral Dumont D'Urville.*

FIG. VIII. *Mount Erebus on Ross Island.*

FIG. IX. *James Clark Ross discovers Mount Erebus, Jan.,*
1841.

FIG. X.
James Clark Ross.

FIG. XI.
Sir Clements R. Markham.

FIG. XII. *Adelie penguin.*

OFFICIAL U.S. NAVY PHOTOGRAPH.

FIG. XIII.
Otto Nordenskjöld.

FIG. XIV. *Nordenskjöld's "Antarctica."*

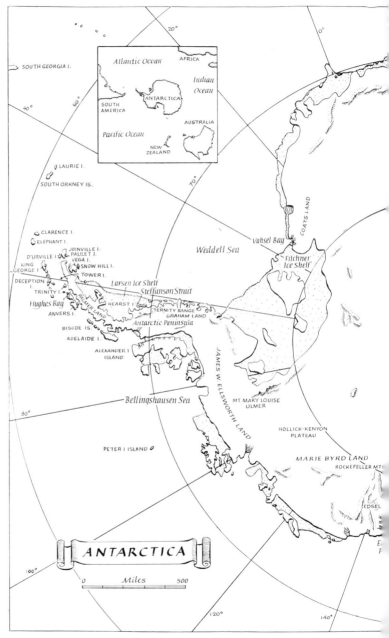

FIG. XV.

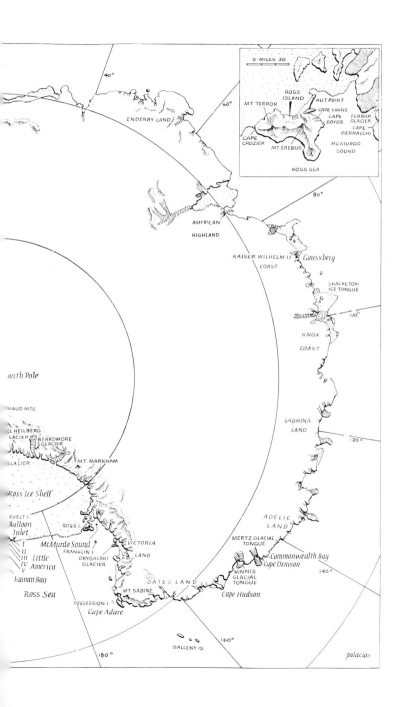

40°

ENDERBY LAND

60°

0 MILES 30

MT. TERROR

ROSS ISLAND

HUT POINT

CAPE EVANS

CAPE ROYDS

FERRAR GLACIER

CAPE BERNACCHI

CAPE CROZIER

MT. EREBUS

McMURDO SOUND

ROSS SEA

80°

AMERICAN

HIGHLAND

KAISER WILHELM II   *Gaussberg*

COAST

SHACKETON ICE TONGUE

100°

KNOX

COAST

uth Pole

MAUD MTS.

EL HEILBERG LACIER

B. FARDMORE GLACIER

GLACIER

MT. MARKHAM

SABRINA LAND

120°

Ross Ice Shelf

EVELT I.
Balloon Inlet

ROSS I.

ADÉLIE LAND

I
II
III *Little*
IV *America*
V

McMurdo Sound

VICTORIA

MERTZ GLACIAL TONGUE

FRANKLIN I.

DRYGALSKI GLACIER

LAND

Commonwealth Bay
Cape Denison

Kainan Bay

NINNIS GLACIAL TONGUE

140°

Ross Sea

OATES LAND

Cape Hudson

MT. SABINE

POSSESSION I.

Cape Adare

BALLENY IS.

160°

180°

palacios

FIG. XVI. *Capt. Robert Falcon Scott.*

FIG. XVII. *The "Discovery" alongside the Barrier.*

FIG. XVIII. *Capt. Scott wearing the wallet in which he carried his sledging journals.*

FIG. XIX. *Scott's hut on Cape Evans, built in 1911.*

OFFICIAL U.S. NAVY PHOTOGRAPH.

FIG. XX. *Sir Ernest Shackleton.*

FIG. XXI. *Lincoln Ellsworth and Roald Amundsen.*

Fig. XXII. *Admiral Byrd at the radio (advance base).*

Fig. XXIII. *The surface of the new Byrd Station; the bulk of the station is in a system of underground tunnels.*

FIG. XXIV. *Sir Edmund Hillary and Sir Vivian Fuchs.*

FIG. XXV. *Emperor penguins at Cape Crozier.*

FIG. XXVI. *Drilling holes in ice at McMurdo Sound to place flags to mark fuel hose leading from ship to storage tanks.*

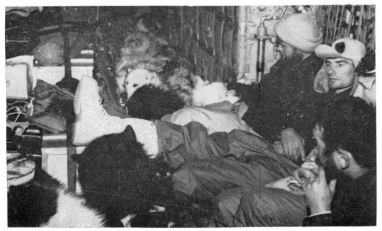

FIG. XXVII. *Scott Base personnel and dogs in transit on a LC–130F Hercules aircraft.*

FIG. XXVIII. *Men of Operation Deepfreeze at the Pressure Ridge at Scott Base.*

FIG. XXIX. *Tractor, sled train and helicopter pass Mount Erebus.*

and shaggy growths of hair added to their grotesque, barbaric appearance.

As Nordenskjöld gaped at the weird apparitions, one of the men held out his hand.

"How do you do, Otto?"

Nordenskjöld was stunned to think that these strange beings—natives of Antarctica, for all he knew—could greet him by name. Automatically, though, he found himself replying:

"Very well, thanks, how are you?"

Jonassen and Nordenskjöld exchanged puzzled glances. An idea occurred: these must be men from the *Antarctic*. Perhaps, when the ship found it impossible to get through to the Snow Hill base, it had put some sort of land party ashore. The explanation, when it came moments later, confirmed that guess. The two shaggy apparitions were J. Gunnar Andersson, a geologist who was Nordenskjöld's second-in-command on the expedition, and Lieutenant Duse, a surveyor. Nearby was a third man, a Norwegian sailor named Grunden.

The *Antarctic*, Nordenskjöld learned, had gone to the Falkland Islands after dropping off the Snow Hill Island party. There, it had picked up Dr. Andersson, who had already had an adventure of his own, getting shipwrecked off the Falklands on his way out from Sweden to join the expedition. From the Falklands, the *Antarctic* had sailed to South Georgia to carry out scientific studies, and then back to the Falklands for refitting and fresh provisions.

The next task was to pick up the Snow Hill Island group. The *Antarctic* had started south on November 9, but was met with unusually severe ice conditions far to the north of the

South Shetlands, and did not reach those islands for two weeks. Finally, the ship broke through, but several attempts to reach Snow Hill Island by different routes were thwarted. Andersson suggested that a small party be put ashore to travel overland to Snow Hill, while the *Antarctic* sailed away to try to find some new channel through the pack that might be open.

Andersson, Duse, and Grunden were landed at Hope Bay, on Joinville Island, with a small supply of food. It was December 29, 1902. They watched the *Antarctic* sail away to the north, and then strapped on their skis and set out along the shores of Erebus and Terror Gulf toward Snow Hill. They had not gone far, however, when they came to a great ice-covered sea that cut them off from Snow Hill. They tried to cross it, but soon they were wading in icy water to the waist, and had to turn back to Hope Bay. The arrangement was that the *Antarctic* would revisit Hope Bay and pick up the three ski travelers if they could not get through to Nordenskjöld.

But the *Antarctic* did not return. By February, Andersson, Duse, and Grunden realized they were stranded for the winter. Although they had scanty rations and no spare clothing, and had not expected to spend a winter in the open, they were undismayed. They slaughtered 700 penguins as a food supply, collected seal blubber for fuel, and built themselves a sturdy stone hut roofed with tent canvas.

It was a Robinson Crusoe adventure—not on a tropical island, though, but in the desolate Antarctic. The stranded trio made fishhooks out of brass buckles, lines out of seal leather; they told each other stories to keep amused; Grunden sang sea chanteys; they collected fossils; and they managed to remain cheerful and healthy.

When winter passed, they set out for Snow Hill Island once again, on September 29, 1903. They took the same route as they had in January, but now, in early spring, the sea was still frozen over, and they were able to cross. Nordenskjöld and Jonassen, meanwhile, had also left their camp, and the two parties met at a point they named Cape Wellmet, on Vega Island—a meeting even less probable than those of Palmer and Bellingshausen, and of D'Urville and Wilkes' *Porpoise*.

Grunden and Duse had suffered badly from frostbite on the trip, and the five explorers hurried back to Snow Hill Island. It must have a strange sight for Nordenskjöld's other companions, when he and Jonassen returned to camp with three strangers who were unrecognizable under the thick grime of six month's soot from a blubber lamp!

One fear troubled all of them now: that the *Antarctic* had met with some disaster. And, though they had no way of knowing it, that was exactly what had happened.

After dropping off the three men at Hope Bay, the *Antarctic* had attempted to reach Snow Hill Island once again through Erebus and Terror Gulf. On January 9, the ship was caught in gathering ice, and the next day a jagged floe ripped a hole in her side and damaged the rudder. The tide changed, and the ice moved away, leaving the hole exposed to the sea. The hold began to fill and the ship started to go down. On February 13, 1903, the end came after a month of attempting to save the ship. Captain Larsen ordered the *Antarctic* abandoned. All hands escaped in open boats, crossing to nearby Paulet Island with the scientific collections, food, and as much of the gear as could be saved.

After sixteen days of rowing and dragging the boats over

perilous pack ice, the castaways reached Paulet Island on February 28, and built a stone hut as a winter shelter. Thus there were three separate parties from the Swedish expedition within fifty miles of one another—but without any way of contacting or reaching one another. Captain Larsen and his men slaughtered 1,100 penguins for a winter food supply, and settled down to endure the long night. One sailor, Wennersgard, died of heart disease during the winter; the others came through safely, though weakened by the cold, lack of fresh air, and shortage of food.

In October, the ice began to break up. It was decided that Larsen and five companions would set out by boat for Hope Bay to find the Andersson party, and then continue on to Snow Hill. Larsen set out on the thirty-first, reaching Hope Bay a few days later. A note from Andersson awaited him in the hut, telling him that the three-man party had set out for Snow Hill at the end of September. Larsen accordingly headed for Snow Hill also.

Meanwhile, back at Snow Hill, Nordenskjöld was entertaining his three new guests. On the morning of November 8, as he sat making entries in his journal, he was surprised to find that four men—or were they penguins?—were coming across the ice toward the camp. They turned out to be men from an Argentinian rescue mission coming to fetch them home!

In that era before radio communications, the outside world could only guess at what was taking place in Antarctica. But the *Antarctic*, which had left late in 1901, had been gone for two years, and many in Europe feared that it had come to harm when it failed to return on schedule in March, 1903. Several rescue missions were organized. Argentina was the country closest to the Antarctic, and Lieutenant Sobral of Nordenskjöld's party was an officer of the Argentine Navy. So the gunboat *Uruguay*, commanded by Captain Julian Irizar, was sent to find the Swedish explorers.

Nordenskjöld, Andersson, and Captain Irizar conferred on how best to search for the survivors of the *Antarctic*. They decided to leave Snow Hill Island and explore Hope Bay, Paulet Island, and other nearby parts. On that same day, though, as the discussion took place, the dogs began to bark, and a sailor rushed into the hut with more surprising news: a *second* group of men was coming toward the camp.

"The next moment," Nordenskjöld wrote, "wild, ear-piercing cheers, mingled with shouts of '*Larsen!* LARSEN is here!!' . . . As a matter of fact we have experienced so much during the last few days that nothing can seem impossible to us, but still I can hardly believe my ears."

The incredible series of coincidences had reached its climax. Larsen and his five men came trekking into the Snow Hill camp only a few hours after the arrival of the Argentinian rescue mission. The three reunited groups—Larsen's, Andersson's, and Nordenskjöld's—boarded the *Uruguay*, and soon they were at Paulet Island to pick up the men Larsen had left there. The *Uruguay* left a cache of provisions at Paulet Island for the benefit of any later explorer who might find himself similarly marooned there. The provisions had been purchased by a young Englishman named Ernest Shackleton—and, strangely, it was destined to be Shackleton himself, on a polar expedition of his own, who would be the next castaway on the floes of the Weddell Sea.

The Swedish expedition was back in Stockholm late in

1903. By then, the bizarre series of mishaps and chance meetings seemed only comic to them. But the Nordenskjöld expedition had achieved more than some Stanley-and-Livingstone meetings in the frozen wastes. It had made valuable geographical and geological discoveries, completing the work of the *Belgica* expedition in charting the Antarctic Peninsula. And the explorers had demonstrated that human beings could survive two successive winters in Antarctica—given perseverance, ingenuity, and a good supply of seals and penguins.

Soon after Nordenskjöld sailed in 1901, a German expedition under Erich von Drygalski was heading toward the Antarctic also. Drygalski, a mathematician and geographer, was chiefly interested in the nature of the Antarctic glaciers, and in making up-to-date magnetic observations. His ship, the *Gauss,* was named for the German mathematician who had first calculated the location of the South Magnetic Pole.

Drygalski's expedition carried on its work west of Victoria Land. He looked for Termination Land, where Wilkes had been forced to end his long cruise, but found no such obstacle in his way. He concluded that the jutting ice peninsula Wilkes had seen had been a mirage. Farther to the west, the Germans discovered previously unknown land at longitude 90° E., and named it Kaiser Wilhelm II Land after the German monarch. Icebergs blocked the approach, so the expedition headed on, and by the middle of February, 1902, the *Gauss* shared the fate of the *Belgica:* it became trapped in swiftly freezing sea ice and was beset for the winter, spending fourteen months frozen in off the coast of Wilhelm II Land. In March, 1902, a party of two sleds crossed the ice shelf to shore, and found an extinct volcano, about 1,000 feet high, which was named Gauss Mountain. That same month, Drygalski took a balloon trip, rising 1,500 feet in a moored captive balloon; he found the air warm at that altitude, almost uncomfortably so.

After a severe but not difficult winter, the *Gauss* expedition managed to free itself from the ice in February, 1903, and by November the German explorers were home. Like the Swedes, they had added greatly to man's scientific understanding of the Antarctic continent, and they had also filled in another blank stretch of the continental coastline.

Many other expeditions swarmed the crowded Antarctic in the years around the turn of the century, now that the fifty-year period of little interest in the southern continent had been broken. A German deep-sea expedition aboard the *Valdivia*, though it did not visit the Antarctic, did settle for all time the question of the existence of Bouvet Island. Since Bouvet's discovery of it, a century and a half earlier, the island had been extremely elusive. Both Cook and Ross had sought it in vain, though several whaling men claimed to have landed there early in the nineteenth century. The *Valdivia* found it—an ice-sheathed volcanic island of about thirty square miles—and charted its location at last.

A Scottish expedition in 1902–03 aboard the *Scotia* entered the Weddell Sea, smashed its way through the pack ice, and got nearly as far as Weddell himself—down to 74° S. in 22° W. Beyond, land was sighted, flat and featureless, with a line of ice cliffs similar to the Ross Ice Shelf on the far side of the continent. This land was named Coats Land, after the sponsor of the expedition.

Another important accomplishment of the *Scotia* expedition was the establishment of a permanent meteorological station on Laurie Island in the South Orkneys, in November, 1903. The Scots hoped that Great Britain would support the station, but the government declined to do so, and so the men of the *Scotia* handed it over to Argentina. The Laurie Island outpost —first weather station south of the 60th parallel—has been in continuous operation ever since.

The French, who had done nothing in the Antarctic since D'Urville's day, now returned with an expedition led by Dr. Jean Charcot. Charcot, a distinguished medical man as well as an explorer, received $15,000 from his government and $30,000 from a French newspaper toward the $90,000 cost of his expedition aboard the small ship *Français;* the rest he raised privately. Sailing in August, 1903, Charcot's first intention was to go to the rescue of the long-missing Nordenskjöld expedition. When he reached Argentina, he learned of the rescue of the Swedish party, and continued on toward the west coast of the Antarctic Peninsula. Between 1903 and 1905, the Charcot expedition prepared a set of charts of the islands making up the Palmer Archipelago.

Of all the many expeditions that entered Antarctic waters during those busy years, the most famous, however, was the much-delayed British one for which Clements Markham had agitated so long. Not the least of its achievements was the fact that it brought to the Antarctic for the first time two men who would write magnificent and imperishable pages in the annals of exploration: Ernest Shackleton and Robert Falcon Scott.

7 SCOTT'S FIRST EXPEDITION

IN 1887, CLEMENTS MARKHAM, VISITING THE WEST Indies, watched a boat race off the island of St. Kitts. Taking part were some young sailors from H.M.S. *Active,* and the race, covering a mile from the starting point to a buoy and back, was a test of strength, boatmanship, and courage. Two midshipmen battled all the way to the finish line, and Markham was so pleased with the race that he invited the winner, eighteen-year-old "Con" Scott, to dine with him. "I was much struck with his intelligence, information, and the charm of his manner," Markham wrote.

Perhaps the young midshipman quickly forgot his meeting with the elderly geographer. Markham, though, never forgot Robert Falcon Scott. Fourteen years later, when the British National Antarctic Expedition, organized by Markham, sailed from London, the man in charge was Scott.

No one, in Scott's youth, had ever expected him to lead an expedition to the South Pole or anywhere else. Born in 1868, he was sickly and frail, and his talk of becoming a sailor brought laughter and jeers. He grew up dreamy and sloppy, disliking hard work and easily provoked to anger—but by the time he was sixteen he had conquered his flaws and turned into a diligent, popular, and active naval cadet.

He could not have known, in 1887, that Clements Markham had already picked him for Antarctic glory. He rose in naval ranks, and by 1899 held the post of lieutenant. Markham, that year, had succeeded in raising $75,000 toward the cost of an Antarctic expedition, and was bombarding the British government tirelessly for official support.

In June, 1899, Markham and Scott met by chance on a London street—the first time they had seen each other since the boat race of 1887. "That afternoon," Scott wrote, "I learned for the first time that there was such a thing as a prospective Antarctic Expedition. Two days later, I wrote applying to command it."

With Markham's backing, Scott got the job. In June, 1900, he was promoted to the rank of commander, once the government decided to yield to Markham's persuasion and sponsor an expedition. Work had already started on the expedition's ship, the *Discovery*, a wooden sailing ship with auxiliary steam engines.

Scott had had no polar experience whatever, and, in fact, had not even been much interested in such exploration. Now, however, he threw himself into his new assignment with as much enthusiasm as though he had been dreaming of Antarctica all his life. He studied the records of earlier expeditions, and went to Norway to visit Fridtjof Nansen, a great Arctic explorer who was the leading authority on polar conditions. Nansen advised him to take a pack of Greenland huskies with him for pulling sledges. Scott, though, had a tendency toward following his own opinions. Somehow he had become persuaded that Siberian dogs would be more useful in the Antarctic, and he took that kind instead.

There were problems in getting the expedition personnel organized. Markham's Royal Geographical Society had gained the support of that other famous learned body, the Royal Society, and now the two groups quarrelled over the make-up of the expedition. After much bickering, Scott put his team together. There were five scientists, including the physicist Louis Bernacchi, a veteran of Borchgrevink's *Southern Cross* expedition, and Dr. Edward Wilson, a biologist and also a talented artist. Among Scott's staff of officers was twenty-year-old Ernest Henry Shackleton, a robust, energetic seaman who had already had a roving and adventurous life.

The *Discovery* was on its way south by August, 1901. Scott's goal was the Ross Sea, that deep indentation cutting into the continent south of New Zealand. Scott was instructed to explore the Ross Ice Shelf and to discover the mountainous land east of it which Ross thought he had seen. After delays caused by the search for a leak somewhere in the hull, the *Discovery* left New Zealand toward the end of December, bound for the Ross Sea. The leak still bothered them, and would to the end of the journey. The ship itself was badly overloaded, carrying a heavy cargo of coal, twenty-three noisy, brawling dogs, and even a flock of forty-five sheep! No expedition had ever gone south so well equipped for scientific research, and hopes were high that important results would be forthcoming.

Scott encountered the ice pack on January 1, and a week later was through it to Cape Adare. The explorers went ashore, visiting the hut Borchgrevink had occupied while wintering over in 1899. Then they set out eastward along the Ice Shelf.

Sailing through iceberg-studded seas, Scott was struck, as so many others have been, by the contrast between the beauty of the scene and the deadly dangers that threatened at all times. "Above us," he wrote, "the sun shone in a cloudless sky. . . . Behind us lay the lofty snow-clad mountains, the brown sun-kissed cliffs of the cape and the placid glassy waters of the bay; the air about us was almost breathlessly still; crisp, clear and sun-lit, it seemed an atmosphere in which all Nature should rejoice. . . . Yet, beneath all ran this mighty relentless tide, bearing us on to possible destruction."

Indeed, destruction threatened that very day. The tide caught the *Discovery* and swept her helplessly toward a group of mighty icebergs. The wooden ship, sturdy as she was, would have been crushed to kindling, but that the tide shifted and the vessel was able to make for the open sea.

They cruised along the edge of the Barrier, which ranged from 70 to 240 feet in height. Careful soundings showed that the Ice Shelf was almost certainly floating on the Ross Sea. Scott hoped to find a "corner" at the east end of the Shelf, around which he could turn to advance southward. Instead, the Barrier ended in a lofty outjutting peninsula that forced the ship to turn north. Scott named it Edward VII Land for England's new king, and turned back.

On the return journey, they came to the inlet where Borchgrevink had been able to ascend the Ice Shelf. Mooring the ship there, Scott went up in a captive balloon, beating Drygalski by about a month to the honor of becoming Antarctica's first aeronaut. It was Scott's first balloon flight anywhere, and, he wrote: "As I swayed about in what appeared a very inadequate basket and gazed down on the rapidly diminishing figures below I felt some doubt as to whether I had been wise in my choice." High above the Barrier, he was able to see that it was not perfectly flat on top, but rolled southward in a series of waves.

Scott named the site of his flight Balloon Inlet, but did not choose it for his winter harbor. For that, he returned to McMurdo Sound, at the western end of the Ross Shelf. There, almost in the shadow of the active volcano, Mt. Erebus, the *Discovery* moored for the winter. Instead of spending the winter ashore, as Borchgrevink's expedition had done, Scott used the *Discovery* as his winter camp, sailing it far up the sound and mooring it at a place he called Hut Point, alongside the southwest corner of Ross Island. It was 400 miles farther south than men had ever wintered before.

A series of sledge journeys were planned for the spring. Scott and his men spent early winter training for their tasks. The dogs posed immediate problems. Arctic dogs are little more than wolves, and when not handled with steady discipline soon turn savage and unruly. Borchgrevink, knowing this, had brought two Finnish dog trainers with him, but Scott had not, and now the inexperienced Englishmen tried desperately to get their dogs under control. So wild and stubborn did they seem that it looked as though they could not be used at all, and manhauling the sledges might be necessary.

Scott sent out three sledging parties in March, 1902—heading south toward the Pole himself with a dog team, and sending other parties west and southwest. One group came down with scurvy and turned back quickly. Scott's party was driven back by cold and dog problems. The third group was caught in a blizzard and, instead of waiting for the storm to blow itself out, tried to walk back to camp while it was still snowing. They blundered onto a steep cliff near the edge of the Barrier and slid helplessly toward the sea; two men, unable to halt their wild slide, shot right over the edge, and one was never seen again. The other, luckily finding a patch of soft snow, was able to check his drop and climb back. He came staggering into camp a day and a half later, weak and hungry but otherwise unharmed.

It was not a promising beginning. "In one way or another," Scott wrote, "each journey had been a failure; we had little or nothing to show for our labors." They had taken the wrong food, the wrong clothing. "Everything was wrong, the whole system was bad," he noted mournfully.

At Hut Point, 720 miles from the South Pole in 78° S., winter came early. The sun set on April 23, 1902, and for the next four months darkness reigned. The explorers spent the winter reviewing the mistakes of the three brief sledge trips, and planning for the spring journeys. The temperature fell to 40° below zero. The ship-bound men amused themselves by publishing a newspaper, the *South Polar Times,* edited by Shackleton and illustrated by Wilson. They put on minstrel shows in below-zero weather, had poetry recitals, and talked endlessly about how good it would be to see the sun again.

"Dawn" came on August 22. The men of the *Discovery*

braved sub-zero temperatures to watch the sunrise. Scott wrote: "For long our blinking eyes remained fixed on that golden ball and on the fiery track of its reflection; we seemed to bathe in that brilliant flood of light, and from its flashing rays to drink in new life, new strength, and new hope."

In spring, preparations were completed for the great effort: a long sledge journey southward over the Ice Shelf. On November 2, 1902, Scott, Shackleton, and Dr. Wilson set out with three sledges and nineteen dogs. Their plan was to go as far south as possible—even to the Pole, perhaps.

Inexperienced, uneasy over the outcome, troubled by the poor results of the sledge trips last March, the three men were far from optimistic as they departed, and even the normally buoyant Shackleton had some misgivings. The dogs pulled well for a while, but, as Nansen had predicted, the Siberian dogs were not as suitable for Antarctic conditions as Eskimo huskies from Greenland. When they came to a stretch of *sastrugi*—ridges of wind-blown snow that turned the ice field into a corrugated, washboard-like surface—the dogs found it hard going. And then some of them became ill, apparently from eating dog food that had spoiled during the *Discovery*'s trip southward.

On November 25, Scott and his companions stood at 80°1' S. Before them lay a trackless white wilderness rimmed with mountains. The South Pole was somewhere beyond. No human eyes had ever beheld this scene before. Wilson, who had been making sketches all the way out—they had not brought a camera—was temporarily unable to see, blinded by the glare of the snow, and as they sledged on toward the mountains, Scott described the scene for him. The snow slope rose ever higher, culminating in a majestic twin peak, 15,000 feet high, which they named Mount Markham.

But they knew they could not continue for long. The South Pole was beyond their reach on this trip. Food was running low—one of the dogs had gnawed himself free of his traces and devoured a week's supply of seal meat—and the fuel oil was diminishing rapidly. The dogs were starting to die. Worst of all, the three explorers were coming down with scurvy.

It had long been known that scurvy resulted from some lack in the diet. No one knew, though, exactly what foods should be eaten to prevent scurvy, and there were many different theories. Captain Cook had shown that eating fresh fruits, particularly limes and lemons, would check the onset of the disease. There were no lemons to be had in the Antarctic, though. Nansen and other Arctic explorers had done without fruit juices, but by eating fresh walrus meat had staved off scurvy. Scott, however, had relied on canned provisions most of the way out, eating fresh seal meat only occasionally.

By December 21, 1902, the sledging party was more than 300 miles from Hut Point, still crossing the Ice Shelf and not yet on the mainland itself. Dr. Wilson, examining Shackleton, saw that his gums were turning red—a sign of scurvy. Scott substituted seal meat for the bacon and canned provisions they had been eating, and Shackleton's health improved, but now all three began to show symptoms of scurvy. On December 30, 380 miles out, Scott realized that they had to turn back. They had reached 82°17′ S., a new farthest south point.

The journey back was a nightmare. The dogs continued to sicken, and one after another had to be shot to put them out of their misery. Scott, a sensitive man who had found the slaughter of seals for food heartbreaking, was deeply distressed at the necessity of killing the tired dogs, and he resolved to try to find some other means of transportation for later polar expeditions.

They battled their way back to the depots where they had cached supplies for their return trip. A storm blew up as they neared the first depot, and they almost failed to find it at all. A good meal buoyed their spirits, but the last two dogs had to be killed, and now it would be man-hauling all the way back. Shackleton's scurvy symptoms returned. He hardly slept, coughed constantly, and, though he tried to hide it, was becoming so weak that he could not do his share of the hauling. On January 16, Scott noted in his journal: "He has been coughing and spitting up blood again, and at lunchtime was very 'groggy.' With his excitable temperament it is especially difficult for him to take things quietly, and at the end of each march he is panting, dizzy, and exhausted." Though troubled with scurvy themselves, Scott and Wilson pulled alone, Shackleton stumbling along with the greatest of effort.

The seal meat was running out—and, since they cooked it too much, most of its scurvy-preventing value was lost anyway. On January 28, they found the second depot, but though it held plenty of food, there was no seal meat. The next day, Shackleton collapsed, coughing and bleeding at the gums and throat. "His face looks pinched and worn," Scott wrote. "His strength is very much reduced, and for the first time he has lost his spirit and grown despondent." Somehow he struggled on, and the exhausted, weakened explorers staggered back into Hut Point on February 3, 1903, after an absence of ninety-three days.

While they were gone, another exploring party had climbed a glacier to the west of Ross Island and, 9,000 feet up, had seen that they were atop a mountain range that connected with the mountains of Victoria Land, farther westward. It began to appear that the interior of the continent was a vast plateau stretching toward the Pole, at heights of as much as 10,000 feet.

Also during Scott's absence, a relief expedition had arrived —the *Morning*, commanded by Captain Colbeck of Borchgrevink's *Southern Cross* expedition. Lying beyond the ice in which the *Discovery* still was frozen, the *Morning* brought provisions and letters from home.

Since the *Discovery* was locked fast, Scott planned to stay in the Antarctic at least another winter, but he gave his men the chance to go home on the *Morning*. Seven accepted the opportunity. An eighth went home with them, but not willingly. He was Shackleton, whose health had given way to such an extent that he could not remain with the expedition. To be sent home as an invalid was a bitter disappointment for Shackleton, a physically powerful man who found it humiliating to return in sick bay. "It has been a great blow to poor Shackleton," Scott wrote. Nursing his wounded pride as well as his health on the homeward journey, Shackleton resolved to return to Antarctica as soon as he was fit. Next time, he vowed, he would wipe out the stain of this disgrace. Nothing less than the conquest of the South Pole itself would serve, Shackleton felt, to atone.

Scott passed a second winter at Hut Point, showing no lingering ill effects from his harrowing journey southward, and in October, 1903, a new series of land journeys got under way. Instead of making another attempt to reach the Pole, Scott

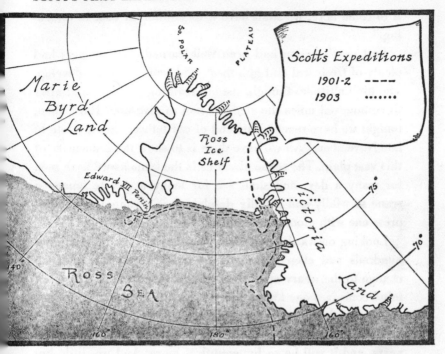

So. POLAR PLATEAU

Marie Byrd Land

Ross Ice Shelf

Edward VII Penin.

Victoria Land

Ross Sea

Scott's Expeditions

1901-2 ----

1903 ....

75°

70°

40°

160° 180° 160°

aimed westward this time, climbing a towering glacier that he named the Ferrar Glacier. Twelve men man-hauled four sledges to the summit of the glacier—the dogs proved of no use—and then, some 9,000 feet above sea level, set out over the high plateau.

Howling winds raked the sledgers. The temperature fell to —40°. The snow was hard and gritty, making progress slow, and an endless zone of *sastrugi* had to be conquered. They got on Scott's nerves; he wrote: "They are shaped like the barbs of a hook with their sharp points turned to the east, from which direction many look high and threatening, and each one now seems to suggest that, however easy we may have found

it to come here, we shall have a very different task in returning."

Last year's lesson had been well learned. The sledgers had
plenty of fresh seal and gull meat, and scurvy did not develop.
The high altitude, though, made breathing a chore, and after
three hundred miles the sledgers had to give up. "Here, then,
tonight we have reached the end of our tether," Scott wrote in
late November. "All we have done is to show the immensity of
this vast plain. The scene about us is the same as we have seen
for many a day, and shall see for many a day to come—a
scene so wildly and awfully desolate that it cannot fail to im-
press one with gloomy thoughts."

Looking outward, Scott knew that beyond the horizon "are
hundreds and even thousands of miles which can offer no
change to the weary eye, while on the vast expanse that one's
mind conceives one knows there is neither tree nor shrub, nor
any living thing, nor even inanimate rock—nothing but the
terrible limitless expanse of snow. It has been so for countless
years, and it will be so for countless more. And we, little human insects, have started to crawl over this awful desert, and
are now bent on crawling back again. Could anything be more
terrible than this silent, wind-swept immensity when one
thinks such thoughts?"

As they started back, Scott was granted a break from the
monotonous whiteness. He caught sight of a second glacier in
a valley just to the north, and, investigating it, discovered that
the river of ice ended midway down the valley. Ahead was a
cleft between the mountains completely bare of snow and ice!
The glacier gave way to streams cutting across thick mud.

Farther on, the valley narrowed to a gorge. Scott and his
men passed through and found a lake, a mile wide and three

or four miles long. It was strangely dreamlike to sit beside a gurgling stream for lunch, running warm sand through their fingers. High above them on the valley wall, they could see the line, 3,000 feet up, where the glacier once had reached. It seemed to Scott that this part of the continent must have grown warmer. Despite its freedom from the eternal ice that blanketed everything around, the valley was lifeless, not even containing the mosses and lichens found elsewhere. The only sign of life was the body of a dead Weddell seal, which had somehow wandered far from the sea. It was in a wondering mood that Scott trudged out of the valley and resumed the journey back to the base.

Food and fuel ran low on the return journey. The explorers dreamed of pork and cream and apples as they struggled on. Scott had sent back all but two of his companions earlier in the march, and now the three remaining men fought their way down a hard glazed surface of ice with the heavy sledges skidding along behind them. Toward the end, with food all but gone and a storm coming up, they realized they were completely lost. Suddenly, stepping out on an icy slope, they began to slip, and went sliding madly downhill, landing in a snowbank. To their surprise and delight, they found themselves back on the right trail again, with the smoke of Mt. Erebus just ahead!

In a few days more, Scott and his two companions were back at the *Discovery* after a fifty-nine day journey that had covered 725 miles. It had been less harrowing than the scurvy-plagued trip of the year before, but also more difficult, because so much of it had been performed in the thin air of the plateau. On his return, Scott found that twenty miles of ice still separated the *Discovery* from the open sea, though it was now January, the height of the Antarctic summer. The crew had started trying to saw through the ice, but it was obviously a hopeless job, and Scott ordered them to stop.

On January 5, 1904, two ships made a surprising appearance at McMurdo Sound: the *Morning* once again, accompanied by a whaling ship, the *Terra Nova*. Unknown to Scott, Clements Markham had asked the government to organize a relief expedition, when he had heard from Colbeck that the *Discovery* was frozen in for the summer of 1903. Prime Minister Balfour, angered by Markham's handling of the whole project from first to last, sent out the two ships with orders to bring back all Royal Navy men involved.

Scott was glad to see the ships arrive, but not at all pleased by the message they brought. He was ordered to abandon the *Discovery* and come home at once. The demand "descended on us like a bolt from the blue," he wrote.

It was painful to have to abandon his sturdy ship—but an order was an order. In six weeks more, summer would be over, and if the *Discovery* did not break free by then, she would have to be left behind. Gloomily, Scott had his instruments and scientific collections carried across the ice—only ten miles of it, now—to the relief ships offshore. Early in February, a thaw developed, and the *Discovery* was able to get within six miles of open water. The crews of all three ships got to work, sawing and hacking at the ice. By February 12 there were just three miles to go. Scott used explosives to smash up the ice, and on February 16 the *Discovery* was at last free. On March 5, 1904, the expedition crossed the Antarctic Circle heading northward, after two years and two months on the mainland of Antarctica.

It had been a fruitful, dramatic expedition. Two great sledge journeys had been made, the first substantial thrust into the heart of Antarctica. King Edward VII Land had been discovered, beyond the eastern end of the Ice Shelf. A new range of mountains had been found, and the plateau of the interior had been explored for the first time. Scott, Shackleton, and Wilson had been 207 miles closer to the South Pole than any other men. The scientific findings, though less romantic, had been of the first rank, and filled many volumes.

Scott returned to more conventional naval duties now. In September, 1905, he married a young sculptress, Kathleen Bruce, and it appeared as if he were giving up the arduous quest of the South Pole in favor of a more settled life as the commander of a battleship. The *Discovery,* though she had been specially designed for polar research, was sold for a fraction of her cost to a commercial shipping company. The members of Scott's expedition went their separate ways. After seven years of intense Antarctic exploration, from the departure of the *Belgica* in 1897 to Scott's homecoming in 1904, a lull seemed to descend.

Nevertheless, Antarctica was far from mastered. All the explorers so far had done little more than scout the borders of the silent continent. What had been accomplished? Patches of coastline had been charted; the Antarctic Peninsula, much of it lying north of the Antarctic Circle, had been explored fairly thoroughly; and Scott had journeyed 380 miles inland without ever getting off the floating bulk of the Ross Ice Shelf.

The heart of the Antarctic still beckoned. The South Pole, the bottom of the world, was the great lure. Scott, for the moment, was not willing to renew the assault. Another man was. Brooding over his ignominious retreat from the Antarctic, simmering with ambition to plant England's flag at 90° S., Ernest Shackleton labored to get a new expedition under way.

8 THE FIRST ASSAULT ON THE POLE

IT WAS MORE THAN MERE PRIDE THAT DROVE ERNEST Shackleton back to the Antarctic, of course. Certainly he stung with shame after having to be invalided home from Scott's expedition. Certainly he burned with the yearning to make up for that display of what he saw as weakness. But his basic reason for renewing the icy quest was the one that has motivated men for untold thousands of years: the desire to know what lies over the next hill, and the next, and the one beyond that.

Shackleton was born in Ireland in 1874. An undistinguished student, an indifferent athlete, he hardly seemed marked for greatness. At sixteen, a big, strong-bodied, good-natured boy who had shown no particular ambition, he left school and joined the merchant service. He moved from ship to ship and from line to line, suddenly coming alive at sea, seeking promotion and responsibility. By the last year of the nineteenth century, he was third officer on a merchant ship working between England and South Africa.

Scott, in putting together his staff for the *Discovery* expedition, had naturally picked mainly Royal Navy men. Shackleton, though only in the merchant service, was chosen for his knowledge of sailing vessels, and because he had several times rounded Cape Horn and so had had a taste of the terrible weather to be encountered in southern waters.

Shackleton and Scott were very different men, with little in common but their bravery and devotion to duty. Scott was precise and methodical, a stickler for small details, a reserved, self-contained man who found satisfaction in the disciplines of military life. Shackleton, full of vitality and charm, was more outgoing, a magnetic personality, happy-go-lucky, a born adventurer with little interest in the niggling detail work that Scott found so congenial. He was more of a romantic than the sober-minded, cautious Scott.

On the voyage home from Antarctica aboard the *Morning*, Shackleton shook off his scurvy, and arrived in England bronzed and fit, already thinking about a new expedition. But he lacked Scott's position in the Royal Navy, and lacked, too, the influential support of Clements Markham. From 1903 to 1906, Shackleton looked without success for backing for his proposed expedition.

Those were busy years for him. He lectured successfully on the adventures of the *Discovery* expedition; he took a wife, in 1904; he ran for Parliament, and lost; he worked as a magazine editor, then as Secretary of the Royal Scottish Geographical Society. When he applied for a naval commission, though, he was turned down—a refusal that he never forgot.

Meanwhile, word came that Dr. Charcot of France was organizing a second Antarctic expedition, and that Belgium was also planning a new attempt to conquer Antarctica. Early in 1907, Shackleton began to fear that one of these other expeditions might forestall him in his dream of reaching the Pole. Frantically, he plunged into one risky business venture after another, hoping to put together enough money to take him to Antarctica. He was involved in an American cigarette factory, a Hungarian gold-mining scheme, an attempt to set up an international news agency. All were failures. He made some valuable business contacts, though, and finally arranged to borrow $100,000 from a group of wealthy industrialists. The money would be repaid, he promised, after his expedition's return, out of the profits from the book he would write and the lectures he would give.

In April, 1907, Shackleton announced that he was assembling an expedition, privately financed, which would have no official government sponsorship. His plan, he said, was to set up camp at Scott's old Hut Point base and then to send out three parties: one eastward over the Ross Ice Shelf into King Edward VII Land; one westward over the mountains of Victoria Land to find the South Magnetic Pole; and one, led by Shackleton himself, due south to the South Geographical Pole. Reaching the South Pole would be the grand goal of the expedition, though Shackleton planned to take scientists along so that it would not be purely an adventure-seeking journey.

No sooner did Shackleton make his plans known then there came a stunning blow from an unexpected quarter. His old leader Scott wrote to him from Gibralter, where he was then in command of H.M.S. *Albemarle,* and asked him not to use the Hut Point base. It seemed that Scott was contemplating a new expedition himself, and needed Hut Point for his own base.

It was a total surprise. Scott had said nothing about such plans before. Shackleton felt himself obliged to yield, and so he agreed to make his camp far to the east, near King Edward VII Land. That meant abandoning the Victoria Land expedition completely, and the South Pole journey would now be riskier and longer. But he felt that Scott had first call on Hut Point.

Shackleton bought a small, elderly sealing vessel, the *Nimrod.* His preparations for the voyage drew heavily on the dismal experience of his earlier failure. Distrusting dogs for transport, he obtained Manchurian ponies to haul the sledges, though at the last moment he took nine dogs as well. He designed much of the equipment himself, and took advice from the veteran Norwegian Arctic explorers, furnishing his expedition with Norwegian sledges, skis, fur garments, and reindeer-skin sleeping bags. A real novelty was the specially adapted automobile that he took along in the hope that the top of the Barrier would be hard-packed enough to support a wheeled vehicle.

Two veterans of the *Discovery* expedition, Frank Wild and P. O. Joyce, went with Shackleton. His scientific staff included a young English geologist, Raymond Priestley, and two Australians, the physicist Douglas Mawson and the geologist Edgworth David. David was almost fifty—an advanced age for

Antarctic exploration—and was taken on for the summer cruise only.

The *Nimrod* sailed from London on July 30, 1907, bound for New Zealand. The forty-year-old ship was so small and slow that she could not carry enough coal for the fifteen-hundred-mile journey from New Zealand to the edge of the Antarctic ice pack, and so Shackleton arranged to have her towed by a larger ship. Even so, he had to leave several of the ponies behind, and the overloaded ship rolled fearfully in the rough seas.

Little ice confronted them in the Ross Sea, luckily. They made for Scott's Balloon Inlet first, but found it greatly changed. The ice walls of the inlet had "calved"—broken off and floated away as icebergs—and what had been a narrow opening now was a huge bay, which Shackleton named the Bay of Whales. Landing there seemed too dangerous now. Suppose they made their camp on the Barrier, only to have it calve again and throw them into the icy sea? The thought of what would have happened if the collapse of Balloon Inlet had occurred after the explorers arrived, instead of before, made Shackleton decide that "under no circumstances would I winter on the Barrier, and . . . wherever we did land we would secure a solid rock foundation for our winter home."

He sailed eastward toward King Edward VII Land, but an enormous pile-up of ice blocked him. It was as though all the icebergs in the Ross Sea had chosen to drift toward the eastern end of the Barrier. With coal running low, Shackleton could not maneuver indefinitely. There was no help for it; he had to go to the one place where he knew safe anchorage could be had—McMurdo Sound at Hut Point. He wrote to his wife, "I have been through a sort of Hell since the 23rd and I cannot even now realize that I am on my way back to McMurdo Sound, and that all idea of wintering on the Barrier or at King Edward VII Land is at an end; that I have to break my word to Scott. . . . All the anxiety that I have been feeling coupled with the desire to really do the right thing has made me older than I can ever say."

Ice still gripped much of the sound, and Hut Point could not be reached. Shackleton had to make his base at Cape Royds, 20 miles farther out at the foot of Mount Erebus. It was another bit of bad luck, for every mile counted in the dash to the Pole. Worse, Shackleton was unable to get over to Ross Island to lay depots for his polar trip, because just after the *Nimrod* steamed away the bay ice broke up and Shackleton was cut off from the far side of McMurdo Sound.

The preliminary depots were of great importance. The sledging season would run from mid-October to early March, at best—little more than four months in which to cover the 1,730 miles from Cape Royds to the Pole and back. Every day would be critical in the race against advancing winter. The polar party would have to average fourteen miles a day, man-hauling much of the time in the thin air of the high plateau. If they could lay down supply depots the season before, it would be that much less that they would have to haul on the actual trip to the Pole. But no depots were laid.

The *Nimrod* left on February 22, 1908, with the winter party living in a hut at Cape Royds. Before winter set in, the explorers got what experience they could by ranging the nearby region. Shackleton tested his equipment and men on short sledge journeys, and was dismayed when four of the ponies died almost at once. Testing out the automobile, Shackleton found that the engine would work in the cold weather—a matter of some doubt—but that the wheels sank into the snow. The motor car was of little use on the expedition and never got far out of the main camp.

In March, Edgworth David—who had decided to stay for the winter after all—and five companions climbed to the summit of Mount Erebus. Though temperatures were near zero and blizzards struck several times, the fifty-year-old David blithely undertook a climb to a peak more than 12,000 feet high. *Sastrugi* blocked the way, but on the first day the party camped at the 2,750-foot level, and the next day reached an altitude of better than 5,000 feet, though the temperature fell to —28°. The crater itself was attained on the sixth day. David wrote:

"We stood on the verge of a vast abyss, and at first could see neither to the bottom nor across it on account of the huge mass of steam filling the crater and soaring aloft in a column 500 to 1,000 feet high. After a continuous loud hissing sound, lasting for some minutes, there would come from below a big dull boom, and immediately great globular masses of steam would rush upwards to swell the volume of the snow-white cloud which ever sways over the crater. . . . Presently a pleasant northerly breeze fanned away the steam cloud, and at once the whole crater stood revealed to us in all its vast extent and depth. Mawson's angular measurements made the depth 900 feet and the greatest width about half a mile. There were at least three well-defined openings at the bottom of the cauldron, and it was from these that the steam explosions proceeded."

The amazing Professor David also led one of the two great

expeditions of the following season—the trek to the South
Magnetic Pole. He was accompanied by the physicist, Douglas
Mawson, and by Dr. A. F. Mackay, a surgeon who, like Maw-
son, had been part of David's Mount Erebus party.

They set out on October 5, 1908—by automobile. The
sputtering car took them only a few miles before the soft snow
became too much for it, and they broke out the sledges and
continued on foot, man-hauling the sledges. For two hundred
miles they hiked over the sea ice fringing the coast of Victoria
Land; it was slow going because of the treacherous crevasses
everywhere. As the first men to set foot on the mainland here,
they raised the flag at Cape Bernacchi, and then crossed the
Drygalski Glacier, a tongue of ice 100 feet high and 20 miles
wide.

Now they had to leave the coast and turn inland, ascending
the mountains that led to the interior plateau on which the
South Magnetic Pole would be found. Ross, Wilkes, and Scott
had all calculated different positions for the Magnetic Pole,
and its exact location would have to be felt out with compass
and dip needle. On December 11, they camped near the far
side of the badly crevassed Drygalski Glacier, while Mawson
loaded some fresh photographic plates. While working in the
tent, Mawson heard Professor David, outside, ask him politely
if he was particular busy. Mawson, who was, said so, and went
back to work. A few minutes later, David asked the same question, and got the same answer. After a while, Mawson heard
the Professor's voice again, ". . . still with infinite politeness
and apology," as Mawson put it.

"I am so sorry to disturb you, Mawson, but I am down a

crevasse and I really don't think I can hold on much longer,"
David said.

Bolting from the tent, Mawson found the Professor, un-
ruffled but nearly exhausted, clinging for his life to the rim of
a crevasse that seemed almost bottomless!

A few days later, as the party scrambled up one of the
glaciers that led inland, it was Mawson's turn to slip into a
crevasse, but he, too, was hauled out in time. The Magnetic
Pole was now about 220 miles away, Mawson computed—but,
as they continued onward along the upward climb, the tantalizing Pole seemed to retreat! Snow blindness struck them. Their
breath froze as it left their nostrils. The skin of their hands
and faces was cracked and peeled. Each time Mawson took
magnetic observations, he found that the Magnetic Pole had
moved farther away. On January 12, he calculated that the
goal lay only four days' journey away. It was not until the
sixteenth that they finally reached it, at 72°25′ S., 155°16′ E.,
atop a 7,000-foot-high plateau. Unlike the South Geographical
Pole, which is permanently fixed—by definition—at 90° S.,
the South Magnetic Pole wanders from year to year as the
earth's magnetic field fluctuates. That explained why the early
explorers of the Antarctic had calculated different positions
for it—and explains, too, why the Magnetic Pole today is not
now where David, Mawson, and Mackay found it in 1909.

Having reached their goal, and made many valuable geological, magnetic, and geographical discoveries along the way,
the David party turned back. The *Nimrod*, which had returned
to Antarctica at winter's end, was supposed to pick them up
at a depot near the Drygalski Glacier between January 15 and

February 1. The return journey was a fatiguing one; they had 249 miles to go, and had to average better than sixteen miles a day or they would miss their rendezvous with the *Nimrod*. Mawson had a sprained leg, which slowed them, and they were also delayed in a stretch of ice later nicknamed "the Devil's Ballroom," where plates of ice set at an angle of 45° created a difficult obstacle. They had one advantage: strong winds swept down the glacier behind them, and they were able to mount a sail on their sledge and glide along. On January 28, they celebrated David's fifty-first birthday, but their mirth was tempered with the fear that they would miss the *Nimrod* and have to trek all the way back to Cape Royds on foot in steadily worsening weather.

They came to the rendezvous point on February 2, 1909. The *Nimrod* was nowhere to be seen. Too exhausted to go on, they set up a tent to rest for a few days, in the hope that the ship would return for them. Two days later, they heard the sound of a gun offshore, and knew the *Nimrod* had arrived.

Gleefully the three men burst from their tent and raced toward the shore, Mawson in the lead by a hundred yards. As David puffed along, well to the rear, Mackay suddenly turned and yelled back, "Mawson's fallen into a deep crevasse. Look out, it's just in front of you!"

Mawson had vanished. David peered forward, over the edge of an oblong sapphire-blue hole in the ice. "Are you all right, Mawson?" he called.

From the depths came a single welcome word: "Yes."

He was hanging on, twenty feet down. David and Mackay fetched the sledge harness and, lowering it to him, tried to pull him out. They nearly pulled themselves in, instead. By this

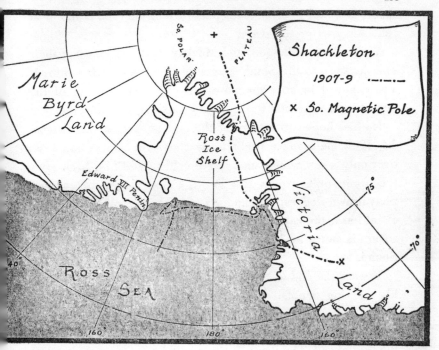

Marie
Byrd
Land

So. POLAR

PLATEAU

+

Shackleton

1907-9 .—.—.—

x So. Magnetic Pole

Ross
Ice
Shelf

Edward VII Penin.

Victoria

75

70

40°

Ross
Sea

Land

160   180°   160°

time the *Nimrod* had berthed and lay to, about two hundred yards away. Mackay cupped a hand and shouted to the men on board, "Mawson has fallen down a crevasse, and we got to the Magnetic Pole!"

A rescue party ran to shore, and in a few moments Mawson had been hauled to safety. In a few days, the explorers were back at Cape Royds. They had been out for 122 days, though carrying rations only for 93; they had covered 1,260 miles of unexplored territory, on foot all the way; they had reached the South Magnetic Pole, had mapped a great span of new land, and had revealed the geological structure of South Victoria Land. It was one of the most remarkable sledge trips ever

made, and that its leader was past fifty at the time is the most
fantastic part of the story.

While David, Mawson, and Mackay were carrying out their
epic journey to the South Magnetic Pole, Shackleton himself
was engaged in an even more grueling trip in quest of the
heart of the Antarctic itself, the South Geographical Pole.

He had hoped to set out at the end of August. On August
12, 1908, he made a preliminary start, but winter had been
over only a few weeks, and severe cold turned him back after
the twenty-mile trip to Hut Point. Using the motor car and
pony-drawn sledges, Shackleton carried his supplies to the Hut
Point base; the car, always troubled by the snow, moved at a
sober six miles an hour over the frozen surface of McMurdo
Sound.

Toward the end of September, Shackleton set up the first of
his outlying depots. A six-man party man-hauled a load of
pony fodder to Depot A, a hundred miles south of Hut Point.
They averaged twenty miles a day, which was a good sign for
the task ahead. The Scott-Wilson-Shackleton sledge journey of
1902 had averaged only about six miles a day, and Shackleton knew that he would have to double and even triple that
pace if he hoped to reach the Pole.

There was no margin for error in his planning. In the four
months of relatively good weather, he would have to trek
across the Ice Shelf to the mainland, ascend steep and hazardous glaciers to the vast interior plateau, and finally march to
the Pole in the thin air of an ice field as much as 12,000 feet
above sea level. Then would come the return journey, which
had to be completed before the winter weather closed in. Any
delay, any unpredicted obstacle, any spell of bad weather,
might be fatal. The odds were against success—but Shackleton

was a man driven by the inner need to make up for an earlier failure, and he paid no attention to the odds.

He took three men with him: Lieutenant Adams, a meteorologist, Dr. Marshall, a map maker, and Frank Wild, the *Discovery* veteran. They allowed themselves food for ninety-one days on the basis of thirty-four ounces a day. Four ponies, each pulling a 600-pound load at the outset, would provide the transport, for Shackleton, like Scott, had little faith in dog-power.

Leaving Cape Royds on October 29, 1908, they were kept at Hut Point by the weather until November 3, and finally got under way then. A supporting party of six men accompanied them for the first thirty-seven miles, which were badly crevassed. By November 6, they were past the crevasses, and the supporting party turned back, having helped all it could.

Progress was slower than expected. Blizzards hampered the four men, and they were troubled by snow blindness, that painful affliction caused by glare, which one explorer described as feeling "as if sand has worked under the eyelids." On November 15, they reached Depot A, but they were behind schedule already, and it was apparent that they would have to be out more than the planned ninety-one days if they were to reach the Pole. Accordingly, they began cutting down on food, but that, too, had its effect since men sledging in bitter Antarctic cold need all the food they can get, and efficiency drops when the food intake goes down.

By November 21, the mountains guarding the Polar Plateau were clearly in sight. But Chinaman, one of the ponies, was weakening badly, and had to be shot. They cut the pony up and cached the meat at Depot B, one hundred miles south of

Depot A, so that some advantage at least could be had from the animal's death. But, Shackleton noted, "Poor old Chinaman was a tough and stringy beast." And now only three ponies remained for the long journey ahead.

Five days later, they passed Scott's farthest south, and made camp at 82° 18′ S. "It falls to the lot of few men," Shackleton later wrote, "to view land not previously seen by human eyes, and it was with feelings of keen curiosity, not unmingled with awe, that we watched the new mountains rise from the great unknown that lay ahead of us. Mighty peaks they were, the eternal snows at their bases, and their rough-hewn forms rising high towards the sky. . . . As the days wore on, and mountain after mountain came into view, grimly majestic, the consciousness of our insignificance seemed to grow upon us. We were but tiny black specks crawling slowly and painfully across the white plain, and bending our puny strength to the task of wresting from nature secrets preserved inviolate through all the ages."

Finding a gap in the mountains, they worked their way upward, and by December 4 stood 3,350 feet above sea level, looking southward toward the distant Pole. "There burst upon our view an open road to the south," wrote Shackleton, "for there stretched before us a great glacier running almost south and north between two huge mountain ranges." The glacier proved to be a colossal river of ice, 15 miles wide and more than 100 miles long. Shackleton named it Beardmore Glacier, after one of his financial backers.

Two more of the ponies had died on the way to the glacier, one at 82° 40′ S. and one at 83° 16′ S. A depot of pony meat had been left at each place. The men had to do most of the hauling as they started to ascend the glacier. Strangely, the explorers stripped to their shirts as the air turned warm, the bare rocks reflecting the sun's heat. Though the temperature was only 22°, Shackleton found himself getting sunburned, and frostbitten as well. "It was quite usual to feel one side of the face getting frozen while the other side was being sunburned."

On December 7, the fifth day of slow, painful climbing up the cracked and crevassed blue ice of the glacier, they lost their last pony, Socks. Adams, Marshall, and Shackleton, man-hauling one sledge, were in the lead, and Wild, guiding the pony, followed. The three men had passed over a snow-covered crevasse without noticing it, but the pony's weight broke the crevasse lid, and poor Socks disappeared. Only luck kept Wild and the sledge from vanishing also, taking half the entire supply of food and fuel.

It was a severe setback. Not only would they have to man-haul the rest of the way and back, but they would not even have the use of Socks for food. They pushed on nevertheless. Near the top of the glacier, Frank Wild found seams of coal, up to eight feet thick—startling evidence that in the remote past Antarctica had been forested and warm. On Christmas Day, the climbers celebrated with cigars and brandy, and two days later they were at the top of the glacier. The South Pole lay 250 miles ahead, across the featureless wasteland of the Polar Plateau.

They were weak from hunger; cold and miserable. Shackleton suffered blinding headaches, the others from nosebleeds. To conserve their strength, they left one of the sledges, one of the tents, and all the extra heavy clothing behind in a depot at

85° S. A little farther on, they cached everything else they could possibly do without, including most of their food. They were at a height of 9,600 feet now. On the last day of 1908, at 86°54' S., the altitude was giving them headaches so severe that it was, in Shackleton's words, "as though the nerves were being twisted up by a corkscrew and then pulled out."

A day later, in temperatures of —14°, they were marching over snow so soft they sank in up to their ankles. Every movement was an effort. "God knows we are doing all we can," Shackleton wrote in his diary, "but the outlook is serious if this surface continues and the plateau gets higher, for we are not traveling fast enough to make our food spin out and get back to our depot in time." He refused to think of failure yet. But, he told himself, "I must look at the matter sensibly and consider the lives of those who are with me. I feel that if we go on too far it will be impossible to get back over this surface, and then all the results will be lost to the world."

Two days later, he wrote: "The end is in sight. We can only go for three more days at the most, for we are weakening rapidly." An observation on January 6 put their position at 88°7' S., 113 miles from the Pole. The temperature was 25° below zero. They still had hopes of making one last rush south to the Pole. But on the seventh, a "blinding, shrieking blizzard" came up, with the wind at eighty to ninety miles an hour, the temperature down to 38° below zero. It kept them in their tent until four in the morning on January 9. Then, leaving sledge and tent behind, they struggled southward for five hours, reaching 88°23' S.

They were ninety-seven miles from the Pole. But they could go no closer. "We have shot our bolt," Shackleton wrote. They

hoisted the British flag and took possession of the Polar
Plateau in King Edward VII's name, and buried a brass cylinder containing documents of their journey and a few postage
stamps. It was disappointing to have to quit this close to the
Pole, but they knew it would mean certain death to go on.
"Whatever regrets may be," Shackleton said, "we have done
our best."

The South Pole was only a symbolic goal, anyway. No new
geographical information would be obtained by reaching the
southernmost part of the earth. Here on the plateau, everything was the same. "We looked south with our powerful
glasses, but could see nothing but the dead white snow plain.
There was no break in the plateau as it extended towards the
Pole."

Now began the terrible journey home. It was downhill,
which was a blessing, but they were weak and hungry, had no
horses, little food. They put a sail on the sledge and coasted
along on a tailwind to Depot E at the head of Beardmore
Glacier in twelve days, making between fourteen and twenty-
nine miles each day. Descending the crevassed glacier was
more difficult: "We fell into hidden crevasses time after time,
and were saved by each other and by our harness," Shackleton
wrote at Depot D on January 27. "I cannot describe ade-
quately the mental and physical strain of the last forty-eight
hours."

February 2 brought a new problem: dysentery, due, they
thought, to eating infected pony meat. Stomach cramps and
diarrhea made the journey hellish now. Blizzards halted them
for days at a time, and they had to fight against sickness and
starvation as they slogged from depot to depot. "It is neck or

nothing with us now," said Shackleton. "Our food lies ahead, and death stalks behind." Biscuits and cheese kept them going. On February 13, they reached the place where they had shot Chinaman on the way out, seemingly centuries ago. They breakfasted on horse meat and set out again, reaching Depot A, a hundred miles from Hut Point, on the twentieth. There was just enough food there to carry them on to the next depot, which should have been laid by a supporting party a short time before. If they could not find the last depot, all would be over. "We are so thin," wrote Shackleton, "that our bones ache as we lie on the hard snow in our sleeping-bags."

Half-starved and all but dead on their feet, they stumbled toward the site of the last depot on February 23. Nothing remained in their packs but a few biscuits. At first, the depot could not be found—but then sharp-eyed Wild spied the sunlight glinting off the lid of a biscuit can that had been placed on top of the depot. Food in abundance was there—fresh mutton, plum puddings! They ate with glorious gluttony. Marshall, the surgeon, was too weak from dysentery to go on, however, and Shackleton left him behind in the care of Adams. He and Wild went on, reaching Hut Point on February 28. There, they found a note telling them that all other parties were back, and that the *Nimrod* would wait until February 26.

But that was two days past! Was it possible that after the seven-week race northward they had missed their ship by two days, and would die here at Hut Point as winter closed in? Frantically, they hoisted flags and lit fires, and in the morning the *Nimrod* appeared. She had waited an extra few days after all. Shackleton went back to fetch Marshall and Adams, and on March 4, 1909, the *Nimrod* sailed for a warmer land with all the sledging heroes safely on board.

The Shackleton expedition had discovered five hundred miles of new mountain ranges surrounding the Ross Ice Shelf; it had found and conquered Beardmore Glacier, the approach to the Polar Plateau; it had come less than a hundred miles from the Pole itself, despite fearful conditions. These accomplishments, and those of Professor David's journey to the South Magnetic Pole, made the *Nimrod* expedition the most successful thus far in Antarctic exploration.

The great prize, the Pole itself, had eluded Shackleton once again. Upon his return to England, where he was greeted as few returning heroes ever have been, he began immediately to plan another attempt. Robert Falcon Scott, too, perhaps relieved at Shackleton's near miss, was readying his second expedition for departure. It seemed certain that one or the other of these bold men would be the first to plant a flag at 90° South.

Soon, indeed, a flag waved there—but not the Union Jack. A man who had never expected to reach the South Pole at all, who longed instead to journey to the opposite end of the earth, entered the picture and carried off the prize.

9 THE CONQUEST OF THE SOUTH POLE

THE SOUTH POLE WAS "SECOND BEST" FOR ROALD Amundsen. Born in 1872 near Oslo, Norway, he had dreamed since boyhood of exploring the Arctic regions surrounding his native land, and of being the first to reach the North Pole. He was also fascinated by the story of Sir John Franklin's quest for a Northwest Passage across the Arctic by sea from the Atlantic to the Pacific, and one of his hopes was to succeed where Franklin had failed.

His mother wanted him to become a doctor. She died when he was twenty-one, and Amundsen immediately gave up his medical studies and turned to the career of an explorer, his first love. Since there is no land around the North Pole, but only drifting floes of ice, Amundsen needed experience as a seaman, and from 1894 to 1896 he served as a sailor aboard an Arctic merchant vessel. A year later, he signed on as first

164

mate of the *Belgica,* going to the Antarctic in order to gain experience for his Arctic projects.

After his return to Norway, he bought the small fishing boat *Gjoa,* and planned an attempt to find the Northwest Passage. The preparations proved expensive, and by 1903, when Amundsen was ready to set out, he found himself heavily in debt. One creditor threatened to halt the sailing of the expedition until Amundsen settled up. There was no way he could find the money; so, with a simple, direct approach that marked his entire career, the Norwegian coolly set out at midnight in a driving rain, slipping off to sea before legal action could be brought. It was, perhaps, not the most honest thing to have done—but otherwise he would never have got under way at all.

It was a superbly planned expedition. Amundsen had studied the records of every voyage that had sought the Northwest Passage since the sixteenth century. He had consulted with Fridtjof Nansen, the leading authority on Arctic exploration. He had plotted a course that looked harder than Franklin's, but was actually much safer. The *Gjoa* headed westward through the complicated island groups of the Arctic, setting up a winter base where Amundsen carried out magnetic observations and obtained sledging experience. In the spring he continued onward, and in October, 1906, the *Gjoa* reached San Francisco after a voyage of almost three years.

The Northwest Passage had little practical value, but it had been sought so long that any man who finally attained it became a world-renowned celebrity. Amundsen, vaulting from obscurity to heroism, was able to pay his debts with the profits from his account of the journey.

He turned now to his next goal: the North Pole.

By 1909, he had raised funds for an expedition, and had obtained the use of Fridtjof Nansen's specially equipped polar exploration vessel, *Fram*. Before he could start out, however, there came news at once thrilling and dismaying: an American, Robert Peary, had reached the North Pole in September, 1909!

Amundsen had no wish to be the *second* man at the North Pole. Here he was, with an outfitted expedition all ready, and Peary had forestalled him. Quietly, Amundsen decided to make a voyage anyway—to the yet unconquered South Pole.

Shackleton had returned, by this time, and Robert Falcon Scott was just about ready to depart on his second expedition. Amundsen feared that if he made his new plan known, it might spur Scott to leave earlier. Amundsen was primarily an explorer, not a scientist, and his chief interest was in having the glory of being first to the South Pole. So once again he began a journey deceptively.

His original plan had been to reach the North Pole from the Pacific, which meant rounding Cape Horn. When the *Fram* set out, on August 9, 1910, no one aboard but Amundsen knew that the destination had been changed. They followed the original southward course, and not until September 9, at Funchal in the Madeira Islands, did Amundsen break the news to his crew that they were bound for the Antarctic.

Scott had also set out by this time, and was in Australia then. Amundsen obligingly sent him a telegram from Madeira: "BEG LEAVE TO INFORM YOU PROCEEDING ANTARCTICA." The secret was out—and Scott, who up till that moment thought he was the only one in the field, came to the stunned realiza-

tion that he was involved in a race against Amundsen to reach
the South Pole.

Amundsen's strategy for reaching the Pole was simple and
straightforward. Scott, who had had his fill of dogs on his first
expedition, was planning to use pony transportation, but
Amundsen brought ninety-seven Eskimo dogs with him. He
felt confident that with his Arctic experience he could handle
dogs, whereas the inexperienced Britishers of the *Discovery*
expedition had failed miserably at that.

Dogs had many advantages. They were light, and were less
likely to break through the snow bridges over crevasses than
ponies. Even if they did fall through, they could be pulled out
by their harnesses; getting a pony out of a crevasse was all but
impossible. Ponies could not climb the glaciers, and would
have to be slaughtered at the foot of the Beardmore. Dog
teams could continue on up to the Polar Plateau. Thus
Amundsen would have dog teams all the way to the Pole and
back; Scott would have to man-haul almost three-quarters of
the journey.

Of course, Amundsen had to find some new base for his
camp. Though he had a head start on Scott, it would never do
for him to steal Scott's site at Hut Point. Amundsen decided
to use the Bay of Whales. Shackleton, two years before, had
felt it too dangerous to moor his ship at that opening in the
Barrier, east of McMurdo Sound. Amundsen boldly risked it.
He felt it was unlikely that the Barrier would calve again
while he was there.

Thus Amundsen started with an immediate advantage. He
was able to put his camp sixty-nine miles closer to the Pole
than Scott, at 78°30′ S. Thanks to fair weather, Amundsen

had an easy journey through the Ross Sea, landing at the Bay of Whales early in January, 1911. He arrived only a week after Scott reached McMurdo Sound, though Scott had set out much earlier for the Antarctic.

Before winter set in, the Norwegians speedily laid down depots at 80°, 81°, and 82° S., for use on their journey the following spring. Dog teams moved at a steady pace of twenty-five miles a day during the depot-laying. Sometimes the Norwegians rode on the sledges; at other times they mounted skis and let themselves be towed along behind. One party, setting up a depot a hundred miles from Amundsen's base, made the return journey in an incredible two-day burst. By April, 7,500 pounds of provisions had been stored at the depots, including large quantities of seal meat to prevent scurvy. Amundsen set up an elaborate chain of snow cairns along the route so none of the depots would be missed on the way back from the Pole. The cairns, every few miles apart, were topped with bamboo poles, and when the supply of bamboo gave out a dried fish from the dog-food supplies was used as a marker.

The depot-laying was so successful that Amundsen decided to reduce the weight of the sledges that would be taken. During the winter, he had the sledges rebuilt and cut down from 165 pounds each to 48 pounds. With lighter sledges, they could move much more rapidly and the dogs would expend less energy.

The Norwegians spent a mild winter at their base—mild by Antarctic standards, that is. Over at Scott's base on the west side of the Ross Sea, the winter was much worse. At the end of winter, when the race for the Pole began in earnest, Scott was held back by severe blizzards, and Amundsen was able to get an early start. He had only nine men, to Scott's fifty-five, and he planned little scientific work. It was simply going to be a dash to the Pole for Amundsen and nothing else.

Amundsen set out poleward on September 8, 1911, at the first hint of spring. It proved to be too soon; en route to the first depot, the temperature dropped to —72°, and the dogs could not take it. Amundsen returned to his base. On October 19, he tried again. Four men went with him; three others set out along the coast of the Bay of Whales toward Edward VII Land. One, the cook, remained behind to look after the base.

The polar party had four sledges, drawn by fifty-two dogs. The men were dressed Eskimo style, in light reindeer-skin garments which kept out the cold without adding to the bulk that had to be carried. The frisky dogs covered 90 miles in the first four days. After a two-day rest at the first depot, they continued on. It was an uneventful journey. The dogs were tireless, and the men had little to do; they donned their skis and let themselves be towed along behind the sledges. "And there I stood," wrote Amundsen, "until we reached 85°5′ S.— 340 miles. Yes, that was a pleasant surprise. We had never dreamed of driving on skis to the Pole!"

Matters became more difficult as they left the Ice Shelf behind and reached the glaciers leading to the Polar Plateau. Unable to find a glacier here as broad as the Beardmore to the west, the Norwegians had to ascend a narrow, steep river of ice that they named Axel Heiberg Glacier. The snow was deep and loose, and the dogs had trouble. Again and again, the way was barred by some impassable chasm or towering ice block, and the explorers had to turn back and try another path.

In the strange summer warmth of the glacier, the men sweated, Amundsen wrote, "as if running races in the tropics."

By December 4, they thought they had reached the Plateau. According to plan, they killed twenty-four of their weaker dogs. The worst of the hauling was over, and some of the dogs could be used as food for the other dogs and for the men. "It was hard—but it had to be so," wrote Amundsen. "We had agreed to shrink from nothing in order to reach our goal." Even so, he could not bear to watch the slaying of the faithful animals, and remained in the tent, hunched over the stove, while the other four carried out the unpleasant work. They named the site the Butcher's Shop, and rested there for two days.

Then it turned out they were not yet on the Plateau at all. Their trail swooped down 2,000 feet, leading them into a tangle of gaping crevasses. They forged onward somehow, even when a blizzard struck. Eighteen dogs still survived, six to a sledge; the fourth sledge had been left behind at the Butcher's Shop. Frostbitten and weary, the men pushed their way ahead, coming next to a zone of angled plates of ice much like the one David had encountered returning from the Magnetic Pole. Amundsen called it the Devil's Ballroom. "Time after time," he wrote, "the dogs fell through, and time after time the men went in. The effect of the open space between the two crusts was that the ground under our feet sounded unpleasantly hollow as we went over it. The drivers whipped up their dogs as much as they could, and with shouts and brisk encouragement they went rapidly over the treacherous floor."

At last they said farewell to the glacier. On December 7, 1911, they passed 88°23′ S., the farthest south attained by

Shackleton. They unfurled a Norwegian flag. Amundsen wrote: "No other moment of the whole trip affected me like this. The tears forced their way to my eyes." They all shook hands, congratulated one another, and pointed toward the goal ahead. Shackleton and his companions had been half dead from starvation and frostbite when they had reached this latitude; Amundsen's party, though taxed by the journey up the glacier, was still relatively fresh and strong. That night, Amundsen wrote in his diary: "Sir Ernest Shackleton's name will always be written in the annals of Antarctic exploration in letters of fire. Pluck and grit can work wonders, and I know of no better example of this than what that man has accomplished."

A week later, the Norwegians were at the Pole.

They had camped on December 13 at 89°45′ S. The weather was fine, but for a few light snow showers. "It was like the eve of some great festival that night in the tent," wrote Amundsen. "I was awake several times during the night, and had the same feeling that I can remember as a little boy on the night before Christmas Eve—an intense expectation of what was going to happen."

The next day, the weather was "of the finest, just as if it had been made for arriving at the Pole." The sky clouded over at noon, but cleared again. At three, the cry of "Halt!" rang out. They were at 90° S.

Amundsen could not avoid a feeling of irony. "The goal was reached, the journey ended. I cannot say—though I know it would sound much more effective—that the object of my life was attained. That would be romancing rather too barefacedly. I had better be honest and admit straight out that I have never known any man to be placed in such a diametrically opposite position to the goal of his desires as I was at that moment. The regions around the North Pole—well, yes, the North Pole itself—had attracted me from childhood, and here I was at the South Pole. Can anything more topsy-turvy be imagined?"

Of course, it was impossible to find the exact location of the Pole in that blank white desert without the help of instruments more accurate than the Norwegians had. To be certain they had been at the Pole, they made a 12½-mile circular trek around their camp. Somewhere within that circle, they knew, was the Pole.

They planted the Norwegian flag and held a brief ceremony. Champagne corks popped that night in their tent. They were in no hurry to return, having reached the Pole well ahead of schedule, and they remained there from December 14 to 17. Then, with the temperature at two below zero and a "mild, summer-like wind" blowing, they started back, after leaving a short message in the tent for Scott.

It was an easy journey back. They had some difficulty finding the Butcher's Shop depot, but after that every depot turned up without problems, and they had so much meat that some of the dogs actually gained weight on the homeward trip. On January 25, at four in the morning, they returned to the home base after a ninety-nine-day journey of 1,860 miles.

There they learned of the experiences of the other party, led by K. Prestrud, which had gone eastward toward King Edward VII Land. Prestrud had unexpectedly met a Japanese expedition under Choku Shirase there; without fanfare, the Japanese had also joined the race for the Pole, but they were unable to get through the Ross Sea ice pack and had to drop out.

Prestrud had explored King Edward VII Land and had claimed it for Norway on December 7, 1911.

The South Pole had been conquered—easily, lightheartedly, almost effortlessly, by five skillful, capable Norwegians. But while Amundsen was making his speedy and triumphant dash to the Pole, stark and tragic events were taking place to the west.

10 THE SCOTT TRAGEDY

WHEN ERNEST SHACKLETON RETURNED TO LONDON from the Antarctic on June 14, 1909, one of his warmest welcomers was Captain Robert Falcon Scott. He felt no jealousy at Shackleton's achievement, and enthusiastically applauded the man who had beaten his own southward record by 366 miles.

As we have seen, Scott himself had been thinking of a second expedition even before Shackleton's departure. Other expeditions were being organized, too. A proposed Belgian voyage had come to nothing, but Dr. Jean Charcot had returned to the Antarctic in 1908 on a two-year expedition to the Antarctic Peninsula. Charcot had no interest in reaching the Pole; he was content to do scientific research of an undramatic kind. The Charcot expedition did introduce such

174

modern innovations as the telephone and the electric light to Antarctic exploration.

Peary's discovery of the North Pole, and Shackleton's near attainment of the South Pole, both in 1909, had stirred tremendous public interest in polar exploration. When Scott announced his new expedition late in 1910, he made the attainment of the South Pole an important objective. He knew that there was little to be gained in the way of knowledge by covering the last hundred miles to the Pole—but he needed public support for his voyage, and the public demanded the Pole. There would also, he said, be an extensive program of scientific exploration east of the Ross Sea in Victoria Land.

Unlike his first expedition, this was a private venture, with no official sponsor and no committees of geographers in charge. Scott received public grants from the British, Australian, South African, and New Zealand governments, but the responsibility for making all decisions on the voyage was Scott's alone.

The expedition left on June 1, 1910, aboard the *Terra Nova*, a converted whaler that had been to the Antarctic in 1904 as part of the *Discovery* relief mission. Accompanying Scott were several veterans of his first voyage, including Dr. Edward Wilson. The scientific staff was extremely strong, with several geologists, an expert on fossils, a physicist, a meteorologist, and others. Once again, Scott refused to take Eskimo dogs. He relied mainly on Manchurian ponies for transport, though he also took three untried motor tractors, and, as a kind of reserve, brought twenty Siberian dogs.

The *Terra Nova* reached Melbourne, Australia, on October 12. Amundsen's stunning telegram was waiting there. The men of the expedition were furious at the sly way Amundsen had concealed the true nature of his voyage until the last minute. Scott himself remained outwardly calm; he refused to get caught up in the frenzy of a race. In his diary he admitted that if Amundsen were to reach the Pole at all, "it must be before we do, as he is bound to travel fast with dogs and pretty certain to start early."

On January 2, 1911, Mount Erebus loomed up. The *Terra Nova* entered McMurdo Sound and passed Cape Royds, Shackleton's 1907–09 base. They continued southward to a small cape about fifteen miles from Hut Point, and made their camp there. Scott named it Cape Evans, after his second-in-command, Lieutenant Edward Evans.

They spent the autumn months laying depots for the polar trek. The key depot was One Ton Camp, about 130 miles from Cape Evans at 79°30′ S., where several thousand pounds of food were stored. (In the Antarctic deep freeze, there were no fears the food would spoil over the months to come!) A smaller depot was set up closer to camp.

The ponies on which Scott had hoped to rely proved disappointing. In one way or another, eleven of nineteen perished before Scott left for the Pole. The motor sledges broke down less than forty miles out of Hut Point. The dogs were as unruly as ever, under the inexpert handling of the English. "Bit by bit I am losing all faith in the dogs," Scott wrote in March. "I am afraid they will never go the pace we look for." It began to look as though the journey to the Pole would be mostly man-hauled.

While the depots were being laid, Scott sent the *Terra Nova* east to explore King Edward VII Land. At the Bay of Whales, they saw the *Fram*, and stopped off to pay Amundsen a visit.

They returned with the report that the Norwegian had made his camp right on the Ice Shelf itself, was many miles closer to the Pole than Scott at the start, and was equipped with a fine team of hardy Greenland dogs. It was not cheering news.

Winter brought an end to depot-laying. But in the dead of the Antarctic night, one of the strangest and most arduous of all journeys of exploration took place.

Ten years before, on the *Discovery* expedition, Dr. Edward Wilson had visited Cape Crozier at the eastern end of Ross Island. He had discovered a penguin rookery there—the nesting place of the Emperor penguin, larger of Antarctica's two penguin species. It had been deserted but for one abandoned chick. Since this was in summer, the penguin must have been hatched the previous June or July—the middle of the Antarctic winter!

It was unbelievable that any creature would bring forth its young at such a ghastly season, and Wilson proposed a sledge journey in the beginning of July to visit the Cape Crozier rookery and study the penguins in their hatching season. No one had ever made a winter journey in Antarctica before, and, though it was only sixty-five miles from Cape Evans to Cape Crozier, Scott was reluctant to let Wilson go. At length, however, he yielded.

Wilson set out with two companions—"Birdie" Bowers, an officer of the *Terra Nova*, and a young zoologist named Apsley Cherry-Garrard. They man-hauled two small sledges, and in the first two days covered the twenty miles to the Ice Shelf via Hut Point, though the temperature was so low that their perspiration froze. In the next fourteen days, they did no better than three miles on any day, and on four days blizzards kept them from moving at all. The temperatures ranged be-

tween 40 and 60 below zero; luckily, there was no wind. The
sledges were so heavy that all three had to haul one, then
leave it and go back for the other, so they had to cover three
miles for every mile of forward advance. For four hours a day,
there was a faint glimmer of light in the sky; the rest of the
time they were in darkness. Sweat dripping inside their
clothing turned to icy armor. Once, Cherry-Garrard wrote: "I
raised my head to look round and found I could not move it
back. My clothing had frozen hard as I stood—perhaps fifteen
seconds. For four hours I had to pull with my head stuck up,
and from that time we all took care to bend down in pulling
position before being frozen in."

Frostbite, optical illusions, hunger, blistered skin—they suffered every kind of torment as they inched toward the penguin
grounds. On July 3, the temperature was —65°, but the next
day it rose to —27°, a "heat wave" that melted the ice in
their clothing and sleeping bags and left them soaking wet. A
few days later, the thermometer was registering 75° below,
and the greatest exertions were needed to advance a mile and
a half in a full day of hauling. Through fog and darkness they
edged down the crevassed zone where the Barrier touched
the land; only a sudden shaft of moonlight saved them from
plunging into a deep abyss.

At last they neared Cape Crozier. After resting in an igloo
of snow and stones, they tried to reach the penguins, but
found an impassable wall of ice before them. Bowers spied a
hole that seemed to lead through. "Well, here goes!" he said,
and wriggled out of sight. At the far end, he found the home of
the penguins, and the other two quickly followed.

A hundred penguins huddled together. Cherry-Garrard

writes that they "made a tremendous row, trumpeting with their curious metallic voice. There was no doubt they had eggs, for they tried to shuffle along the ground without losing them off their feet." (Penguins hatch their eggs by keeping them warm between the upper surfaces of their feet and a fold of their bellies.) The hardy explorers observed the penguins for a while, then collected five eggs to bring back for study. Stumbling, Cherry-Garrard broke two of them as they started back.

A violent hurricane whipped their tent away as they camped on the return journey, leaving them unprotected from the elements. Without the tent, wrote Cherry-Garrard, "we were dead men." They went without food for thirty-six hours, huddling miserably in their sleeping bags while hurricane winds ripped down. During a lull in the storm, they left their bags and numbly searched for the tent—and, to their astonishment, found it, hardly damaged, half a mile away. By August 2, 1911, after a winter journey lasting more than a month, they were back at Hut Point. On the trip, the weight of their sleeping bags had grown from 47 to 118 pounds through the accumulation of ice. But they had seen the midwinter hatching of the Emperor penguins, and they had brought back three eggs, which reached England eventually for microscopic examination.

They had made "the worst journey in the world"—not to the South Pole, but to a nearby penguin rookery. It received fewer headlines than the long treks of Shackleton, Scott, and Amundsen. In many ways, it was far more difficult than those, because made under incredibly bitter winter conditions. And its scientific yield was great, producing invaluable information about those strange, primitive, flightless birds of the

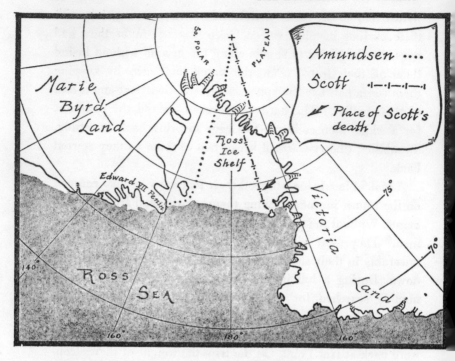

South Pole. The journey could have been made at no other time of the year because it was now *known* that Emperors hatch their young only in the polar winter, so that they can go out on their own when the sun returns.

Scott's polar journey began from Cape Evans on November 1, 1911, the earliest that weather would permit. Amundsen, having a milder winter at his base 450 miles to the east, had been able to get started for the Pole two weeks before.

Scott planned to use motor, dog, and pony transport. Three four-man parties would carry supplies to the foot of Beardmore

Glacier. There, the ponies would be shot and the dogs sent back with the Russian boy who was in charge of them. At the top of the glacier, one party of men would turn back; and a second group would be sent back halfway to the Pole, leaving only Scott's team to finish the journey.

The motor sledges had to be abandoned not far from Hut Point. The dogs performed surprisingly well, reaching their destination and delivering the provisions they hauled. The ponies, one by one, were shot and their meat used for food, though Scott found this a sad task. The returning parties would depend for their nourishment on the caches of pony meat, and on the depots laid down the previous autumn.

The trip across the Ice Shelf was slower than expected. The explorers were held up by blizzards and warm air that melted the snow into sledge-slowing slush. From December 4 to December 9 it was impossible to march at all. The same blizzard bothered Amundsen, who was already high on the glacier, but he was able to make some progress where Scott, with his ponies and Siberian dogs, could not.

Scott was racing now, but not against Amundsen. He was racing against the coming winter and against the timetable of Shackleton's journey to 88°23′ S. in 1908–09. Scott carried the diary of Frank Wild, who had been with Shackleton on his march, and drove himself and his men mercilessly in order to keep pace with Shackleton's timetable. For Shackleton, not quite reaching the Pole, had returned with hardly a day to spare before winter. Scott, who was following Shackleton's route, knew he must better that pace.

He was behind Shackleton's schedule as they reached the foot of the glacier. Here, the last pony was shot and a depot of meat established. Man-hauling now, the sledge parties began to toil up the crevassed glacier, and managed not only to catch up with Shackleton's timetable but to get three days ahead of it. It was done, though, at a cost in strength that would be crucial later. Where Amundsen was moving at a leisurely pace, resting often even when it did not seem necessary, Scott was furiously prodding onward.

On December 22, another depot was set up 8,000 feet up the glacier, and the first supporting party turned back. Many of the men were visibly weakening, less than halfway to the Pole. But on January 1, 1912, Scott felt optimistic, writing in his journal: "Only 170 miles to the Pole, and plenty of food."

Three days later, at 87°34′ S., 146 miles from the Pole, Scott sent the second support party back, but for one man. The four-man polar team had originally consisted of Scott, Dr. Wilson, a sailor named Edgar Evans, and an army officer named Lawrence Oates, nicknamed "Titus" or "Soldier." Surprisingly, Scott now added a fifth man to the party on the spur of the moment—Bill "Birdie" Bowers, one of the three men who had made the penguin trip in July.

Bowers was a man of immense strength, and Scott thought he would be useful on the grueling man-hauling journey ahead. But including him posed great problems. Everything—tent, rations, equipment—had been planned for a four-man team. Now the food and living quarters would have to be shared with a fifth. Worse, Bowers had left his skis behind at the depot below the glacier, so he would have to plod along through the snow on foot for hundreds of miles, while the others could run on skis.

As they camped, Scott jotted down a few of his impressions of the Antarctic wastes:

"The small green tent and the great white road.

"The drift snow like finest flour penetrating every hole and corner—flickering up beneath one's head covering, pricking sharply as a sand blast.

"The sun with blurred image peeping shyly through the wreathing drift giving pale shadowless light.

"The eternal silence of the great white desert. Cloudy columns of snow drift advancing from the south, pale yellow wraiths, heralding the coming storm, blotting out one by one the sharp-cut lines of the land."

The peril that underlies Antarctica's eerie beauty soon showed itself. A blizzard held up the polar team again on January 8, and the soft snow that remained afterward made man-hauling an agony. They made no better than ten miles a day, dropping behind schedule again. On January 12, Scott wrote that he and his men were feeling chilled though the temperature was fairly mild—a sign of growing physical weakness.

Two days later, Scott noted: "I think Wilson, Bowers and I are as fit as possible under the circumstances. Oates gets cold feet." And, soon after, "I don't like the easy way in which Oates and Evans get frost-bitten." Scurvy was beginning to take them.

On January 15, they were within striking distance of the Pole. "It ought to be a certain thing now," Scott wrote, "and the only appalling possibility the sight of the Norwegian flag forestalling ours. . . . Only twenty-seven miles from the Pole. We ought to do it now."

Next day came the shock. "The worst has happened, or nearly the worst," wrote Scott. "Noon sight showed us in Latitude 89°42′, and we started off in good spirits." Then sharp-eyed Bowers spotted a black speck ahead. They marched on and "found that it was a black flag tied to a sledge bearer; near by the remains of a camp; sledge tracks and ski tracks going and coming and the clear trace of dogs' paws—many dogs. This told us the whole story. The Norwegians have forestalled us and are first at the Pole. It is a terrible disappointment, and I am very sorry for my loyal companions. . . . Tomorrow we must march on to the Pole and then hasten home with all the speed we can compass. All the daydreams must go; it will be a wearisome return."

On January 17, 1912, there was this entry:

"The Pole. Yes, but under very different circumstances from those expected. Great God! this is an awful place and terrible enough for us to have laboured to it without the reward of priority. . . . Now for the run home and a desperate struggle. I wonder if we can do it."

At the Pole, they found Amundsen's tent, with the Norwegian flag flying high, and letters addressed to Scott. There was no time to linger, as the Norwegians had done. Sadly, the second polar party raised the Union Jack, and started back. They were already badly weakened from the journey out, and this new blow to their spirits, though not unexpected, left them dejected and morose.

All five were frostbitten and had some degree of scurvy by now. Evans seemed the worst. On January 23, Scott wrote: "There is no doubt that Evans is a good deal run down—his fingers are badly blistered and his nose is rather seriously congested with frequent frost bites. He is much annoyed with himself which is not a good sign. . . . Oates gets cold feet. . . ." Crossing the Polar Plateau, Wilson strained a tendon; Scott fell and injured his shoulder; Oates' toes began to turn black from frostbite; Evans' hands were so badly frozen that the fingernails began to drop off. Yet, at the top of Beardmore Glacier, they camped on February 8 and spent a day "geologizing." "It has been extremely interesting," Scott wrote. They were under sandstone cliffs, from which Wilson "has picked several plant impressions, the last a piece of coal with beautifully traced leaves in layers. . . . In one place we saw the cast of small waves in the sand." Science was not forgotten, even with death nipping at their heels.

The next day they stopped again. "Too tired to write geological notes," Scott scrawled in his diary. Descending the glacier Evans fell twice, injuring his head, and became dazed and incoherent. "Evans has nearly broken down in brain, we think," Scott observed. "He is absolutely changed from his normal self-reliant self."

On February 17, they were at the bottom of the glacier. All five men were cracking under the strain as their health continued to give way, but now Evans began to drop behind the group, and at lunchtime they had to go back to find him. "He was on his knees with clothing disarranged, hands uncovered and frostbitten, and a wild look in his eyes," Scott wrote. Brought back to the camp, Evans lapsed into a coma, and died that night.

They were saddened by Evans' death, but they could not help admitting that with the sickest man gone, the other four had a better chance of surviving the trip. They struggled

along, dragging sledges now weighted with 35 pounds of geological specimens, and soon it was Oates' turn to weaken.
His hands and feet were frozen, and he could no longer pull
the sledges, but simply trudged along beside them. Scott, Wilson, and Bowers, still in fairly good shape, were forced to do
extra work as a result, and the daily marches became shorter
and shorter as fatigue overtook them.

As they came to their depots, unpleasant surprises greeted
them. The leather stoppers of their oil cans had shrunk from
cold, and the oil had mostly evaporated. With fuel short, they
could have fewer hot meals, and had to cut down on drinking
water because they would have less opportunity to build snow-
melting fires. And now the weather turned unpredictably cold.
It was well into February, and at night the mercury dropped
below —40°. Oates suffered new torments from frostbite. On
March 2 Scott wrote: "This morning it took 1½ hours to get
our foot gear on. . . . The surface is simply awful. In spite of
a strong wind and full sail we have only done 5½ miles. We
are in a very queer street since there is no doubt we cannot
do the extra marches and feel the cold terribly."

There was only one real hope, now: that a relief party would
come out from Cape Evans to meet them. But in these low
temperatures, with frequent blizzards, no relief party was able
to set out.

On March 3, the weakening men made only 4½ miles, and
the next day, just 3½. Oates lost strength from hour to hour.
On the fifth, Scott wrote that Oates was "nearly done," and a
day later put down, with brutal honesty, the statement, "If
we were all fit I should have hopes of getting through, but the
poor Soldier has become a terrible hindrance."

There was no question of leaving him behind. They were about forty miles from the next depot on March 4, and had food for a week, but fuel for only three days. "Shall we get there?" Scott wondered. "Such a short distance it would have appeared to us on the summit!" Cold and hungry, they reached that depot six days later, and prepared to go on to the next one.

By March 10, Oates himself seemed to realize that he was endangering the life of the entire group, and asked for advice. "Nothing could be said," wrote Scott, "but to urge him to march as long as he could." A day later, Scott worked out a grim piece of arithmetic. They were fifty-five miles from the One Ton Camp depot now, and had seven days' food. Since they were doing, at best, 6 miles a day, "six times seven equals forty-two, leaving us thirteen miles short of our distance, even if things go no worse."

On the seventeenth, Oates came to the end of his tether. He had asked to be left behind, and Scott refused. With the party huddled in the tent during a blizzard, and the temperature 40° below zero outside, Oates staggered to his feet and said calmly, "I am just going outside and may be some time." He walked off into the storm and was never seen again. Scott wrote:

"We knew that poor Oates was walking to his death, but though we tried to dissuade him, we knew it was the act of a brave man and an English gentleman. We all hope to meet the end with a similar spirit, and assuredly the end is not far."

With three men instead of four now, the arithmetic of the food was a little better. The survivors struggled ahead through the terrible cold, shambling like walking corpses, and by March 21 they were within eleven miles of One Ton Depot. To save weight, they had left their camera and other instruments behind, but were still hauling their precious bag of geological specimens.

A blizzard came up and they had to make camp. Day after day the snow fell, turning the outer world into a blinding landscape of whirling whiteness. It was impossible to move on. For eight days the blizzard pinned them into their tent, and they slowly starved and froze with thousands of pounds of food waiting for them only eleven miles away. As death approached, Scott wrote twelve superb letters, to his wife, to Wilson's wife and Bowers' mother, and to some of his close friends. "We are showing," he wrote to playwright James Barrie, author of *Peter Pan* and godfather of Scott's son, "that Englishmen can still die with a bold spirit, fighting it out to the end." Now that there was no longer hope of survival, Scott, Wilson, and Bowers were calm, tranquil, and resigned. Scott composed a magnificent message to the public, explaining why the disaster had occurred. It was not poor planning, he said, but a series of unexpected misfortunes: the death of many ponies early in 1911, the bad weather on the journey outward, the incredibly cold weather on the return.

"I do not think human beings ever came through such a month as we have come through," Scott said. Yet, he insisted, they would have made it if Evans and Oates had not sickened, and if the fuel shortage at the depots had not developed, and if a blizzard had not kept them from reaching One Ton Camp when it was only a two-day march away.

"Had we lived," he concluded, "I should have had a tale to tell of the hardihood, endurance, and courage of my companions which would have stirred the heart of every English-

. man. These rough notes and our dead bodies must tell the tale, but surely, surely, a great rich country like ours will see that those who are dependent on us are properly provided for."

On March 29, 1912, Scott made the final entry in his journal:

"Since the 21st we have had a continuous gale. . . . We had fuel enough to make two cups of tea apiece and bare food for two days on the 20th. Every day we have been ready to start for our depot *eleven miles* away, but outside the door of the tent, it remains a scene of whirling drift. I do not think we can hope for any better things now. We shall stick it out to the end, but we are getting weaker, of course, and the end cannot be far.

"It seems a pity, but I do not think I can write more.

"R. Scott.

"For God's sake look after our people."

In October, after the winter had passed, a search party went out to find the dead men. Eleven miles beyond One Ton Camp, they came upon what looked like an igloo, but it was the tent, covered with snow. The bodies lay within. Apsley Cherry-Garrard, who was in the party, wrote: "Bowers and Wilson were sleeping in their bags. Scott had thrown back the flaps of his bag at the end. His left hand was stretched over Wilson, his life-long friend. Beneath the head of his bag, between the bag and the floor-cloth, was the green wallet in which he carried his diary. The brown books of diary were inside; and on the floor-cloth were some letters. . . . We never moved the bodies. We took the bamboos of the tent away, and the tent itself covered them. And over them we built the cairn. . . ."

On January 18, 1913, the *Terra Nova* returned to Cape Evans. Aboard ship, all was ready for a great feast to celebrate the reunion with the shore party. The engines stopped, and the ship's captain stepped to the deck.

"Is everyone well?" he called.

A man on shore replied, "The southern party reached the South Pole on the 17th January last year, but were all lost on the return journey—we have their records."

There was a great silence, broken by the splash of the falling anchor. Aboard the ship, the steward silently began to remove the cheerful decorations. There would be no feast of celebration this year.

11 MAWSON AND BLIZZARDS, SHACKLETON AND "ENDURANCE"

THE SEASON OF 1911–12 HAD SEEN THE SOUTH POLE conquered twice. Amundsen, a second exploring triumph stowed away, was making plans for more Arctic research; Antarctica held no more interest for him. Scott lay buried under the snows of the harsh continent that had taken his life, while volume after volume of his last expedition's scientific reports poured from the presses. Covering such subjects as geology, biology, glaciology, meteorology, and geophysics, they formed perhaps the finest possible memorial to a brave and noble man whose mistakes and bad luck had ended in tragedy.

"The discovery of the South Pole," Ernest Shackleton wrote in March 1912 upon hearing of Amundsen's success, "will not be the end of Antarctic exploration. The next work of importance to be done in the Antarctic is the determination of the whole coastline of the Antarctic Continent, and then a

191

transcontinental journey from sea to sea crossing the Pole."

Even while the Scott drama was playing toward its final curtain, an Australian expedition was adding to man's knowledge of the Antarctic coast. Its leader was Douglas Mawson, born in England in 1882 but raised in Australia. On Shackleton's *Nimrod* expedition, Mawson had been among the group that climbed Mount Erebus, and then had been a member of the party that reached the South Magnetic Pole. A physicist and geologist, he was a pioneer of radio study, and the first explorer to make use of long-distance radio communication in Antarctica.

His target was what is now called Wilkes Land, directly to the south of Australia. D'Urville had seen part of it, which he called Adelie Land, and Wilkes had coasted it, but no one had been ashore. Mawson intended to make scientific and geographical investigations of as much of the coastline as he could, in the almost unknown territory that ranged westward from Victoria Land to Wilhelm II Land.

He set out in 1911. His ship was the *Aurora*, a Newfoundland sealer. The expedition was equipped with radio and even an airplane. (The airplane crashed on a trial flight and was never used, but its engine was installed in a motor sledge.) In January, 1912, a land base was established at Commonwealth Bay, about 144° E., and the *Aurora* took a separate party led by Frank Wild, who had been on both the *Discovery* and *Nimrod* expeditions, to the west. It was Wild who gave Wilkes Land its name; and, coming to a glacier stretching far into the sea, named it Shackleton Ice Tongue. Quite probably it was the "Termination Land" barrier that had stopped Wilkes in the 1840's.

During 1912 and the early months of 1913, these two parties carried out important explorations in the coastal areas.
Mawson's Commonwealth Bay base, at a point he called Cape
Denison, was nicknamed "The Home of the Blizzard," because of the fierce weather conditions. There was no coastal
range of mountains to break the force of the cold winds coming off the Polar Plateau. An unbroken ice sheet rose in a
steady but gradual slope to a height of more than 7,000 feet,
and down this slope there roared the savage wind out of the
south. During July, 1912, the average wind velocity, twenty-
four hours a day for thirty-one days, was 63.6 miles an hour.
There were gusts of up to 200 miles an hour, and one day in
the winter of 1913 the wind blew at 107 miles per hour for
eight hours straight. In these screaming gales, the men had to
wear shoes with spikes an inch and a half high, lest they be
swept away. They learned to lean into the wind, and sometimes, when the wind dropped abruptly, they fell on their
faces. Once a 3,000-pound tractor was lifted and tossed fifty
yards. The wind whipped up towering banks of drift snow.
"Intervals of many days together passed," Mawson wrote,
"when it was impossible to see one's hand held at arm's length.
The drift snow became charged with electricity and in the
darkness of the winter night all pointed objects and even one's
clothes, nose, and finger tips glowed with the pale blue light of
St. Elmo's Fire."

In any sort of weather, someone had to make frequent visits
from the hut to the nearby meteorological station, a few yards
away, to record weather observations. This is how Mawson
described such a trip:

"A howling, whirling wall of grey hits him, and he does

not rise from his hands and knees lest he should be blown
away. . . . Ice at once begins to form on the face and in a few
seconds small icicles dangle from the eyebrows and eyelashes,
and bind the beard to the helmet. Carefully he rises to his feet,
bracing himself against the wind, and step by step guides himself along the slope of the hut roof. Now he is round the corner, a few yards and he has turned again and is fighting his
way up wind. . . . Now comes the plunge into the unknown. At
right angles he makes a rush. . . . As he clings to the screen
with one hand, the wind plucks at him and tries to tear him
away, but he hangs grimly on, and at last with his free hand
successfully prizes open the door. He inserts his head in the
aperture and fumbles for the electric switch connected with a
battery in the hut. A flicker of light falls on the thermometer,
but first he must break the ice from his eyes and peer forward
to within a couple of inches before he can read the temperature. . . ."

When summer came, Mawson sent out several sledging parties to map the nearby shores. He led one himself, to the east,
and though he was seeking only scientific knowledge and not
adventure, he became enmeshed in a journey as grueling as
any taken by Shackleton or Scott.

Mawson set out with two companions: Lieutenant B.E.S.
Ninnis, a young English army officer, and Dr. Xavier Mertz,
a Swiss lawyer whose hobbies were skiing and exploration.
Leaving on November 10, 1912, with three sledges and seventeen dogs, the Mawson party crossed two gigantic glaciers, "a
solid ocean rising and falling in billows two hundred fifty feet
in height," which Mawson named for his two comrades. Each
was some thirty miles wide. Beyond them lay three hundred

miles of easily tracked shoreline. Crossing the two glaciers, Ninnis, Mertz, and half a dog team all fell into crevasses at different times, but were rescued without much difficulty. On November 28, one of the sledges dropped into crevasse, threatening the loss of much of their food, but they managed to haul it out and continue.

A blizzard halted them from December 6 to 8. During the storm, the dogs snuggled warmly into the snow, which they found more comfortable than remaining exposed. When the party got going again, they abandoned the damaged sled and loaded their supplies onto the remaining two. Most of the food was put aboard the sledge to be drawn by the strongest dogs, Ninnis in charge. They set out across another heavily crevassed area.

On December 14, the sun was bright and the sky fair, and they decided on one last eastward dash before turning back. Mertz led the way, skiing along and bellowing German student songs. Mawson followed aboard one sledge, and Ninnis brought up the rear with the other. About midday, Mertz held up one ski pole, a prearranged danger signal to warn that they were passing over a crevasse. Mawson halted his sledge to inspect the snow, but he found no sign of a crevasse and proceeded, deep in calculations of their latitude. Suddenly he noticed that Mertz had halted and was looking worriedly back. Mawson swung round to see how Ninnis was coming.

"Behind me," he wrote, "nothing met the eye but my own sledge tracks running back in the distance. Where were Ninnis and his sledge?"

Hurrying back, Mawson found a gaping hole, eleven feet wide. Ninnis' heavily laden sledge had broken through. As

Mertz came rushing up, Mawson leaned into the depths and shouted. "No sound came back but the moaning of a dog, caught on a shelf just visible one hundred fifty feet below. . . . Another dog lay motionless by its side. Close by was what appeared to be the remains of the tent and a canvas tank containing food for three men for a fortnight." For three hours they shouted into the crevasse, but no answer came from Ninnis. The injured dog died. A chill wind blew out of the abyss.

Mawson read a short burial service. The situation was desperate, now. They had lost all the dog food, the tent, the strongest dogs, and even Mertz' windproof trousers, which he had not been wearing because of the calm weather. The two men had food for a week and a half, with nothing for the dogs. They were three hundred miles from the base and had laid no depots. There was only a slim hope that they could get back, rushing at top speed and eating the dogs when their own food was gone.

They were so close to the South Magnetic Pole that their compasses were useless, and cloudy weather hid the sun, forcing them to set their course by guesswork. They fed the dogs on worn-out fur mitts and shoes, flogging them mercilessly and killing them one by one for food. Snow blindness and starvation assailed them. They dreamed of feasts and banquets. Mertz began to weaken; they ate the last dog and man-hauled the sledge, but by January 1 Mertz could no longer pull, and Mawson dragged him along as a rider. His own strength was ebbing, and he could make no more than two or three miles a day. The weather turned bad, and they had to halt, using up their precious food without making progress. "Both our chances are going now," Mawson wrote on January 6. He refused to abandon the totally helpless Mertz, dragging him along a few miles, but the next day Mertz became delirious, fell into a deep sleep, and died.

Mawson was alone, more than a hundred miles from Cape Denison, with little food and no depots. Few men have ever known such terrible isolation. At least Scott, on his fatal last trek, had had beloved companions with him, and the dream of One Ton Camp just a few short miles ahead.

Not until January 11 was Mawson strong enough to go on. He cut the sled in half to reduce his toil, and discarded everything but the barest necessity. His feet were so badly frostbitten that the skin of the soles had dropped away. "There is little chance of my reaching human aid alive," he wrote in his log. He could do five or six miles a day, at best.

Crossing Mertz Glacier on the seventeenth, he dropped into a crevasse and fell fourteen feet, swinging in mid-air over an abyss while his sled slowly edged toward the rim. If it slipped over, it would carry him to his death, but miraculously it halted just short of the edge. Mawson clambered up the harness that bound him to the sledge. Just as he reached the surface, a section gave way, dropping him the full length of the harness again. Bare-handed, half frozen, he dangled there. "It would be but the work of a moment to slip from the harness, then all the pain and toil would be over," he wrote later. But he found the strength to climb the harness again; this time the crevasse lid held, and he crawled to safety, lying exhausted for an hour before he could move.

He had almost no food left now, but incredibly he marched on. On January 28, he found a snow cairn that had been set up by a search party out looking for him. They had left a bag of food, and a note telling him there were additional supplies at a point called Aladdin's Cave, twenty-three miles farther on.

The food gave Mawson new strength. He trekked on to Aladdin's Cave. Now he was only five miles from Cape Denison. A blizzard held him there from February 1 to February 8, and he rested, gathering his forces for the final stretch. Meanwhile, the expedition ship *Aurora* had reached Cape Denison to take the shore party back. It had waited as long as possible. When Mawson failed to arrive, the *Aurora* had picked up the men at the base and put out to sea, leaving five who volunteered to spend another winter there in the hope of finding their leader.

On February 8, Mawson tottered into camp, seeing human beings for the first time since Mertz' death a month before. He had successfully completed an astonishing one-man journey against the most formidable odds. The *Aurora*, he learned, had sailed that very day! Quickly Mawson had a radio message sent to the ship: "Mawson arrived. Mertz and Ninnis dead. Return at once and pick up all hands."

The *Aurora* tried to get back, but a hurricane kept her from landing. A new problem developed: if the ship waited off Cape Denison for a break in the weather, it might be too late to get through the newly forming ice to Frank Wild's party to the west. Mawson's group could survive another winter at Cape Denison; Wild's, without proper shelter or provisions, could not.

It was a bitter decision to make. The *Aurora* left Mawson and his party and went to pick up Wild, reaching him on February 27, 1913. Mawson had backed the decision, even though it forced him to spend another winter in "The Home of the Blizzard" after his punishing journey. The marooned men made the best of it, settling in for another year of weather observations. They had radio contact with Australia, and learned belatedly of the death of Scott. In December, the *Aurora* returned, and Mawson reached Australia early in 1914. Though badly broken in health, he recovered fully, and eventually visited Antarctica again—in 1929, using Scott's old ship, the *Discovery*.

Thanks to Mawson's expedition, a great arc of Antarctic coast had been mapped at last, and the discoveries of Wilkes, D'Urville, Drygalski, and Scott had been linked. At about the same time, a German expedition under Wilhelm Filchner had been at work on the other side of the continent, breaking through the Weddell Sea ice pack and discovering an ice shelf at the shore similar to the Ross Shelf. Filchner was able to land on this barrier, which now bears his name. Afterward, his ship, the *Deutschland*, was beset in the ice and drifted for nine months before it could be freed.

Filchner had found an opening in his ice shelf, which he named Vahsel Bay after the *Deutschland*'s captain. It promised to be a gateway to the continent's interior, playing the same role that the Bay of Whales and McMurdo Sound did in the Ross Ice Shelf. When Filchner returned home, he tried to promote a new expedition that would land at Vahsel Bay and cross Antarctica via the Pole to the Ross Sea.

His timing was poor. In 1913, Filchner's native Germany was mobilizing her resources for war, and not a pfennig could be spent on something so impractical as a trans-Antarctic expedition. It was Ernest Shackleton who made the attempt instead.

Since the attainment of the South Pole, Shackleton had been at loose ends, restlessly looking for new worlds to conquer. The return of Filchner in 1913, with word of the discovery of Vahsel Bay, spurred Shackleton to action. He planned a grandiose expedition that would trek clear across Antarctica.

One party would brave the Weddell Sea and land at Vahsel Bay on the Filchner Ice Shelf. While this team headed inland, a second party, starting from the Ross Shelf, would lay a trail of depots up to Beardmore Glacier for the use of the trans-Antarctic group. Neither of these parties would do any scientific work; that would be carried out by two other teams, one going eastward from Vahsel Bay toward Enderby Land, the other westward toward the Antarctic Peninsula.

Shackleton's Imperial Trans-Antarctic Expedition had a budget of $250,000. Half the money came from a Scottish industrialist, Sir James Caird; the rest was made up by public and private donations. Shackleton bought two ships: Mawson's *Aurora*, which would land the Ross Sea party, and a specially constructed vessel that he named *Endurance*, after his family motto—an apt name indeed, as it turned out.

In August, 1914, just as the *Endurance* was about to sail, war broke out in Europe. A polar expedition seemed somewhat frivolous to Shackleton at such a time, and he wired the Admiralty, offering to put his ships and crew at the service of the war effort. Within an hour Shackleton had a one-word answer from Winston Churchill, First Lord of the Admiralty: "Proceed." An hour later came a more formal explanation; Britain was grateful for the offer, Churchill said, but the expedition should not be interfered with even in wartime.

The only event of note on the journey southward was the

discovery of a nineteen-year-old stowaway. He had tried to
sign on in Buenos Aires, but Shackleton had refused to hire
him; finding the boy now, he kept him on as a steward. On
December 5, 1914, they left South Georgia, and two days later
began to hit ice. Shackleton was dismayed at finding ice this
far north—at 58°30′ S.

For the next 480 miles, they could advance at a mere 1 mile
an hour. The result was the *Endurance* fell well behind Filchner's schedule, though Shackleton was able to get as far south
in the Weddell Sea as 76°34′ S. by January 19, 1915. That
day, the pack closed around the ship and she began to drift
helplessly. At one point she came within 60 miles of Vahsel
Bay, and all hands frantically tried to saw the ship free, but
the ice froze as fast as they cut it. Like Filchner's *Deutschland,*
Endurance was a prisoner of the pack. But she was destined
never to be free again, nor would Shackleton make his
dreamed-of landing on the Filchner Ice Shelf.

The ship was frozen into a slab of ice three miles long and
two and a half miles wide, drifting toward the northwest. The
dogs were kenneled on the ice in what the crewmen called
"dogloos," and dog races were held to while away the time.
After three months of peaceful drifting, strange sounds began
to come from the floe—squeaks and groans, and later a sound
like thunder. Other floes were jostling against it, creating pressure ridges where the big floe began to buckle. On August 1,
the floe cracked in half, and now the ship, sheltered by the
borders of the floe so long, was directly exposed to ice pressure.

The ice tightened its grip. "The pressure-ridges," Shackleton wrote, "massive and threatening, testified to the overwhelming nature of the forces that were at work. Huge blocks

of ice, weighing many tons, were lifted into the air and tossed
aside as other masses rose beneath them. We were helpless
intruders in a strange world. . . ." It seemed certain that the
ship would be crushed, and Shackleton made plans to abandon
her and try to sledge to safety across the drifting ice floes.

New ridges rose. Shackleton heard "the creaking and groan-
ing of her timbers, the pistol-like cracks that told of the starting of a . . . plank, and the faint, indefinable whispers of our
ship's distress." Millions of tons of ice hemmed them in. On
October 26, Shackleton ordered the boats, sledges, and provisions moved to a safe position on the flat ice. Eight Emperor
penguins appeared from nowhere and watched this operation
gravely, "and after a few ordinary calls proceeded to utter
weird cries that sounded like a dirge for the ship."

The next day, the *Endurance* had to be abandoned. "At
last," Shackleton wrote, "the twisting, grinding floes were
working their will on the ship. It was a sickening sensation to
feel the decks breaking up under one's feet, the great beams
bending and then snapping with a noise like heavy gunfire. . . .
I cannot describe the impression of relentless destruction
which was forced upon me as I looked down and around. The
floes, with the force of millions of tons of moving ice behind
them, were simply annihilating the ship."

They were castaways in the frozen Weddell Sea, 573 miles
from the point where the *Endurance* was beset in February.
They had had one last sad meal aboard ship, "Taken in silent
gravity, whilst the crushing is in progress and an ominous
sound of splintering timbers arises from below." Now they
were on the ice, looking back at the crumpled wreck of the

ship in which Shackleton had "centered ambitions, hopes, and desires."

The nearest point where they might find shelter was Paulet Island, 346 miles away. Captain Larsen of the Nordenskjöld expedition had built a hut when cast away there in 1903, and the hut contained provisions left by the Argentinian relief ship that picked Larsen up. Shackleton knew all about those provisions, for he had purchased them in London "on behalf of the Argentine Government when they asked me to equip the relief expedition."

They salvaged what they could from the ship, which finally vanished, crushed and shattered, on November 21. There were twenty-eight men, forty-nine dogs. The plan was to sledge across the floes as far as possible, crossing open water, when they came to it, in their three small boats. Everything that could be spared was discarded. Shackleton set the tone by throwing away his valuable gold watch, a gold cigarette case, and some gold coins—just useless dead weight here. Not even the Bible, a gift of the Queen, was spared, though Shackleton tore out and kept the fly-leaf with its inscription, and a page from the Book of Job, containing this verse:

Out of whose womb came the ice?
The waters are hid as with a stone,
And the hoary frost of Heaven, who hath gendered it?
And the face of the deep is frozen.

On December 23, they set out for Paulet Island. Dogs pulled the supplies on sledges, and the men hauled other sledges on which the boats had been mounted. But the floes were drifting away from Paulet Island even as they marched toward it. After seven days, they found they had advanced in a straight line just seven and a half miles. At that rate, it would take almost a year to reach Paulet Island. They had food for a month and a half.

They decided to wait for the ice to break up, and make the journey by boat. Settling on a floe they named Patience Camp, they waited for three and a half months, shooting penguins and seals for food. Back and forth they drifted, exposed to gales and blizzards and even that Antarctic rarity, rain. Icebergs occasionally charged down on their floe, missing it by the narrowest of margins. Sea leopards, vicious seals that will eat anything they can catch, lurked at the edges of the floe, and once a sea leopard charged right into their camp in hot pursuit of one of the men. It was shot dead by Frank Wild, Shackleton's second-in-command, who was making his fourth Antarctic expedition. The sea leopard joined the store of provisions.

The drift had taken them north of the Antarctic Peninsula. Early in April, 1916, they found themselves only a hundred miles from Clarence Island and Elephant Island of the South Shetland group. The pack began to break up on April 9, and they piled all they had into the boats and put to sea. After a hard day's rowing, the castaways camped for the night on a large floe. When they had settled down for the night, the floe split in two, the crack passing right under one tent. Shackleton saw a man drop into the water, still in his sleeping bag, and hauled him out a moment before the edges of the crack slammed violently together again. A little while later, Shackleton himself discovered that he was floating away in the dark on a small platform of ice. A boat had to be sent to fetch him back.

Hauling ice-encrusted oars through stormy water, they put to sea again on April 13, and reached Elephant Island two days later, suffering from thirst because they had left the pack too quickly to collect fresh-water ice for melting. Shackleton allowed the stowaway steward to be the first to go ashore, after they had found a small, rocky beach on the mountainous, ice-covered island. But the boy was so frostbitten that he collapsed in the surf and had to be hauled ashore. Another man had been so badly frostbitten that five toes had to be amputated, in a makeshift hut on shore.

They had reached solid land, but they had no way of communicating with the outside world, and no one would think of looking for them on this barren, uninhabited island so far from the Weddell Sea. The nearest place to seek help was South Georgia, 870 miles away across the stormiest seas in the world. There was but one thing to do. Someone had to try to reach South Georgia.

Shackleton picked five men to go with him, including Thomas Crean, a member of the supporting party in Scott's fatal polar journey, and Frank Worsley, who had been captain of the *Endurance*. The rest of the men remained on Elephant Island under the charge of Frank Wild.

It was a journey that seemed hopelessly impossible. Their boat, the *James Caird*, was only 23 feet long, and open to the elements; 6 feet wide, 3½ feet deep, it would hardly be a comfortable craft for the grueling trip. A carpenter roofed the deck over to provide place for sleeping and cooking meals, and one of the smaller boats sacrificed its masts and sail to give the *Caird* a better chance of making it.

On April 24, 1916, the six men set out on the most extraordinary boat trip in history. Worsley navigated, and the men took turns sleeping, cooking, and bailing. Half the time they stood ankle-deep in water. Gale after gale raged over them. Ice froze in chunks on the deck and sails, threatening to drag the frail boat under with its weight, and the voyagers crawled out on the icy deck, wedging their feet into chipped-out toe-holes to hack away at the accumulated ice. "A thousand times it appeared as though the *James Caird* must be engulfed; but the boat lived," Shackleton wrote later. The men lived on sledging rations and hot milk. Toward the end of the journey, the water ran short, and they had to limit themselves to half a pint a day. On the eleventh day out, all their effort seemed to have been wasted when drowning threatened:

"At midnight I was at the tiller," Shackleton wrote, "and suddenly noticed a line of clear sky between the south and the south-west. I called to the other men that the sky was clearing, and then, a moment later, I realized that what I had seen was not a rift in the clouds but the white crest of an enormous wave. During twenty-six years' experience of the ocean in all its moods I had not encountered a wave so gigantic. It was a mighty upheaval of the ocean, a thing quite apart from the big white-capped seas that had been our tireless enemies for many days. I shouted, 'For God's sake, hold on! It's got us!' Then came a moment of suspense that seemed drawn out into hours. White surged the foam of the breaking sea around us. We felt our boat lifted and flung forward like a cork in breaking surf. We were in a seething chaos of tortured water; but somehow the boat lived through it, half-full of water, sagging to the dead weight and shuddering under the blow. We bailed with the energy of men fighting for life, flinging the water over the sides with every receptacle which came into our hands; and after ten minutes of uncertainty we felt the boat renew her life beneath us. She floated again and ceased to lurch drunkenly as though dazed by the attack of the sea. Earnestly we hoped that never again would we encounter such a wave."

On May 6, the sun appeared. Worsley was able to take their position, and reported that they were less than a hundred miles from the northwest corner of South Georgia. It was good news indeed, for their thirst was becoming intense; Shackleton wrote: "The salt water in our clothing and the salt spray that lashed our faces made our thirst grow quickly to a burning pain. . . . That day and the following day passed for us in a sort of nightmare. Our mouths were dry and our tongues were swollen."

On the eighth, they spied two birds on a floating mass of seaweed—a sign that land was near. And at noon on the tenth, they saw South Georgia, and landed later that day, just as dusk was gathering. A fresh-water stream came down to the sea at the beach where they had landed, and as soon as the boat was safely tied the men were on their knees, gulping the ice-cold water.

The ordeal was not over. They were on the opposite coast from South Georgia's one inhabited spot, a whaling station. It would be a 150-mile journey by boat around the island, and they doubted that the battered boat would survive the trip. The only other route was across a range of mountains that were unsurveyed and unexplored and had never been crossed before.

Though exhausted by the three-week boat trip, Shackleton set out with Worsley and Crean to cross the mountains, leaving the other three with the boat. They took compass and chronometer, a stove, three days' provisions, and fifty feet of rope. With only a vague idea of the direction of the whaling station, they climbed the glacier-covered foothills on May 19, 1916, and started out on the third leg of the incredible journey from the floes of the Weddell Sea to the safety of South Georgia's whaling station.

Fog masked the route on the way up, lifting to reveal a vast crevasse into which they nearly had plunged. Time and again, they climbed ridges only to find the way hopelessly blocked by chasms or precipices, and had to retrace their steps and find another route. At last, three thousand feet up, they could look over the crest of the island and see the open sea beyond, on the far side. "My eyes searched vainly for a way down," Shackleton wrote. "The hot sun had loosened the snow, which was now in a treacherous condition, and we had to pick our way carefully. Looking back, we could see that a fog was rolling up behind us and meeting in the valleys a fog that was coming up from the east. The creeping grey clouds were a plain warning that we must get down to lower levels before becoming enveloped." They had no sleeping bags, and if they were caught and had to spend the night at such an altitude, they would probably freeze to death.

Cutting steps in the ice, they hacked a way down, until they came to an icy slope whose bottom was hidden in fog. To save time as night approached, they coiled their rope into a pad, on which they locked themselves into a tight huddle, and slid down the slope. "We seemed to shoot into space," Worsley wrote. "For a moment my hair fairly stood on end. Then quite suddenly I felt a glow and knew that I was grinning! I was actually enjoying it. . . . We were shooting down the side of an almost precipitous mountain at nearly a mile a minute."

They landed in a snowbank, unharmed. One more obstacle remained on the very last lap before the whaling station: as they came to the bottom of the mountain, making their way through a narrow gorge, they heard, in Shackleton's words, "an unwelcome sound that might have been musical under other conditions. It was the splashing of a waterfall, and we were at the wrong end. When we reached the top of this fall, we peered over cautiously and discovered that there was a drop of 25 or 30 feet, with impassable ice-cliffs on both sides. To go up again was scarcely thinkable in our utterly wearied condition. The way down was through the waterfall itself." They made their rope fast at one end to a boulder, and swung down, coming out of the icy fall gasping and chilled. The whaling station was only a mile and a half away over level shore, and soon the thirty-six-hour journey across the island was at its end.

The whaling men, tough as they were, gasped in shock at the sight of the three newcomers. "Our beards were long and our hair was matted. We were unwashed and the garments that we had worn for nearly a year without a change were tattered and stained. Three more unpleasant looking ruffians could hardly have been imagined." Shackleton told the unbelievable story of the death of the *Endurance* and all that had happened since, and soon a relief mission was under way to pick up Shackleton's marooned men.

It took not one but four relief expeditions before the Chilean ship *Yelcho* got through the ice to Elephant Island, on August 30, 1916. The men had suffered through a severe winter, and were at the edge of starvation when rescue arrived. They had been stranded on the barren island almost twenty weeks.

While Shackleton's Weddell Sea party was making its magnificent stand against unbelievable hazards, his Ross Sea team was having its own share of hardships. The *Aurora* had put ten men ashore at Cape Evans, McMurdo Sound, and they had set out at once to lay the depots for Shackleton's party. The *Aurora* was supposed to remain frozen in for the winter, serving as a base for the shore party. But in May, 1915, just as the worst part of winter began, a gale broke up the ice and blew the ship out to sea. The ten men ashore were stranded with only meager supplies, while the *Aurora*, damaged and rudderless, drifted in the ice of the Ross Sea for nine months with low fuel and food stores. Scurvy struck the shore party, and several men died. The *Aurora* survived her buffeting and reached New Zealand in April, 1916. She was repaired, and set out in December, with the by-now-rescued Shackleton on board, to pick up the survivors at Cape Evans.

The expedition had been a failure. Men had suffered and men had died. There had been no trans-Antarctic crossing; Shackleton had not even reached Antarctica before his ship was beset. But, though no other Antarctic expedition ever failed so completely to achieve its goals, none had so superbly demonstrated the powers of human courage and endurance.

Among the monuments of perseverance and fortitude, Shackleton's boat trip must stand forever with such other great achievements as Mawson's lonely sledge journey, Scott's ill-fated trek to the Pole, and Shackleton's own polar attempt.

It was 1917 when Shackleton and his men returned to England. The First World War was in its third year. Every man of the Antarctic expedition enlisted at once; three were killed in action and five were wounded. After the war, Shackleton organized yet another Antarctic voyage. He set out from London in September, 1921, aboard a new ship, the *Quest*. His purpose was to map the unknown Antarctic coast south of the Indian Ocean, from the Weddell Sea eastward to Enderby Land. With him once more went his old companions, Worsley and Frank Wild. The outward journey was slow and stormy, and Shackleton was in a depressed, pessimistic mood. Near South Georgia, at quarter to three on the morning of January 5, 1922, he felt a sudden stabbing pain in his chest. It was a heart attack, and death came suddenly. He was forty-seven years old.

He was buried on South Georgia, not far from the place where he had come ashore at the end of his epic boat trip. Like Scott, he went to his final rest in that stormy, ice-bound part of the world he loved so dearly.

Amundsen, who had carried off the prize sought by Scott and Shackleton, also found a chilly grave and a hero's death. He had never returned to the Antarctic. Instead, he turned to his first love, Arctic exploration, making pioneering flights by plane and dirigible over the North Pole. In 1928, the Italian pilot Umberto Nobile crashlanded his dirigible in the Arctic, and Amundsen, though he had quarrelled bitterly with Nobile only a short time before, joined the search for him. A Swedish plane found Nobile; but Amundsen's small aircraft disappeared in the Arctic Ocean. Fragments of the plane were found off the Norwegian coast in September, 1928, but the great explorer, first man to stand at the South Pole and first to navigate the Northwest Passage, was never seen again.

12 BYRD— ADMIRAL OF THE ENDS OF THE EARTH

THE DEATH OF SHACKLETON SEEMED TO SIGNAL THE end of an era in Antarctic exploration. The time when men hauled sledges through the trackless ice desert, cut off completely from civilization, was over. Motor transport, radio communication, and the airplane took much of the peril from the work. There would still be Antarctic adventures and Antartic heroes, but nothing quite to compare with the ordeals of Shackleton and Scott.

In the years between the two World Wars, a new figure joined the company of Antarctic heroes, taking his place on the roster that began with Cook. He was Richard Evelyn Byrd (1888–1957), America's greatest Antarctic explorer since Wilkes.

Byrd came from a well-known Virginia family. (His elder brother, Harry, has been Senator from Virginia since 1933).

213

When he was fourteen, he set down in his diary that he would someday explore the North Pole; a year later, he thrilled to the news of the Wright Brothers' pioneering airplane flight. The themes of aviation and polar exploration remained entwined in Richard Byrd's life to the end of his days.

He served in the United States Navy just before World War I, but a severe ankle injury took him out of active service in 1915, and as a retired officer he filled several desk jobs. When the United States entered the war in 1917, Byrd became an aviator, but was not allowed to see action; he was used as an instructor for other pilots instead. Developing an interest in long-range flights, Byrd invented several instruments that played important parts in the first successful crossing of the Atlantic by air, in Navy planes in 1919. Six years later, he was assigned to the MacMillan Arctic Expedition in Greenland, and got his first experience in polar exploration. He flew thousands of miles over the Arctic region, and in 1926 he and another naval aviator, Floyd Bennett, made the first flight over the North Pole.

"I cannot but marvel at the superiority of the airplane," Byrd jotted in his log as the flimsy three-engine plane leveled off at an altitude of 2,000 feet for its polar flight. "To think that men toiled for years over this ice, a few hard-won miles a day; and we travel luxuriously a hundred miles an hour. How motors have changed the burdens of man!"

Soon, Byrd would experience the same emotions at the other end of the earth. At a dinner in Byrd's honor after his return from the Arctic in 1926, Roald Amundsen had asked him, "Well, Byrd, what shall it be now?"

Byrd's reply, half-humorous, half-serious, was, "The South Pole."

The decade after the end of World War I had seen several Antarctic expeditions. One was the *Quest* expedition of 1921-22, on which Shackleton died; it had continued to Antarctica after his funeral, making scientific discoveries but no major new land finds. Another British expedition in 1920-22 under J. L. Cope had made minor discoveries along the Antarctic Peninsula. In 1923, Captain C. A. Larsen, a thirty-year veteran of Antarctica, had led a whaling expedition in the Ross Sea; other German, British, and Norwegian whaling voyages had followed.

In 1928 came the first successful use of the airplane in Antarctica. Sir Hubert Wilkins, an Australian who had been south with Cope in 1920 and with the *Quest* a year later, was the polar pioneer.

Wilkins hoped to fly south down the Antarctic Peninsula to the Weddell seacoast, and then to continue across the continent to the Bay of Whales. He brought two Lockheed Vega planes to Deception Island in the South Shetlands, and cleared a rough landing strip for his take-off and return. On November 16, 1928, Wilkins made the first flight in the Antarctic regions, though it was only a trial hop that did not take him to Antarctica proper. On December 20, he flew down the east coast of the Antarctic Peninsula to 71°20'S., roughly the point where the 800-mile-long peninsula joins the Antarctic mainland. Finding no place to land, Wilkins turned back, reaching Deception Island ten hours after he had set out.

From the air, it seemed to Wilkins that the peninsula was really an island group, divided by four channels. The largest of these, 20 miles wide and 100 miles long, he named Stefansson Strait after the great Arctic explorer, Vilhjalmur Stefansson. Beyond Stefansson Strait, Wilkins saw the continent itself, covered by a great ice sheet, and he named the nearby mainland Hearst Land for the American newspaper publisher who had sponsored his expedition. (Later exploration showed that what Wilkins thought were channels were only deep valleys cutting across the peninsula.)

Another flight on January 10, 1929, was troubled by low-lying clouds, and once again Wilkins had to turn back without finding a base from which he could launch his proposed flight to the Ross Sea. Several later attempts had no better luck, and Wilkins gave up in 1930—though he did not abandon the idea of making a trans-Antarctic flight, and eventually saw it carried through.

Byrd, meanwhile, was getting his own Antarctic expedition under way at almost the same time as Wilkins'. He was doubly famous now, not only for his flight to the North Pole, but for a flight in 1927 nonstop from New York to Paris with Floyd Bennett and a third companion. Riding the crest of his fame, Byrd was able to organize the most ambitious Antarctic expedition yet, at a cost of about $800,000. The year 1928 was one of booming prosperity in the United States, and many wealthy industrialists, notably Edsel Ford and John D. Rockefeller, Jr., were glad to contribute to Byrd's expedition fund.

Byrd took forty-two men, and four airplanes, equipped with special cameras for surveying purposes. The expedition also carried powerful radio transmitters, a motor tractor, ninety-five Greenland huskies ("the infantry of polar exploration," Byrd called the dogs), and a correspondent of the *New York*

Times—the first newspaperman to take part in an Antarctic expedition.

Four ships brought the 665 tons of Byrd's expedition cargo to his base at the Bay of Whales on the Ross Ice Shelf. Two of the vessels were whalers bound to the Antarctic anyway; two were Byrd's: a venerable Norwegian whaler of wooden construction that he named *City of New York*, and the steel-hulled steamer *Eleanor Bolling*, named for Byrd's mother. The ships left New York in August, 1928, meeting at Dunedin, New Zealand, in November. On December 2 they set out for the Bay of Whales, the *Bolling* towing the *City of New York* to save fuel. They reached the Ross Ice Shelf on Christmas Day, 1928. The *City of New York* was moored to the ice in the Bay of Whales, and dog teams carried the equipment eight miles inland to the chosen site of Byrd's camp, three miles from where Amundsen's base had been in 1911.

It took more than a month to transfer everything from ship to base. At one point Byrd nearly lost the *Bolling*, also moored to the Barrier, when a great chunk of ice calved out of the wall and fell on the ship's deck. Several men were knocked overboard, but no lives were lost and, amazingly, little damage was done.

No mere hut, but a veritable village, began to grow on the Ross Ice Shelf. Byrd named it Little America. There were three main buildings—the Administration Building, the Mess Hall, and a dormitory that was called Norwegian House because there were seven Norwegians in the party. Surrounding these were more than a dozen smaller huts, aircraft hangars, and the 70-foot wire-stayed radio towers. The main buildings were placed several hundred feet from one another so that a fire in one of them would not endanger the others.

Little America, wrote Byrd, "was a beautiful and eerie location. Out beyond the orange shacks, the tall wireless masts, resembling the spidery derricks in an oil field, and the spectral shapes of the anchored planes, were the vast stretches of the Barrier. The long, sweeping lines of the hills were tinted with hues that constantly changed. Overwhelming solitude and a terrible stillness brooded over that immobile, frozen scene."

Yet they were anything but cut off from civilization. Each day, the reporter sent an account to *The New York Times*. Byrd and his men made regular radio broadcasts to the public. After the 1929 stock-market crash, one member of the expedition sent instruction via wireless from the Bay of Whales to his stockbroker in New York. It was all quite different from the days of Scott and Shackleton.

On January 5, 1929, less than three weeks after their arrival, the first trial flight was made at the base. Twelve days later, Byrd, accompanied by pilots Bernt Balchen and Harold June, made a more extensive flight eastward along the Ice Shelf. They carried extra rations in case they were forced down and had to return on foot. They flew to King Edward VII Land, and saw beyond it to frozen-over ocean—the first hint that Edward VII "Land" needed to be renamed Edward VII Peninsula. Snowstorms ahead halted the eastward flight, but they turned south and saw fourteen noble mountain peaks. Byrd named them the Rockefeller Mountains. They reached from 500 to 2,000 feet above the ice sheet that gripped them. "One could not resist the impression," wrote Byrd, "that the peaks were struggling to lift their heads above the eternal snows."

There were other exploring trips before winter arrived. On March 7, Balchen, June, and the geologist Lawrence Gould, Byrd's second-in-command, flew 130 miles to study the geology of the Rockefeller Mountains. A freak accident destroyed their plane; they had made a safe landing, but a 120-mile-an-hour wind had ripped the plane from its mooring, carried it through the air for a mile, and hurled it to pieces against a glacier. So Byrd and two other men had to fly a rescue mission on March 19.

Then it was winter. The *Bolling* and the *City of New York* had left for warmer climes, and Byrd's group was on its own. In their comparatively spacious base, with its gymnasium and well-stocked library, there were fewer psychological problems than had been experienced by earlier, less comfortable winter parties. The sun set on April 18, and months of darkness followed, the men keeping busy with scientific observations, making the most of their modern equipment. Every few hours, it was somebody's task to duck out into the fierce cold to take down a weather reading or repair a recording mechanism. On July 3, the radio brought news of a heat wave in New York— but the temperature at Little America was −64°. A few days later, it was −71°, and in the extreme cold the Barrier ice below the camp began to contract. "All about us we could hear the ice snapping and cracking," wrote Byrd. "Then, as large cracks occurred, the bay ice began booming like distant guns." But the base was not endangered.

The average temperature in August was 27.8° below. September's average was a numbing 44° below! On September 3, it was −63° at Little America, 94° at New York City—a span of 157 degrees!

When the cold relented in October, exploration began again. A geological party under Laurence Gould set out on November 4 for a sledge journey to the Queen Maud Mountains, which Amundsen had crossed on his way to the Pole. Dog teams had laid down a depot several weeks earlier at the foot of the Axel Heiberg Glacier. The motor tractor had helped in the depot-laying, traveling at 25 miles an hour when the surface was smooth and hard, but it broke down in soft snow 80 miles from Little America, and its crew had to walk back.

Gould's party was gone seventy-seven days and covered 1,300 miles. They discovered one of Amundsen's camping places at the foot of the glacier, where he had left a page of his diary behind. The geologists found that the mountains were topped by sandstone cliffs containing coal formations, and were connected with the chain of mountains that Shackleton and Scott had explored to the west.

The most spectacular event of the expedition was Byrd's flight to the South Pole. The Ford tri-motor plane could not make the trip non-stop, and so on November 19 Byrd set out to fly to the base of the Axel Heiberg and establish a depot there for use on the polar hop. On the 440-mile flight, the plane passed over Gould's geological party, looking like a slow moving procession of ants as it sledged along, 2,000 feet below. Byrd's pilot, Dean Smith, made a safe landing at the foot of the glacier, and they deposited gasoline, oil, 350 pounds of food, a stove, and other equipment. On the return trip to Little America, the plane ran low on gas and had to make a forced landing 100 miles from the base. For thirty-six hours Byrd, Smith, the photographer, Ashley McKinley, and the radio engineer, Harold June, were stranded on the Ice Shelf until Bernt Balchen could fly gasoline to them.

On November 28, clear weather conditions made possible the poleward flight. Byrd was accompanied by McKinley, Balchen, and June. Once again, they passed over Gould's toiling geological party, this time dropping a map and photographs that had been taken on Byrd's first flight. Then the plane began to strain for altitude as the great mountain wall of the Polar Plateau drew near.

Weighted down with a heavy load, including a 100-pound aerial camera, four men, and their supplies, the plane could not climb above 11,000 feet. Amundsen had said that the pass atop the Axel Heiberg was 10,500 feet high, which left a bare 500 feet of clearance. And the glacial pass was bordered by steep mountains. If the plane entered the pass and then found it could not make the grade, it would have no room to maneuver or turn back.

Nearby lay a second glacier, the Liv, that had never been explored. The route over the Liv looked more promising, and Byrd ordered Balchen, at the controls, to alter the planned course. The plane soared upward into the mountains, which Byrd wrote were "majestic—colossal shapes carved into amazing jagged and rounded forms by untold centuries of creeping ice." The air was turbulent, and the little craft bounced around wildly. The plane grew sluggish and refused to climb. Ahead lay the narrow mountain pass, with mighty peaks towering on each side. Suddenly Balchen turned. They had to drop 200 pounds of weight, he said, or they would never make it over the pass.

The plane had a dump valve through which gasoline could be jettisoned if necessary. Harold June sprang to the valve. A touch of his hand and 600 pounds of fuel would go over. But then they would not have enough fuel to reach the Pole and return. They would have to turn back as soon as they cleared the pass.

"Wait," Byrd told June.

What else could be jettisoned? The food!

"A bag of food overboard!" Byrd yelled, and McKinley shoved 150 pounds of food out of the plane. If they had to make a forced landing now, they might starve to death. The plane soared higher, but the pass was still above them.

"Quick!" Balchen shouted. "Dump more!"

Another bag of food went through the trap door. They had only 500 pounds left, and could spare no more. If the plane still failed to rise, they would have to dump gasoline next, and that would mean the end of their hopes to reach the Pole. Slowly, it edged upward, while the four men waited tensely— and then it cleared the pass with a few hundred yards to spare. They had reached the Plateau. The Pole lay ahead.

Flying at about 1,500 feet above the roof of the Plateau, they made a beeline for the Pole. When they reached it, they did not attempt to land, but were content to circle it while Byrd dropped an American flag weighted with a stone from the grave of his Arctic flying companion, Floyd Bennett. There were curious effects as they flew around the Pole. Since all times zones met there, they were traveling, in effect, twenty-four "hours" in the few minutes it took to circle the Pole. When they crossed the meridian of 180°, the International Date Line, they were passing from today into tomorrow, and then back into today as they reversed course.

Even more confusing was the effect on directions. All the

way out from Little America, they had been flying southward, toward the Pole. The moment they passed the Pole, though they had not changed course, they were heading north, since any route away from the South Pole must be northward by definition. East and west also changed places, so that "one moment we were looking eastward out of the port window, and the next we had crossed the Pole and were looking westward out of the same window." Byrd noted that "to try to think in terms of north and south, noon or midnight, or even today or tomorrow" at the Poles "is to become hopelessly involved in meaningless, contradictory phrases."

They turned back, heading for their depot at the base of the Axel Heiberg. There were strong air currents that "tossed the plane about like a cork in a washtub." But they were able to descend without serious difficulty, making a neat landing on the hard ice. They loaded fuel aboard and took off again, arriving at Little America at 10:10 A.M. on November 29, 1929. They had made the round trip to the South Pole by air in fifteen hours and fifty-one minutes. It had taken Amundsen three months.

A week later, Byrd was in the air again, flying eastward into the unexplored territory beyond 150° W. There, beyond King Edward VII Peninsula, he discovered another new mountain range, which he named for Edsel Ford, and a vast ice-shielded plateau beyond. "North, east, south, and west," he wrote, "everything that was there was unseen and untrodden and unknown. . . . To the new land I have given the name Marie Byrd Land after my wife, who has backed and helped me every foot of the way, who has shouldered much of the burden of the expedition and whose understanding has made my many expeditions possible." Gould's geological party entered Marie Byrd Land on foot soon after, claiming it for the United States.

When it was time to depart, 400 miles of pack ice girdled the Ross Sea, and the *Eleanor Bolling*, with her steel hull, could not get through. The *City of New York*, whose wooden hull could rebound under the impact of the ice where a steel ship's brittle, inflexible frame could not, cleared the pack by February 7, 1930. But as she headed through the Ross Sea to Little America, a particularly nasty storm came up, and frozen spray clung to the decks and rigging until 150 tons of ice weighted the ship down. She was driven three hundred miles off course, almost to McMurdo Sound. When she finally reached the Bay of Whales, the Byrd expedition loaded all it could in ten hours, leaving much behind, including Byrd's Pole-reaching plane, the *Floyd Bennett*. On February 19, 1930, they sailed away, after fourteen months in the Antarctic.

A hero's welcome awaited them all. Byrd—promoted to Rear Admiral Byrd—was personally greeted by President Hoover when his ship arrived at the Washington Navy Yard. It was considerably different from the homecoming of Charles Wilkes ninety-two years before.

Byrd knew that he had left unfinished work in Antarctica. He wanted to explore Marie Byrd Land by air and by land. The whole Pacific Quadrant of Antarctica, from King Edward VII Peninsula to the Bellingshausen Sea region and Alexander I Island, was unknown. Raising the funds for his second expedition proved a difficult task, though. In the boom year of 1928, money was easily come by. Now, in the wake of the stock-market crash, the United States was deep in economic

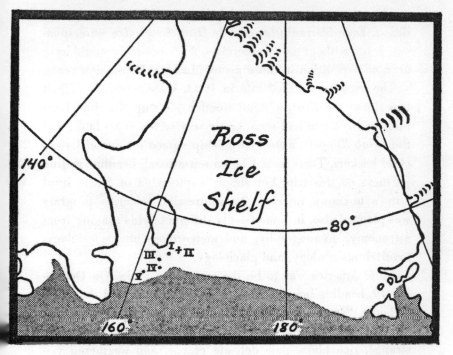

Ross
Ice
Shelf

140°

80°

160°

180°

I + II
III.
IV.
V.

Byrd's Little Americas

depression. The tycoons who previously had contributed so generously were feeling some financial pinch themselves. In 1933, when Admiral Byrd began collecting funds for the new voyage, he was able to raise only $150,000 in cash. By sending out thousands of letters, he managed to get the free use of much equipment on loan, but with strings attached—Byrd had to agree to let the lenders advertise the fact that such-and-such an oil company had donated fuel for the planes, that the so-and-so airline had contributed a plane.

Thus there was a commercial tinge to Byrd's second expedition. Even his radio broadcasts from Antarctica were sponsored. But without the commercials, there probably would have been no expedition in those penny-pinching Depression years.

The expedition sailed late in 1933. Once again, Byrd had two ships: the *Bear*, a small wooden ice ship that had been built in 1874 and had seen Arctic service ten years later, and the *Jacob Ruppert*, a steel cargo ship named for one of Byrd's chief backers. There would be no sensational, headline-getting journeys on this trip, but simply exploration of Marie Byrd Land's unknown interior. An impressive scientific program was planned also, in some twenty different fields ranging from astronomy, oceanography, and meteorology to bacteriology, invertebrate zoology, and glaciology.

Little America was to be the main base again. On December 19, heading into the Ross Sea, the ships sighted their first icebergs. "In the fractured sides of the bergs," Byrd wrote, "in the grottoes and caves worn at their water-line, were strange, rich blues, pale delicate greens, and weathered yellows and greys. The sea surged over their submerged spurs, and exploded in shining puffs of surf." In a single day, they saw an estimated 8,000 icebergs.

Fog made the trip through the ice deadly—a "sleet-oozing, dripping, oppressive fog, so thick that the bow at times was lost from the view of the bridge. . . . And through that smoking pall, like phantom fleets, proud icebergs past numbering, with the sea sobbing in their basement grottoes. Like a cornered thing, the ship stood among them, stopped and drifting, or maneuvering . . . to evade towering cliffs, emerging with formidable clarity out of the gloom which bore down upon her."

The coast was invisible. On January 3, 1934, Byrd flew toward land without sighting it in the fog. The plane crossed one iceberg 20 miles wide, and so long the men could not see from end to end of it. Two Emperor penguins were in the middle of the berg—"the loneliest couple on earth," Byrd commented.

A later flight found an open channel through the pack, and soon the *Ruppert* reached the Bay of Whales; the *Bear*, delayed by a storm at sea, would not arrive for several more weeks. A party went ashore and found Little America in good condition, though clogged with four years of drift snow. Now came the hard work of unloading and moving in. The *Ruppert* could get to within two miles of Little America if she moored along the Barrier. Byrd studied the place where the *Bolling* had unloaded in 1929. While he discussed the possibilities of mooring there, "One moment we saw that wonderfully fine cliff face, seemingly as solid as the Palisades. Next moment there was a sound like a skyscraper collapsing. A quarter mile of Barrier was streaming downward, spilling and tumbling into the sea. The impact rocked the ship, and several hundred thousand tons of ice came spreading out fanwise, covering the water."

A man standing on deck next to Byrd turned to him and said, "Admiral, I don't think I should care to tie up there."

The ship moored in the bay, and dogs, tractors, and men were employed to haul supplies over the 40-mile trip from the *Ruppert* to Little America and back. The *Bear* arrived on January 30, and a week later both ships left. A new Little America was built, right above the old one. Eight new buildings rose, with connecting passages to the lower level. Little America II included a machine shop, a tailoring establishment, a carpentry shop, a radio station and broadcasting plant, and even a dairy housing three cows and a bull! The wintering party included fifty-six men this time.

Byrd had brought four aircraft with him, including the first helicopter to reach Antarctica. He also had a 6-ton tractor called the Cletrac, two "snowmobiles" with tractor treads and skis mounted on a truck chassis, and three smaller trucks designed the same way. They spent February and March testing out this equipment on short hauls before winter arrived.

Winter could arrive none too soon to suit them, either. This year, the ice shelf on which Little America rested was cracked and fissured and in danger of calving into the sea. For a while, there was a good chance that the whole base would be dumped into the icy waters, but when winter came the cold weather cemented the cracks and crevasses and ended the danger.

One of Byrd's pet projects on this expedition was to set up what he called an "Advance Base" on the Polar Plateau, where weather observation could be made during the winter. A prefabricated cabin had been brought for use in this project. Because it was so late in the season, there was no time to carry the cabin inland to the Plateau, or even to the foot of the Queen Maud Mountains. On March 16, 1934, Byrd set out with the Cletrac and three small trucks to establish the base as far south as possible.

The Cletrac broke down after 67 miles, and so Advance Base was set up only 123 miles south of Little America. For protection against wind and cold, the cabin was set in a pit dug in the ice, flush with the surface. A trap door in the roof gave access to the open air.

Because of the breakdown, it had not been possible to bring enough supplies to last for the three men who were supposed to man the cabin through the seven months of winter. No more than two could stay. On the spur of the moment, Byrd decided that two men were bound to get on each other's nerves. Three might offer enough variety to offset the nervous strain. But, he said, "two men, jammed together at arm's length in a tiny shack in this strange environment, living by the dim light of a lantern in a state of perpetual congestion and intrusion, staring at each other for seven months. . . . What man's nerves could stand the irritation?"

So Byrd announced he would make the vigil alone.

He felt a desire, he said, "to taste peace and quiet and solitude long enough to find out how good they really are." On March 28, with the temperature at 60° below zero, Byrd bade farewell to the other men for the winter. He would have radio contact with Little America, but otherwise he would be completely alone—as alone as any man had ever been.

He posted a notice in the shack: "There will be no gossiping."

Each day, he took weather readings, made observations of the Aurora Australis, and, when the weather permitted, went for short walks outside. He did a great deal of reading, watched the stars in the winter night, cooked more or less successfully. The solitude and silence did not trouble him through March, April, and May.

Toward the end of May, he began to feel his health giving way. He discovered that his oil stove had a faulty burner; carbon-monoxide fumes were leaking into the hut. Also, the fresh-air ventilators of the cabin had become clogged with snow. He cleared the vents and patched the cracks, and his mood of irritability, brought on by gas poisoning, cleared away.

Then, on May 30, he spent an hour and a half sending radio messages to Little America, until he realized something was wrong again. The gasoline generator that powered his radio was malfunctioning, and the tunnel leading from the generator to his cabin had filled up with exhaust gases. Byrd dropped to his knees as the poisonous fumes entered his lungs. Groggy and half-conscious, he managed to crawl back to the radio and sign off, and then to shut down the generator before its fumes killed him.

The worst of the winter lay ahead. Byrd, farther south than any man had ever wintered, had to face four months of darkness in poor health. For weeks, he showed the effects of his gas poisoning, barely able to eat, struggling up the ladder out of the cabin to make weather observations in 80°-below-zero weather. To fight the cold, he had to run the stove—but the stove let more fumes into the cabin. "This fire was my enemy," he said. "But I could not live without it."

Three times a week he made contact with Little America, and deliberately pretended that all was well. He knew that if he admitted his condition, a rescue party would be sent out in dead of winter—and he did not want to jeopardize any lives but his own. In July, though, his second-in-command, Dr. Thomas Poulter, radioed that he would like to come to Advance Base to make meteor observations. Byrd gave him permission to make the trip safely, but told him to turn back if he found he could not follow the marked trail in the winter darkness.

While these discussions were going on, Byrd's generator broke down. For radio contact now he had to rely on a hand-cranked generator. He had hardly strength enough to work it. On July 7, he wrote in his diary: "I am still in wretched condition. My brain seems unspeakably tired and confused. Last night was agony. This morning was one of my worst. The gloom, the cold, and the *evenness* of the Barrier are a drag on the spirits. . . ."

Poulter could not set out until July 20. When he did, he lost the trail and had to turn back. Byrd, his strength ebbing from day to day, dragged himself through his round of work, despite weather so cold that "you can hear your breath freeze as it floats away, making a sound like that of Chinese fire-crackers."

His messages from Advance Base were so ragged now that the men at Little America suspected something was wrong. On August 8, Poulter set out again, and two days later the rescue party reached Byrd. Poulter reported that Byrd was "emaci-ated, hollow-cheeked, weak, and haggard," but greeted them calmly. Byrd's first words were, "Come on down, fellows. I have a bowl of hot soup for you."

He was so feeble that the three men of the rescue party had to remain at Advance Base with him for two months before he was strong enough to return to Little America.

In the spring, sledging parties got under way. One team went eastward into Marie Byrd Land with dog teams, and found an almost fertile area at the Edsel Ford Mountains, with flowing streams and colorful ice stained by the presence of microscopic plants and animals. Another party made a 525-mile round trip venture by tractor into the region south of the

Rockefeller Mountains, while other groups went southward past Advance Base to the Queen Maud range. Byrd himself explored by plane, flying far inland and adding new mountain ranges to the rapidly filling map of the Antarctic interior. In January, 1935, the ships returned, and early in February the expedition left for home.

Except for Byrd's unique and voluntary ordeal in the lonely cabin, there were no dramatic exploits on this second expedition. As on Byrd's earlier voyage, not a man lost his life. A vast inland region had been explored by plane for the first time, and men had entered it on foot and by tractor. Scientific studies had revealed new information about the depth of the Antarctic icecap, the geology of the underlying land, and the biology of the frozen continent. A wealth of new scientific information came back with Byrd. And, as before, he came home feeling that his work in the Antarctic had only just begun.

13 ELLSWORTH— ACROSS THE CONTINENT BY AIR

WHILE BYRD, OPERATING OUT OF LITTLE AMERICA ON the Ross Ice Shelf, was probing at the borders of the unknown, another man was attempting a flight clear across the continent —and succeeded where Sir Hubert Wilkins, in 1929–30, had failed.

He was Chicago-born Lincoln Ellsworth, son of a millionaire coal-mine operator. Ellsworth, born in 1880, had every advantage of wealth, but, though sent to the best schools, he failed to develop much interest in his studies. Athletics, yes— rowing and wrestling. "Purely physical endeavor is an inborn passion with me," Ellsworth once wrote. He took up geology and mineralogy, though, worked as an engineer in his father's mines, took long hikes through the rugged country of South America and the Rockies, and sought hardship and adventure in many parts of the world. In 1913, while in London, he

233

attended a memorial service for Robert Falcon Scott, and began to feel the lure of the Antarctic.

Ellsworth's first polar exploits were made in the Arctic. Though thirty-seven when the United States entered World War I, he had taken up aviation with the hope of seeing military action, and after the war joined forces with Roald Amundsen for the aerial exploration of the North Pole. The elder Ellsworth attempted to block what he considered a dangerous adventure, but finally relented and put up $85,000 to finance his son's flight with Amundsen. In 1925, Ellsworth and Amundsen made two unsuccessful attempts to reach the North Pole by plane. They then teamed with the Italian, Umberto Nobile, on a dirigible flight that did take them over the North Pole in 1926. (On a later flight, Nobile was forced down, and Amundsen lost his life in search of him. Ellsworth was not aboard on this trip.)

In the course of his wanderings, Ellsworth had become friendly with Sir Hubert Wilkins. After Wilkins failed in his attempt to fly across Antarctica, Ellsworth took up the challenge in 1933. He bought a Norwegian sealer that he named the *Wyatt Earp*, in honor of the frontier marshal who had been his boyhood hero, and left New Zealand in November, 1933, bound for the Bay of Whales. With him were Wilkins and the pilot, Bernt Balchen. They hoped to fly the 31-foot-long *Polar Star* from the Ross Sea to the Weddell Sea and back. That would decide a question long in doubt: whether or not a strait linked the two big Antarctic seas.

Reaching the Bay of Whales on January 9, 1934, they unloaded the plane on the bay ice and made a few trial runs. Then, unexpectedly, the ice began to break up in a storm; the

plane was damaged and had to be brought back to New
Zealand for repairs. It was too late in the season to try again.

In September, 1934, Ellsworth made his second attempt.
This time, he tried to perform the flight in the other direction,
from the Weddell Sea to the Ross Sea, following Wilkins'
original 1929 plan. They landed on Deception Island in the
South Shetlands, but a warm spell melted the hard-packed
snow of their runway, and the plane could not take off. Looking for a better base, they searched the Antarctic Peninsula
for forty-four days, coming at last to Snow Hill Island.

Nordenskjöld had wintered here more than thirty years
before. They found his hut, still intact though filled with ice.
"A pair of ice skates lay near the door," Ellsworth wrote.
"Against the cabin were several boxes of cans of sardines,
pepper and mustard, and cakes of chocolate. The chocolate
tasted all right, but the thought of fish of a vintage of 33 years
ago was too much for us."

The weather remained bad. In two months, there were but
twelve continuous hours of cloudless flying weather, and Ellsworth's single flight covered only a few hundred miles before
he had to call it quits once again.

He returned in November, 1935. In three years, the *Wyatt
Earp* had carried him 48,000 miles in search of a place to take
off for a twenty-hour flight across Antarctica. A friend told
him, "Your *Polar Star* has traveled farther and flown less than
any other plane!"

This time he was accompanied by a new pilot, Herbert
Hollick-Kenyon. November 21 saw them take off in perfect
weather, only to turn back after ten and a half hours when a
fuel gauge bulged and threatened to burst. Two days later,

they tried again. There was no thought of attempting a non-stop flight, of course. Ellsworth planned to fly until the weather grew poor; then he would try to find a flat spot on the ice sheet where he could land and wait for clearing skies. It was a wild scheme that seemed doomed to failure, but he refused to listen to anyone who tried to discourage him.

They flew 600 miles down the Antarctic Peninsula and onto the continental mainland. At an altitude of 13,000 feet an unknown mountain range rose ahead of them: "Bold and rugged peaks, bare of snow. . . . We were indeed the first intruding mortals in this age-old land, and, looking down at the rugged peaks, I thought of eternity and man's insignificance," Ellsworth wrote. "So these first new mountains we saw I named Eternity Range."

Beyond lay a vast plateau, broken only by a few *nunataks*, or rocky outcroppings. When they had traveled a thousand miles, the radio broke down, and they would have no contact with the outside world after that. They were nearly at the half-way point, though. Little America was 1,300 miles ahead.

New mountains appeared to the right and left as they advanced over the plateau. Ellsworth named the highest peak Mount Mary Louise Ulmer, for his wife. Farther on, clouds began to form, and they decided to land. They had been in the air nearly fourteen hours. "We climbed out of the plane rather stiffly and stood looking around in the heart of the Antarctic," Ellsworth wrote. "There we were—two lone human beings in the midst of an ice-capped continent two-thirds the size of North America."

They spent nineteen hours there, on a plateau 6,400 feet above sea level. They were at 79°12′ S., 104°10′ W. The

South Pole was 750 miles ahead in one direction, the Bay of Whales 750 miles in another. Ellsworth raised an American flag at the camp, and claimed the entire 350,000-square-mile region between 80° W. and 120° W. for the United States, naming it James W. Ellsworth Land for his father. The immediate plateau he called Hollick-Kenyon Plateau.

They fixed a meal—oatmeal and bacon—and then crawled into their sleeping bags, but were too tense to sleep. On November 24, they took off again. After half an hour thick clouds forced them to land, and they waited three days for good weather before they could take to the air. This time, they were able to make only 90 miles before fog forced them to land once more.

Blizzards and 50-mile-an-hour gales struck them. For seventy-two hours they huddled in their tents, with the temperature below zero. Then the storm abated, but not enough to let them take off. For eight days, until December 4, they camped on the ice while drift snow piled up around them. With their radio gone, their fuel and food ebbing, and the weather so cold the plane's engine would not start, the situation began to look critical. When the weather cleared, they found that the entire tail of the plane had filled with snow. Ellsworth spent a whole day bailing it out with a bucket, using a teacup to scoop the snow away from the fragile controls.

They made it aloft and the sky turned clear, the day sunny. After nearly four hours of flight, they landed again to find out where they were, and to check their fuel.

They found that they had left the Plateau and were on the Ross Ice Shelf, only 125 miles from the Bay of Whales. The unexplored territory was all behind them now. But their fuel was lower than they had anticipated; they had burned a great deal of gas in climbing over the Eternity Mountains and making three take-offs. It seemed doubtful that they would make it to Little America by plane.

At 5:58 A.M. on December 5, they took off again. In four hours, they reached a point where "from the air we saw the ice-free waters of the Ross Sea—the goal of my three years of endeavor." But then the engine began to sputter and miss. At 10:30 the last of the gasoline was exhausted, and the *Polar Star* glided gently to the snow.

They knew they were near the Bay of Whales. Hollick-Kenyon thought he could make out Little America's snow-covered buildings and windmill generator about four miles away. They loaded three weeks' food onto a sledge and, leaving their tent and sextant at the plane, set out on foot.

What Hollick-Kenyon had seen turned out to be fifteen miles away, not four. Nor was it Little America. The "buildings" were ridges of ice, and the "generator" was a cake of ice turned on end and standing above the ridges. So they had to trek back to the plane, having wasted time, energy, and valuable food in a 30-mile round trip to nowhere and back.

At the plane once again, they took position readings that showed them to be actually twelve miles south of the Bay of Whales. Wearing snowshoes and hauling a sledge, they set forth once again—more prudently taking the tent with them this time.

Fog descended, so that they could see no more than 100 feet ahead, and had to travel by compass and guesswork. They pulled the sledge fifteen minutes at a time, rested four minutes, pulled fifteen. Six hours of sledging a day was the best they could manage. Ellsworth had developed a frozen foot, and progress was slow. Eventually they came to a ridge, and heard an odd booming sound that they thought was the wind against the far side of the ridge. When they looked over, they were startled to see the Ross Sea, two hundred feet below! The "wind" was the sound of waves lapping against the Ice Shelf.

They had found the Bay of Whales, but somehow had overshot Little America. So they camped that night a mile back from the edge of the Barrier, remaining there two days, until December 15. Then, in clear weather, they followed the edge of the Bay of Whales until they came to Little America. They had been wandering on the Ice Shelf for ten days. After making a 2,300-mile flight across the continent with unerring accuracy, they had had endless problems in covering the last 16 miles, from their final landing point to Little America!

Byrd's second expedition had left the base in February, 1935. Now, the following December, it was deserted and snow-covered, with masts and poles and pipes jutting above the snow. Ellsworth and Hollick-Kenyon found a skylight, pried it open, and climbed down to find themselves in Byrd's radio shack.

They had been out of radio contact with the *Wyatt Earp* for two weeks. Three times a day, they had cranked their hand-operated radio set and tried to get a message through. But though they could hear the ship, the ship could not hear them, and the only word they ever got from the *Wyatt Earp* was the sentence, "We can't hear you." Now, they wanted to send word that they were safe—but Byrd had left no radio equipment behind! All they could do was settle in and live off

Byrd's leftover provisions until Wilkins and the *Wyatt Earp* came to the Bay of Whales to look for them.

On January 15, they heard the roar of a plane overhead. Rushing out, they saw a parachute descending, bearing packages of chocolate, raisins, orange juice—and a note from Captain Hill of the Royal Research Ship *Discovery II*, sent out by Australia as a rescue mission when Ellsworth's radio had failed. A few days later, men of the *Discovery II* arrived at Little America. Soon afterward the *Wyatt Earp* pulled into the Bay of Whales. Ellsworth returned to Australia aboard *Discovery II*, while the men of the *Wyatt Earp* hiked out to recover the abandoned plane sixteen miles away.

Ellsworth and Hollick-Kenyon had achieved a history-making flight. They were the first to cross Antarctica from the Atlantic (Weddell) side to the Pacific (Ross) side. They had discovered mountains and plateaus never before seen by human eyes, and they had seen no sign of the much-debated strait cutting across from sea to sea. They had proved that a small plane, using skis instead of wheels as landing gear, could come down and take off again and again on the hard ice fields of the continent's interior.

Ellsworth, though, had only flown across a corner of Antarctica. He dreamed of making a flight through the continent's heart, from the Indian Ocean side of Antarctica to the Bay of Whales. In October, 1938, he sailed from Cape Town in the *Wyatt Earp* with two planes. Once again Sir Hubert Wilkins accompanied him. Unusually heavy ice conditions met them; it took forty-five days to struggle through the ice pack to the coast, and by that time it was three weeks too late to attempt the mid-continent flight. Ellsworth had to be content with a much shorter flight in the unknown area between Wilkes Land and Enderby Land. He flew on a looping course for 250 miles inland, over territory never before explored. There were no mountain ranges here, he found; only a broad, featureless sheet of ice that apparently rose steadily as it led toward the Pole. Ellsworth gave the name of American Highland to the 77,000-square-mile region he explored.

The flights of Ellsworth and Byrd had taken the mystery from hundreds of thousands of square miles of the frozen continent. Where dog teams and tired men once had labored for months to cover a few hundred miles, the new explorers could venture deep into Antarctica in a matter of hours, penetrating regions far beyond the dreams of the pioneers.

An age of wonders was at hand—and soon even the early expeditions of Byrd and Ellsworth would come to seem puny and small of scale.

14 TOWARD THE ATOMIC AGE

MANY NATIONS NOW LOOKED TO THE SOUTH. THE gathering world tensions of the late 1930's pointed toward war, and in war even the loneliest outpost could have strategic value. In the First World War, important naval battles had been fought off the tip of South America; perhaps the second might see combat even in the frozen Antarctic. With new means of transportation making the polar regions more accessible, Antarctica became the target of many expeditions.

The Norwegians were the most active, after the United States, in the 1930's. For Norway, the Antarctic was an important commercial territory, the heart of the still-active whaling industry. Norwegian whalers, mostly owned by the Christensen family of Sandefjord, were busy in the coastal region westward from the Weddell Sea to Enderby Land, and —in the Enderby Brothers tradition—combined exploration

242

with their quest for profit. In 1935, one Norwegian expedition made history of a sort when it landed at a rocky, ice-free shore in the American Highland sector. A party of eight went ashore, including the ship's captain, Klarius Mikkelsen, and his wife, Caroline—the first woman ever to set foot on Antarctica.

In 1938 and 1939, Germany returned to the Antarctic, in search of a strategic foothold for the war soon to break out. The Germans made three landings in what was considered the Norwegian sector of Antarctica, raised the swastika on the ice field, and greeted puzzled penguins with a brusque "Heil Hitler!" Several years later, during the war, German raiders used sub-Antarctic islands such as Kerguelen as bases, and harassed Allied shipping until driven out.

With the Antarctic situation growing increasingly tense, Admiral Byrd persuaded the United States government to set up a continuing United States Antarctic Service that would be, essentially, a permanent American expedition. In that way, the United States would be able to claim "settlement" of Antarctica in case matters came to an actual dividing up of the continent into national zones. France had already claimed Adelie Land, New Zealand the regions south of the Ross Sea, and Great Britain the Antarctic Peninsula. None of these claims had been strictly enforced as yet, and the United States did not recognize any of them. Even Byrd's and Ellsworth's claims on behalf of the United States had not met with official approval in Washington. So far as the U.S. was concerned, Antarctica was international territory—but, to be on the safe side, President Roosevelt decided on semipermanent occupation of Marie Byrd Land, which could be declared an "American zone" if necessary.

Byrd, of course, was put in command of the new expedition. The assigned task was to explore the coastline between 78° and 148° W., and to penetrate as far into the interior as possible. Hearst Land, seen by Wilkins in 1930, was also to be explored.

Congress set aside $350,000 for Byrd's third expedition, and the War and Navy Departments donated equipment valued at $327,000. Another $240,000 came from private contributors. Byrd reached the Bay of Whales in January, 1940. He found that the old Little America site could not be used; the ice sheet had shifted and the buildings had caved in. Little America III was constructed not far away.

Byrd sailed eastward in the *Bear*, getting through the pack and coasting Marie Byrd Land 140 miles farther east than anyone had gone before. Aerial exploration added to the knowledge of the interior. The winter season was enlivened by a fire at Little America; a tub of blubber, being melted down to be used as dog food, caught fire and threatened to take the lives of the expedition's dogs, in a hut nearby. With the temperature far below zero, Byrd's men turned out to rescue the dogs—needed for the summer sledge journeys— and to keep the fire from spreading. Luckily, there were no casualties, either canine or human—and one of the dogs calmly gave birth to six pups during the confusion!

After extensive scientific studies and geographical work, Byrd's third expedition came home in 1941. Much of the world was already at war, and the United States soon was drawn in. Admiral Byrd returned to active duty in the navy. From 1942 to 1945 he headed important missions in the Pacific and on the fighting front in Europe. One of his responsibilities was the surveying of remote Pacific islands for airfields. He was decorated several times, and was present at the Japanese surrender in 1945.

Within a year after the end of the war, Byrd was organizing a fourth expedition—the biggest ever. The United States Navy's "Operation Highjump" brought thirteen ships, six planes, and 4,000 men to the Antarctic. Through all of history, only about 600 men had set foot on Antarctica before Operation Highjump.

Highjump's chief task was to circumnavigate the 16,000-mile Antarctic coastline and map it thoroughly. The existing maps, Byrd said, had "little more relation to reality than some of the grotesque sixteenth-century maps of America used by pioneer explorers who crossed the Atlantic." Seaplanes based at various points would explore the coast and the immediate inland region, while ski-equipped landplanes would make long photo-reconnaissance journeys deep into the interior.

The attack on Antarctica was three-pronged. An eastern force of ships would start from the Balleny Islands, south of New Zealand, and head westward. A western group would begin at 90° W. and move toward the meridian of Greenwich (0°), in Queen Maud Land east of the Weddell Sea. These two groups were to meet. A central group, based at the Bay of Whales, would explore the remaining coastline.

World War II had provided a host of dazzling new tools and weapons. There were new techniques for making aerial photographs and maps; instruments for determining the depth of the ice and the structure of the land beneath it; fantastic new ice-breaking ships that could knock down a 30-foot wall of ice in an hour; long-range planes that could soar effortlessly for thousands of miles without refueling. Many of the problems faced by the old explorers were trivial now. When Byrd's ships approached the Bay of Whales and found it blocked by ice floes, the icebreaker *North Wind* smashed up 15,000,000 tons of ice in three days, making it possible for the squadron to enter and unload.

They found that the Bay of Whales' entrance was less than 300 yards wide. In 1940, the entrance had been a mile and a half across; in Amundsen's time, it had been ten miles. Study showed that the Bay had formed at a place where two independent sections of the ice walls met. Between them was a submerged island, Roosevelt Island. To the west lay the 160,000 square miles of the Ross Ice Shelf; to the east, the smaller Prestrud Shelf, discovered on the Amundsen expedition. The Ross Shelf moved northward and the Prestrud Shelf westward at about four feet a day, both curving around Roosevelt Island. Regularly—about every fifty years, the scientists decided—the two ice shelves met. There was a fearful collision, and a great section of the Barrier crashed free and drifted away.

Amundsen had arrived early in the cycle, while the Bay of Whales was still wide open. In the thirty-five years that followed, the two shelves had gradually been moving toward each other, closing the mouth of the Bay of Whales. When Byrd arrived, he found that Little America III, on the Prestrud Shelf, had moved a mile and half to the northwest between 1941 and 1946. Another collision was due in about six months, and then once again the Bay of Whales would be wide open. For safety's sake, Little America IV was built two miles north of Little America III, well back from the edge of the ice.

One of the journeys carried out by the central group of Operation Highjump was a trip to Cape Evans, 300 miles west of the Bay of Whales. Scott's 1911 camp was still there, containing provisions good to eat, matches that still struck, seal carcasses from which fresh steaks could be cut. Fifteen miles away at Hut Point they found Scott's 1901–04 base, also well preserved. A hitching rope that Scott had used for ponies was in such good condition that it was used to moor a helicopter— and how that would have astonished Scott! A British magazine lay embedded in a block of ice. "Paper and print," wrote Byrd, "looked as if the publication had come from the press only a few days before. But this journal had been printed in 1892."

A feature of the expedition for Admiral Byrd was a second flight to the South Pole. It was quite different from his daredevil 1929 visit in the rickety *Floyd Bennett*. Now he had the benefit of JATO—Jet-Assisted Take-Off—and there were no problems of jettisoning food or fuel to get the ship onto the Polar Plateau. They flew southward, "into the strange sunset of the Antarctic's late-summer midnight. The sun was low, a great ball like a red wheel rolling along our horizon just a few feet above it." On the plateau, they flew at altitudes of 11,500 to 14,000 feet above sea level, with the flat white surface about 2,000 feet below them. Soon the Pole appeared, and Byrd became the first man in history to reach it twice. It was only the fourth time men had seen the Pole—Amundsen and Scott by land in 1911–12, Byrd by air in 1929 and again in 1947.

"Below us," Byrd wrote, "the snow had a slight metallic sheen. Where the sun struck at angles it was tinged with gold.

I dropped a cardboard box containing multicolored little flags of the United Nations."

Then they flew on for 100 miles, into the unvisited land beyond the Pole, seeing "only the rolling white desert from horizon to horizon." By noon, they were back at Little America, after an 1,800-mile flight that had lasted twelve hours.

Meanwhile, Highjump's western group was at work off Wilkes Land. A stretch of coast as long as the United States' West Coast lay between Adelie Land and the Shackleton Ice Shelf, virtually unexplored since Wilkes had sighted it in 1840. Since then, Byrd wrote, "this has been an elusive coast. Broken segments appear across the ice pack in green and smoky-yellow mirages and vanish in blizzard-driven snow and low cloud. At only rare intervals have the curtains lifted to allow brief real glimpses of the continent or landings upon it." Only Mawson had done any systematic exploring inland here, and he, trekking on foot, had covered only a few hundred miles at the eastern end of the region.

Now, exploratory mapping flights entered the rugged inland strip, following the coast and finding new glaciers and mountains everywhere. Deeper inland, Wilkes Land turned out to be a flat ice sheet 6,000 to 9,500 feet above sea level, with no peaks high enough to thrust through.

Nearly 1,500 miles of coastline were mapped accurately—a geographical achievement of high order. But the accomplishment that drew the most attention was the discovery of a strange sheltered ice-free "oasis" that contrasted powerfully with the eternal whiteness surrounding it.

A plane piloted by Lieutenant Commander David Eli Bunger made the discovery on February 11, 1947. Following the eastern cliffs of Shackleton Ice Shelf inland, Bunger and his crew were 110 miles from the sea when they came upon a land of blue and green lakes and brown hills hidden in the expanse of white. It was a region of about 300 square miles, containing three large open-water lakes and about twenty smaller ones, of all shapes and hues. Between the lakes were jumbled masses of barren reddish-brown rock. The only life in the oasis was microscopic—algae and bacteria. Penguins and seals seemed to shun the place, though the lakes teemed with blue-green, green, red, and brown algae. The water of the lakes was warm—by Antarctic standards, at least. Evidently the entire oasis was an area left bare by a retreating glacier; why the glaciers are retreating in some parts of Antarctica is a question that still remains unsettled.

Another novelty of Operation Highjump was the first deliberate swim ever taken in Antarctic waters. Now and then, men had fallen in by accident, but had always hurried out as fast as possible, since those chill waters could draw the warmth out of a man's body and kill him in minutes. During the Second World War, though, rubber suits for cold-water swimming had been developed, and they were tested in the Bay of Whales on February 4, 1947. After a wary look around for such unpleasant offshore denizens as killer whales and sea leopards, fifteen "frogmen" clad in green rubber suits and flippers entered the water. The air temperature was 27°, the water temperature 29°. Three men had leaky suits, and beat a quick retreat, but the rest, their body heat kept in by the rubber garb, stayed in as long as twenty-one minutes without discomfort.

When Operation Highjump ended, in February, 1947, it

could claim to be the most successful exploring mission so far in Antarctica: 70,000 aerial photographs had been taken on sixty-four flights; 60 per cent of the continent's coastline had been photographed, including hundreds of miles never seen before. The newly discovered land had an area of 350,000 to 700,000 square miles—greater than the areas of Germany and France combined. Hundreds of new mountains had been seen, in eighteen separate mountain ranges.

The next major Antarctic expedition was a joint Norwegian-Swedish-British one, directed by Norway's John Giaever. This, the first international Antarctic expedition, concentrated on Queen Maud Land on Antarctica's Atlantic side. From January, 1950, to February, 1952, they explored this little-known area. They, too, came upon an "oasis." Not far inland, they discovered a hill "bright with lichens of various colors—black and white, yellow and grey, orange and red—an absolute jungle for people who had seen no plant life whatever through the year 1950." So wrote a glaciologist of the expedition, Valter Schytt. "As well as the lichens, there was a green moss, almost luxuriant in growth and sometimes nearly an inch high."

Another group of the same expedition found two species of tiny spiders living on a barren rock heap. For much of the year, the spiders were frozen solid, it appeared—but when the thaw came, they returned to life, unharmed by their long chill.

The early 1950's also saw French, British, Argentinian, and American expeditions to Antarctica, all of them minor. The nations of the world were simply warming up for that monu-

mental scientific enterprise, the International Geophysical
Year.

The IGY, as it was called, was first suggested in 1950. It
was planned as a joint international effort to carry out simul-
taneous scientific observations in many fields—research into
cosmic rays, the earth's weather, the nature of the aurora, and
much else. Most of the world's major nations, including the
United States and the Soviet Union, agreed to take part.

Antarctica was selected as a key area for IGY studies. Late
in 1954, the IGY countries met in Rome to plan the Antarctic
phase of the operation, and twenty-eight Antarctic observation
sites were selected, ten on the mainland. The United States
agreed to set up three of them—one at Little America, one in
Marie Byrd Land, and one, astonishingly, at the South Pole
itself. Australia had already established Mawson Station, near
Enderby Land, and planned to set up others. So did Japan,
France, New Zealand, South Africa, and several other countries—including Russia, which had done nothing in the Antarctic since Bellingshausen's time. The Russians intended to
put a station on the Knox Coast, in the western part of Wilkes
Land, and to build other stations inland. One Russian station
was to be set up at the "Pole of Inaccessibility"—the unexplored heartland northwest of the South Pole, so named
because it is the point in Antarctica farthest from the sea.

All these bases were to be begun in the 1955–56 season. The
IGY itself, not really a "year," would run for eighteen months,
from July, 1957 through December, 1958.

The United States' IGY program bore the name of "Operation Deep Freeze"—headed, of course, by Admiral Richard E.
Byrd. The first contingent of Operation Deep Freeze—1,800

men—sailed late in 1955. Thousands of other men followed
the next year as work proceeded on the construction of the
new bases. An airstrip was laid out near Hut Point at
McMurdo Sound, and in December, 1955, eight planes flew
nonstop from New Zealand to Antarctica—the first time that
the icebound continent had been reached in a direct hop by
plane.

The Bay of Whales had broken out, since 1947, and the
Barrier looked unsafe. For the site of Little America V, Byrd
chose Kainan Bay, 30 miles to the northeast, and here rose
the seventeen bright orange buildings of the seventy-three-man
station.

The McMurdo Sound airstrip was the base for several awe-
some flights. The first was a 3,000-mile journey across Wilkes
Land to the Knox Coast and back. The plane passed near the
Russian IGY base then being built. A later flight, even more
impressive, was a 3,200-mile aerial survey flight from the Ross
Sea to the Weddell Sea and back.

Admiral Byrd made his third flight to the South Pole early
in 1956. He took off from McMurdo Sound, circling the Pole
three times—"the first time any of us had made three round-
the-world trips in ten minutes," he joked. The homeward flight
took the plane directly over the route on which Scott had perished in 1912. "What changes two generations had wrought!"
Byrd later commented. "Where Scott and his ill-fated trail
mates man-hauled heavy sleds, we rode past at three and a half
miles a minute with the security of four engines and magical
new electronic navigating equipment. Tea was served at
intervals."

On other flights, between January 3 and 14, 1956, long-range United States Navy planes made aerial surveys of 800,000 square miles never before seen by human eyes—an area equal to one-fourth the continental United States.

Of all the achievements of Operation Deep Freeze, probably the most spectacular was the establishment of a permanent base at the South Pole. How incredible that would have seemed to Shackleton or Scott! The first step was a reconnaissance flight on October 31, 1956. Byrd did not go along; he had returned from the Antarctic earlier that year, and chose not to go south with the second Deep Freeze contingent in late 1956. The man in charge on this flight was Byrd's successor, Rear Admiral George J. Dufek. With six companions, he flew to the Pole in a Navy R4D plane and landed on the Polar Plateau.

No one had set foot at the Pole since Scott's tragic journey of 1912. The seven Deep Freeze men spent forty-nine minutes there, in temperatures down to 58° below zero. They chopped a hole in the snow and set up an American flag at the Pole. Then they beat a quick retreat, hampered when the plane's skis froze fast to the ice, and fifteen JATO charges had to be fired to get aloft.

When the weather grew warmer, three weeks later, the job of constructing the base got under way. Giant Air Force Globemasters dropped 760 tons of packaged building material, fuel, and supplies at the Pole, making eighty-four round trips in all. Two dozen Navy men, working in midsummer temperatures that ranged between 5° above and 25° below, put up the seven tunnel-connected buildings. The polar outpost was named Amundsen-Scott Station, after the leaders of the only two expeditions that had ever reached the South Pole overland.

During the Antarctic winter of 1957, eighteen Americans occupied Amundsen-Scott Station. Their leader was Dr. Paul A. Siple, who in 1928, as a nineteen-year-old Eagle Scout, had accompanied Byrd on his first expedition. Dr. Siple, who has probably logged more time in Antarctica than any other person, guided the occupants of the snug polar base through six sunless months of the coldest temperatures human beings have ever braved. There were 169 consecutive days of temperatures below —40°. One month the *average* temperature was —80°! The coldest day of all was September 17, 1957, when the thermometer recorded a temperature of —102.1°. Through this coldest and darkest of winters, the men carried on a full program of work, and discovered that they could even go outdoors without harm. One man stayed outside in temperatures close to —100° for four hours, without ill effects. The thin air gave many men headaches, though, and some were troubled by an arthritis-like stiffness of the joints. Nearly everyone lost weight during the long night.

It would require a healthy-sized book in itself to describe the many IGY Antarctic activities. Thousands of men in more than three dozen stations built by eleven countries subjected the southern continent to a detailed investigation that dwarfed all previous research. Sadly, Admiral Byrd did not live to see this massive effort commence. He died on March 11, 1957, several months before the IGY's official opening.

With the coming of the machine age to Antarctica, much of the drama inevitably departed. Now that a radio network provided reliable communication, now that planes could fly nonstop to the Antarctic from the outside world, now that men could calmly dig in for permanent occupation of the South

Pole itself, there could be few more great adventures such as Shackleton's boat trip or Mawson's trek across the glaciers. Yet the IGY did produce one superb exploit that ranked with the earlier heroic deeds. It was the first overland crossing of Antarctica from the Weddell Sea to the Ross Sea.

As early as 1912, Ernest Shackleton had called for such a trip. Two years later, in the *Endurance* expedition, he attempted to carry it out—but, as we have seen, did not succeed even in reaching the mainland. For a generation thereafter, the trans-Antarctic land crossing remained an unfulfilled dream.

Now it became part of Great Britain's IGY program. The old Shackleton idea was revived in 1950 by Dr. Vivian Fuchs, now Sir Vivian, an English geologist who had explored Africa and the Arctic. Fuchs mentioned the project to J. H. Wordie, the president of the Royal Geographical Society and a former shipmate of Shackleton's, in 1953, and soon the British government agreed to support it.

In November, 1955, the thirty-seven-year-old Fuchs led an advance party to the Weddell Sea aboard the Canadian sealer *Theron*. Delayed by bad ice conditions, they did not get through the pack until January 30, 1956, when they landed at the foot of the ice shelf near Vahsel Bay, and, one mile inland, set up a base named for Shackleton.

It was too late in the season to build a hut, and so the eight men of the advance party used as their winter shelter a packing crate, only 21 by 9 by 8. When spring came, they set up their hut and began to scout the route that the trans-Antarctic team would take.

The plan was the same as Shackleton's: the main party

would travel from Vahsel Bay to McMurdo Sound on the Ross Sea, while a supporting party, starting out from the Ross Sea side, would lay food and fuel depots along the route. Instead of dog-drawn sledges, though, they would use trucks with tractor treads, aircraft dropping supplies from above.

Fuchs himself would lead the main party. The Ross Sea party was to be led by Sir Edmund Hillary, the gallant explorer who in 1953 had been the first to climb Mount Everest. The purpose of the expedition was to explore the unknown area between the Weddell Sea and the Pole, and to map the western side of the mountains Shackleton and Scott had seen from the east in their polar treks.

In 1956, the advance party established an inland base 300 air miles south of Shackleton Base. It was called South Ice, and was built as the South Pole station would be, by shuttling men and supplies out by air. Not until October, 1957, did a party try to reach South Ice by land. Fuchs and three companions set out, driving four American-made snow vehicles, three Weasels and a Sno-Cat.

Crossing the crevassed Filchner Ice Shelf was a risky business. "From beneath us," Fuchs wrote, "often came startling sounds caused by movement of the ice below. In one crevasse the staccato metallic sound of breaking ice made us liken it to two men building a metal shed in the dark depths beneath. Another, about five feet from our tents, was even louder, sounding as though boilermakers were at work." For safety, they drove with the vehicles roped together "like climbers on a mountain," and in the most dangerous stretches the men went ahead on foot to probe the surface with chisels and picks in search of hidden crevasses.

Even with the use of snow vehicles, and with the aid of aerial support, it took thirty-seven days to cover the 400 trail miles to South Ice. The return trip—by air—took two and a half hours!

All was ready now to begin the trans-Antarctic trek. On November 24, 1957, Fuchs set out, leading his convoy of snow tractors. They were plagued by crevasses that had not been spotted on the reconnoitering trip in October, and three times in the first week Sno-Cats dropped out of sight and had to be laboriously pulled from the chasms. This time, it took twenty-nine days to reach South Ice, and Fuchs radioed ahead to Hillary on December 21, telling him that the worst part of the trip was probably over.

He continued on with four Sno-Cats, three Weasels, and a Canadian-made Muskeg tractor. Two dog teams went ahead to mark the trail. On Christmas Day, the convoy set out again, bound now for the South Pole, 555 miles away. Hard *sastrugi* lay before them, but the tractors slowly ground over the sharp, iron-hard ridges. Every three hours, the party paused for scientific observations. One Weasel broke down and had to be abandoned. All the vehicles were badly strained by the *sastrugi*, which were as high as five feet. "It was impossible to go round the high, ice-hard ridges, for they formed a great field that extended out of sight in all directions," Fuchs wrote. "Each driver had to judge the course for his own particular type of vehicle, and often we found ourselves scattered a mile or two apart."

Hillary, meanwhile, had finished the depot-laying job on December 20. Now he was on his way to Amundsen-Scott Station at the South Pole, with three tractors and four companions. He got there on January 4 to wait for Fuchs' arrival.

Since Fuchs was behind schedule because of the high and almost impassable *sastrugi*, Hillary suggested by radio that Fuchs halt at Amundsen-Scott Station and let the Americans fly the party out. The trans-Antarctic trek, he said, could be completed the following year.

Fuchs had only come 200 miles beyond South Ice by January 4. Nevertheless, he felt that the worst was behind him, and that his party could beat the oncoming winter to McMurdo Sound. He told Hillary that "there was no question of abandoning the journey." Newspaper reporters interpreted this exchange of messages as a quarrel between the two leaders of the expedition, though there was never any real disagreement.

The next day, the zone of *sastrugi* was left behind. The convoy now began averaging thirty to thirty-five miles a day. On January 9, they were 240 miles from the Pole. Observations made that day showed the ice to be 6,500 feet thick at that point.

Several of the explorers developed high fever, nausea, and stomach disorder a few days later. It was mysterious, because in the germ-free Antarctic such diseases are rare. Eventually, everyone but Fuchs and one other man came down with the bug. They never did learn what the cause was.

On January 17, two American planes flew over the convoy and radioed greetings. Aboard were Hillary, Rear Admiral Dufek—and a squad of reporters! Antarctic exploration had never been like this in Shackleton's day! The tractors rolled on, and by January 19 they were at Amundsen-Scott Station. (Fuchs had not crossed the date line on his trip. But the

Americans at the Pole had arrived from the other direction, and so for them it was January 20.)

Hillary and Fuchs shook hands at the Pole. The new arrivals got some rest, changed over to South Pole time, and were guests of honor at a party on January 22. Two days later, Fuchs and his men were on their way again. They had come 900 miles from Shackleton Base, and still had 1,250 miles to go.

Though they had been traveling in a straight line, their course now shifted as they passed the Pole. Instead of going south, they were now on a northward course. Twenty-five miles beyond the Pole, they took a reading that showed the ice depth at about 2,000 feet. They had found the same depth 25 miles on the other side of the Pole. At the Pole itself, though, the ice was about 8,000 feet. So it seemed that the Pole was located on a great ice-filled basin about 50 miles wide, rimmed by hidden mountains some 6,000 feet high.

On January 28, when they were 142 miles north of the Pole, an emergency developed. One of the men slumped unconscious in his Sno-Cat, a victim of carbon-monoxide poisoning. In the rarefied atmosphere of the Polar Plateau, he needed oxygen urgently, but the expedition carried only a five-hour supply. What might have been a polar tragedy years before was readily averted, though. Fuchs radioed for help, and soon two American planes took off from McMurdo Sound, carrying oxygen bottles. It was too cloudy to make a landing, but they parachuted the oxygen down, and soon the sick man was back on duty.

The last Weasel broke down soon afterward. The Sno-Cats were also showing signs of wear. But the convoy moved ahead steadily, making good time as it journeyed from one of Hillary's depots to the next. From Shackleton Base to the Pole, they had averaged only 19 miles a day; now they were averaging 35 miles a day. On March 1, 1958, they rolled up a remarkable 75 miles. The next day, they came rolling into Scott Base at McMurdo Sound. They had covered 2,158 miles from Shackleton Base to Scott Base, in ninety-eight days. (Ninety-nine by the calendar, since they had gained a day when crossing the International Date Line.) The expedition assembled on the sea ice for photographs and speeches of welcome. The trans-Antarctic crossing had been made.

It had originally been planned that when the International Geophysical Year ended in mid-1958, most of the new bases would be closed down. By the time the finish of the IGY was actually at hand, though, it was obvious that too great an investment had been made in Antarctic research to halt now. Though some of the stations were closed, others were given permanent status. Today, many parts of the Antarctic are inhabited all the year round. As Rear Admiral David M. Tyree, who headed Operation Deep Freeze from 1959 to 1962, put it, "We are in Antarctica to stay." Between 1960 and 1962, American ships steamed 750,000 miles through Antarctic waters. American planes flew almost 8,000,000 miles; 12,000 miles were covered in overland traverses. In 1962 alone, 4,000 men took part in the United States' Antarctic work, using eleven ships and forty-one aircraft. Nine tons of scientific records and specimens were the haul of that single summer's work.

The Soviet Union, too, has an active Antarctic program,

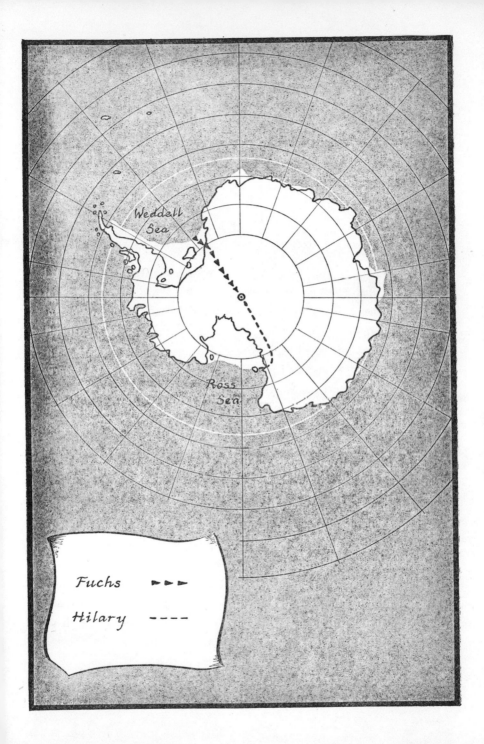

Weddell
Sea

Ross
Sea

Fuchs ▶ ▶ ▶

Hilary - - - -

with several permanent bases along the coast and deep in the interior. Great Britain, Chile, Argentina, France, New Zealand, and other countries are represented.

Antarctica today has changed in many ways that the early explorers would find unbelievable. Motor toboggans have replaced the faithful dogs at almost all stations. Tractors, planes, and powerful icebreakers aid the explorers. The sometimes bitter political feuds over possession of Antarctic territory have given way to an international agreement, signed in 1959, which sets Antarctica aside as a continent of peaceful scientific research. The various national claims have not been renounced, but they are no longer put forth with much conviction. The Cold War has not reached the coldest continent.

The atomic age has, however. Though the 1959 treaty bans all atomic explosions in Antarctica, the peaceful use of atomic energy is permitted. Atomic power came to Antarctica in July, 1962, when a nuclear reactor went into operation at McMurdo Sound. A core of uranium produces heat that creates steam, which turns generators that yield 1,500 kilowatts of electricity. With atomic energy providing power, it will no longer be necessary to haul many thousands of gallons of fuel oil to Antarctica. Soon an atomic-powered water-desalting plant will go into operation at McMurdo Sound also; water from the Ross Sea will be pumped up and distilled for drinking, replacing the laborious method of melting snow. Eventually, all of the American stations in Antarctica will run on atomic energy—and, no doubt, so will the Russian ones. The result will be a startling transformation and expansion of the growing "cities" of Antarctica.

Nearly two hundred years ago, Captain Cook sailed south until ice would let him sail south no more. Men like Bransfield, Palmer, and Bellingshausen found ways to get past the ice and sight land beyond. Wilkes, D'Urville, and Ross greatly increased man's knowledge of the Antarctic coast. Finally, in the most heroic age of Antarctic exploration, such men as Shackleton, Scott, and Amundsen defied the elements to venture onto the Antarctic mainland.

Over these two hundred years, a continent has taken shape —the loneliest continent, inhabited only by penguins, seals, and micro-organisms until the human invaders came. We know a great deal about that continent today. Its coastline has been mapped, its most remote areas have been seen by air and visited on foot. We know that 22 quadrillion tons of ice cover Antarctica—in some places, 9,000 feet thick. That is 90 per cent of all the ice in the world. Including its ice shelves, Antarctica has an area twice that of the United States. Much of Antarctica is included in the largest high plateau in the world, at an altitude of 3,000 to 10,000 feet. It has many mountains fifteen thousand feet and more above sea level. It is the coldest place in the world, where temperatures as low as $-120°$ have been recorded.

Beneath the ice, there may be coal, gold, iron, uranium, and other valuable minerals. As of now, though, Antarctica has little economic value, since mining operations are impractical there. It was only fifty years from Scott's death to the start-up of the first nuclear reactor in Antarctica, though, and it is unsafe to try to guess how much progress the next half-century may see.

At the moment, Antarctica's chief value is as a vast laboratory. Seismologists study earthquakes there, and have learned much about why and how they are produced. Weather experts have gathered voluminous data on temperatures, humidity, storm formation, and solar energy. Physicists are at work on studies of the aurora and on research into the earth's magnetic field. Entomologists are collecting the incredibly durable insects of Antarctica; botanists ponder the lichens and mosses; zoologists are busy with the penguins and seals and whales. Here in the last outpost of the Ice Age, there is plenty of work for all.

Many mysteries remain. Outcroppings of coal tell us that Antarctica once had forests and a much warmer climate. Why did it turn cold? Did the earth once spin on a different axis? Or—as one theory has it—have the continents drifted over the face of the earth, taking Antarctica from near the Equator to the South Pole? The next few years may provide an answer.

Even the structure of the continent beneath the ice holds puzzles. The latest studies seem to indicate that much of what is now called West Antarctica is not part of the mainland at all, but only a group of islands covered by a great sheet of ice. According to this view, if the ice sheet were peeled away, the Ross Sea would join the Weddell Sea; the Antarctica Peninsula would become an archipelago; much of Marie Byrd Land and Ellsworth Land would disappear entirely, leaving isolated mountainous islands. East Antarctica, on the other hand, is thought to be a stable continental shield. All this, too, remains to be determined.

Once, men went south in search of a mythical continent of fertile fields and friendly natives. Captain Cook showed there was no such place. Then, men went south to hunt seals and whales, and found a southern continent after all, buried in ice, wrapped in bitter cold. There is little money to be made in sealing and whaling today, but men still go south.

Why?

What drove Robert Falcon Scott to find death on the ice? What sent Shackleton southward again and again? What led Byrd to spend a six-month night in a lonely cabin? What sends thousands of men to Antarctica today?

It is the same motive that is now sending men toward that other dark frontier—space. It is the need to *know*—the fierce, driving curiosity that brooks no obstacles. It is impossible, perhaps, to try to explain that curiosity to anyone who does not feel it himself.

The best and simplest explanation of the force that drives men to the ends of the earth, I think, was offered many years ago by the Arctic explorer, Fridtjof Nansen. Curiosity—that burning urge to roll back the barriers of the unknown—is a basic characteristic of mankind, he said. "The history of the human race is a continuous struggle from darkness toward light. It is therefore of no purpose to discuss the use of knowledge. Man wants to know, and when he ceases to do so he is no longer man."

BIBLIOGRAPHY

I. HISTORIES OF DISCOVERY AND EXPLORATION

BROWN, LLOYD A., *The Story of Maps*. Little, Brown, Boston, 1950.

CARAS, ROGER A., *Antarctica: Land of Frozen Time*. Chilton, Philadelphia and New York, 1962.

CHRISTIE, E. W. HUNTER, *The Antarctic Problem*. George Allen & Unwin, London, 1951.

HOBBS, WILLIAM HERBERT, *Explorers of the Antarctic*. House of Field, New York, 1941.

KIRWAN, L. P., *A History of Polar Exploration*. Norton, New York, 1960.

MILL, HUGH R., *The Siege of the South Pole*. Alston Rivers, London, 1905.

MITTERLING, PHILIP I., *America in the Antarctic to 1840*. University of Illinois Press, Urbana, 1959.

MOUNTEVANS, ADMIRAL LORD, *The Antarctic Challenged*. John de Graff, New York, 1956.

NEWTON, A. P., (editor), *Travel and Travellers of the Middle Ages*. Routledge & Kegan Paul, London, 1926.

STEVENS, HENRY N. (editor), *New Light on the Discovery of Australia*. The Hakluyt Society, London, 1930.

SULLIVAN, WALTER, *Quest for a Continent*. McGraw-Hill, New York, 1957.

II. ACCOUNTS BY THE EXPLORERS

AMUNDSEN, ROALD, *South Pole*. John Murray, London, 1912.

———, *My Life As an Explorer*. Heinemann, London, 1927.

BELLINGSHAUSEN, FABIAN GOTTLIEB VON, *The Voyage of Captain Bellingshausen to the Antarctic Seas, 1819–1821*. Translated from the Russian and edited by Frank Debenham. The Hakluyt Socicty, London, 1945.

BYRD, RICHARD E., *Alone*. Putnam, New York, 1938.

———, *Discovery*. Putnam, New York, 1935.

———, *Little America*. Putnam, New York, 1930.

CHERRY-GARRARD, APSLEY, *The Worst Journey in the World*. Chatto & Windus, London, 1922.

COOK, DR. F. A., *Through the First Antarctic Night*. Heinemann, London, 1900.

COOK, JAMES, *Voyage Towards the South Pole*. London, 1777.

COURTAULD, AUGUSTINE (editor), *From the Ends of the Earth: an Anthology of Polar Writings*. (Many explorers.) Oxford University Press, London, 1958.

FUCHS, SIR VIVIAN and HILLARY, SIR EDMUND, *The Crossing of Antarctica*. Little, Brown, Boston, 1958.

MAWSON, SIR DOUGLAS, *The Home of the Blizzard*. Heinemann, London, 1915.

ROSS, JAMES CLARK, *A Voyage of Discovery and Research in the Southern and Antarctic Regions*. John Murray, London, 1847.

SCOTT, ROBERT FALCON, *The Voyage of the* Discovery. Scribner's, New York, 1905.

SCOTT, ROBERT FALCON, *Scott's Last Expedition* (edited by Leonard Huxley). Dodd, Mead, New York, 1913.

SHACKLETON, ERNEST H., *The Heart of the Antarctic*. Lippincott, Philadelphia, 1909.

———, *South: The Story of Shackleton's Last Expedition*. Macmillan, New York, 1920.

STEFANSSON, VILHJALMUR (editor), *Great Adventures and Explorations*. (Many explorers.) Dial, New York, 1947.

WEDDELL, JAMES, *A Voyage Towards the South Pole*. Longmans Green, London, 1825.

WILKES, CHARLES, *Narrative of the Exploring Expedition, by Authority of Congress, during the years 1838–1842*. Lea & Blanchard, Philadelphia, 1845.

III. MAGAZINE ARTICLES

BYRD, RICHARD E., "The Conquest of Antarctica by Air," *National Geographic Magazine*, August, 1930.

———, "Exploring the Ice Age in Antarctica," *National Geographic Magazine*, October, 1935.

———, "Our Navy Explores Antarctica," *National Geographic Magazine*, October, 1947.

———, "All-out Assault on Antarctica," *National Geographic Magazine*, August, 1956.

DUFEK, GEORGE J., "What We've Accomplished in Antarctica," *National Geographic Magazine*, October, 1959.

ELLSWORTH, LINCOLN, "My Flight Across Antarctica," *National Geographic Magazine*, July, 1936.

———, "My Four Antarctic Expeditions," *National Geographic Magazine*, July, 1939.

FRAZIER, PAUL, "Across the Frozen Desert to Byrd Station," *National Geographic Magazine*, September, 1957.

McDONALD, EDWIN A., "Exploring Antarctica's Phantom Coast," *National Geographic Magazine*, February, 1962.

SIPLE, PAUL A., "We Are Living at the South Pole," *National Geographic Magazine*, July, 1957.

———, "Man's First Winter at the South Pole," *National Geographic Magazine*, April, 1958.

TYREE, DAVID M., "New Era in the Loneliest Continent," *National Geographic Magazine*, February, 1963.

Scientific American, September, 1962. Entire issue devoted to Antarctica.

INDEX